Levels of Knowing and Existence

Levels of Knowing and Existence

STUDIES IN GENERAL SEMANTICS

HARRY L. WEINBERG

TEMPLE UNIVERSITY

HARPER & BROTHERS, PUBLISHERS,

NEW YORK

To Blanche

    without whom . . .
    without whose . . .

CONTENTS

Contents

x   Contents

PREFACE

IN 1933 I received my B.S. in chemistry from C.C.N.Y., utterly convinced that the only useful subjects were the natural sciences. English composition and literature were of some value, but nothing approached chemistry. Especially philosophy. I had had only one course in it and had cut all the classes. The professor was an unworldly soul who never took attendance and I easily outsmarted him. How I squeaked through the final exam I will never know. It was not until twenty years later that I realized what an utter fool I had been and how much I had missed. The professor was Morris R. Cohen.

In 1934 the University of Pennsylvania bestowed upon me an M.S. in chemistry; shortly after I went to work as an industrial research chemist and continued in this until 1940. I was still convinced that science, as I understood it—a bundle of facts and some theories and techniques for manipulating them—was the only worthwhile knowledge. But a crack had appeared in my shell—quite by accident. One day in 1939 my wife came home with a book from the lending library, *The Tyranny of Words* by Stuart Chase. She had selected it more, as she explained, from an interest in words than in tyranny. For some reason, I also read it—probably to make sure we got our money's worth. Chase had been inspired to write the book by his reading of *Science and Sanity* by Alfred Korzybski. I bought this book and haven't been the same since.

It was the most difficult book I had ever read and it took me almost four months to go through it the first time. Why I stuck it out I don't know; something in it appealed to me. I have the suspicion that my

complete ignorance of logic, psychology, philosophy, and the canons of
good literary style saved me from passing judgment too quickly. It
is so easy to demonstrate that it is a dogmatic, pretentious, terribly
written, philosophically naïve, psychologically unsound work. Many
are the critics who hold this view. They are absolutely correct, but
only if we start from *their* premises and criteria. Unfortunately, I think
most of the critics of general semantics have assumed that their
premises and assumptions are the only ones which are sound or even
conceivable.

But the essence (if I may use that dirty word) of *Science and Sanity*
is that other assumptions are not only possible but desperately needed.
Yet one cannot "see" this until he has read and thoroughly understood
the book. In fact, one must first read the book in order to learn how to
read it. It was here that my ignorance of everything but chemistry
came to my aid. I swallowed it whole—the book, the line, the thinker.
All of which proves that everything happens for the best in this best
of all possible worlds.

In the spring of 1940, with the war looming closer and closer, my
wife and I decided to have one last fling. We quit our jobs, bought a
canoe, loaded it with 350 pounds of mostly useless camping equipment
and started on a trip that lasted four months and covered about a
thousand miles. Neither of us had ever been in a canoe before and so
our progress at first was slow. Even slower was my reprogress through
Science and Sanity. Each morning I would read a page or two and
spend the rest of the day thinking about them while paddling. I like
to think that my understanding and my biceps improved at about the
same rate.

In December of 1940, I attended one of Korzybski's seminars and
it did much to clarify his book. During the next few years, I more or
less neglected my study of general semantics until one September
morn I found myself aboard an ammunition ship headed for Guadal-
canal with a copy of *Science and Sanity* in my duffel bag. Naturally,

since I had been a chemist, the obvious position for me aboard ship was that of chief pot washer and potato peeler.

There is nothing more conducive to meditation than potato peeling. One morning, in mid-Pacific, I was sitting under the forward gun deck peeling my way through the daily quota of 100 pounds. Suddenly the sun came up and there spread before me the most beautiful sunrise I had ever seen. So great was its effect that for a full five minutes I stopped peeling the potatoes and neglected to scratch the fungus infection on parts unmentionable. The next morning, under what seemed identical circumstances, the sunrise affected me hardly at all. Why? For the next ten months my reflections on this and related problems occupied my mind and resulted in a bundle of notes which later formed the basis for a paper titled, "Some Functional Patterns on the Non-Verbal Level." Part of it appears in this book.

After the war I sent the paper to Korzybski who thought it was good enough to have published in *ETC.: A Review of General Semantics*. He sent a copy to Professor Irving J. Lee of the School of Speech of Northwestern University who offered me a graduate assistantship in speech. So a-wondering I wandered into a field entirely new to me.

Professor Lee was one of the most magnificent teachers I have ever encountered and I owe him an unpayable debt. From him I learned whatever good teaching techniques I may now possess and with his encouragement and prodding I read widely and intensively in philosophy, logic, psychology, rhetoric, and anthropology. It was only then that I began to understand some of the many philosophical, psychological, and linguistic factors involved in what we call the scientific method. Is it not absurd that I had to leave the field of science in order to learn what patterns of talking and action are involved in scientific behavior! Yet, as of this date, natural science majors in most universities are still receiving the same kind of lopsided education I received more than twenty-five years ago.

This book is not supposed to be a general semantics primer. I suggest that the reader who is unfamiliar with the subject read Irving J. Lee's *Language Habits in Human Affairs,* Wendell Johnson's *People in Quandaries,* and S. I. Hayakawa's *Language in Thought and Action.* With these as guides he might then, if he is courageous, attempt *Science and Sanity.* After a few years he may begin to realize what an impressive achievement it is.

I have attempted to indicate that general semantics can be used as a tool for analyzing and understanding almost every area of human endeavor, and have tried to apply it to a variety of what I consider nontrivial problems in order to show that its wide applicability is due, primarily, to its being a metalinguistic system—a pattern for talking, thinking, and feeling about talking, thinking, and feeling. If I have failed, the failure is mine and not, necessarily, Korzybski's. Of course, there is the possibility that the system has inherent flaws, weaknesses, and contradictions which neither I nor its other vendors have discovered. I hope I have demonstrated that this is not true.

I have not attempted an extensive bibliography but have simply listed the works referred to throughout this book. The reader will find that *en masse* they constitute a comprehensive compendium of essential and peripheral material. I thank the publishers and individuals who granted permission to quote from the publications cited in the text.

In closing, I gratefully acknowledge the help of M. Kendig, Director of the Institute of General Semantics, whose critical reading of the manuscript led to many improvements.

H. L. W.

Havertown, Pennsylvania
May, 1959

Introduction

THIS has been called the age of anxiety, the age of the hollow man lost in a lonely crowd. It is the age of the drifting man, the man without a purpose, without any clear philosophy of life other than to "get by" or to "succeed"—succeed meaning to conform to the crowd, to keep up with the Joneses, to be accepted. Many reasons have been advanced to explain this phenomenon. Modern man, it is said, is rootless. He has no tradition to guide him. The old faiths, the traditional guides, have been rejected and no acceptable new ones have arisen.

One result of this aimless, meaningless existence which has neither past nor future is a sense of panic; and a common means of escaping the terrible anxiety thus generated is a headlong, irrational drive to lose oneself in the crowd. The goal of life is "to be adjusted," that is, to be accepted by and identical with the crowd. Writers such as Erich Fromm, David Riesman, Rollo May, and Ralph Lindner have vividly described this panic to conform. It represents, says Fromm, a flight from individual freedom which has become intolerable. Individual freedom implies responsibility for actions and decisions and because the individual has no tradition or philosophy to guide him, his decision-making generates unendurable anxiety. The ability to make important decisions without provoking neurotic anxiety takes a clear sense of one's own identity as a person similar to, yet distinct from, any other person and the ability to accept the essential and inescapable loneliness that this uniqueness implies.

I shall not spend more time delineating the plight of modern man as these authors view it, nor shall I attempt to estimate just how true or widely applicable these generalizations may be. All such generalizations must necessarily be stamped "handle with care," but I have a hunch that there is much truth in what they say.

It seems to me that many of the people these authors describe have gone from the one extreme of complete acceptance of traditional ethical, moral, and religious doctrines to the other extreme of complete cultural relativism. Claiming that all ethical and moral judgments are relative only to the culture in which they are made, that what is considered good and valuable in one society may be judged bad and useless in another, these people find themselves unable to build any kind of relatively stable ethical code. For if these codes are relative to societies, they are also relative to parts of societies and to smaller parts of these, and they must necessarily vary with the date. Consequently, it becomes almost impossible to make moral and ethical decisions with any degree of certainty and security. One result, then, is a slavish dependence on the majority opinion of the group within which they function. These groups seem to offer the only standards for making value judgments. In short, having lost or never having found standards of their own, individuals become what has been called "outer-directed men"—the hollow men swaying in the winds of ethical fashions, clinging to the group for a security bought at the price of intellectual freedom and self-actualization.

I do not mean to imply that one must necessarily adopt either of these extreme positions. I suppose most people can be spotted somewhere between, accepting parts of both philosophies in a makeshift patchwork which, being so much of a compromise of contradictory points of view, gives little comfort to them and lends credence to

Santayana's caustic observation that "the philosophy of the common man is an old wife that gives him no pleasure, yet he cannot live without her, and resents any aspersions that strangers may cast on her character."

Is it possible to formulate a "comfortable" philosophy? I believe it is, provided it can operate on all levels of abstraction. The meaning of this will be made clearer, I hope, in the body of this book. Briefly stated, it means that such a philosophy must have both static and dynamic elements. The static will contain relatively unchanging, invariant answers to questions of this nature: What should be the goals of life? How does one face the certainty of death and the uncertainty and insecurity of living? What is the use of struggling and competing if the grave is the inevitable end? What ethical principles should form the basis of comparison for all value judgments? The answers given here will be in the nature of value statements and prescriptions for conduct. Only if taken in this sense can these questions be considered answerable; if we are looking for verifiable knowledge, e.g., what is the chemical constitution of water, these questions are unanswerable and meaningless. But if properly understood as value questions, they become meaningful and answerable; indeed, in a way, they are among the most important questions one can ask. And the failure to ask them can have a stultifying effect upon the full development of one's intellectual and emotional life.

Any answers given to questions of this type, while in themselves not in the realm of verifiable knowledge, should be based upon the best verified generalizations science has produced to date, and the data on which the ethical generalizations are based should be made as explicit as possible.

When we turn to the lower, dynamic levels of abstraction, we find, not answers that apply in general, but methods for getting answers to very specific problems such as: How can I get the boss to give me a raise? For which candidate shall I vote? Shall I buy a new car or a used one? How can I keep from blowing my top when Joe needles me? What shall I tell my 12-year-old daughter about sex? What our philosophy will contain on this level will be tools of analysis and methods for evaluating situations. All value judgments at this level should, of course, be consistent with and derivable from the more general ethical standards given on the higher levels of abstraction. On this lower level, each answer is applicable to each particular situation and can be devised only by the person involved. The answers given on the higher level are, by definition, applicable by all men and need not be devised by each person using them.

In this book I shall attempt to present a "comfortable" philosophy, using comfortable in the sense already stated, i.e., usable on many levels of feeling, thought, and action. I am a little unhappy about calling it a philosophy because of the associations that usually cluster about this term. Perhaps "program for living" would be better; but this seems to have a prissy, preachy air about it. So rather than risk the communication road-blocks which some terms in common usage may set up, we shall not give it any specific label or attempt to define it. Rather, we will descend to a lower level of abstraction and simply try to describe what we are advocating—what we shall later call "patterns of proper evaluation."

The technical terms such as "levels of abstraction" which have already crept, undefined, into our discussion come from the general semantics of Alfred Korzybski [1] which forms a foundation for the material presented in this book. And if you ask, as most people do when they hear the words "general semantics," what is it, I shall be unable to give a meaningful answer and will have to put you off with the statement, "Read the book, and then perhaps you will know something about it." Any definition at this point would be practically

[1] Alfred Korzybski, *Science and Sanity: An Introduction to Non-aristotelian Systems and General Semantics*, International Non-aristotelian Library Publishing Company, distributed by Institute of General Semantics, Lakeville, Conn., 1st ed. 1933; 2nd ed. 1941; 3rd ed. 1948; 4th ed. 1958.

useless. What we need are descriptions. And what is the difference between definition and description? We shall come to that. For to understand the significance of the difference, we have to know what we mean by meaning. More precisely we have to know about the meanings of meaning, that is, about the different kinds of meaning. But this immediately brings up the problem of knowing—how we know what we know and, just to complicate matters, how knowing that we know affects what we know. And the moment we tackle that problem, the floodgates open. Is what I am saying factual? Before I can attempt to demonstrate that it is, you ought to know what I mean by a factual statement, how it is distinguished from a fact and, moving in the other direction, how it differs from an inferential statement.

But meaningful talk about facts, factual statements, and inferences cannot be made without discussing the problem of verification, the criteria used by the scientist for checking his theory. The most obvious criterion is reality. And immediately the question arises, What is reality? What is a thing really? The answer to the latter question is quite sharp and unequivocal. Whatever you say it is, it is not. No, this is not double talk. It is a statement of a profound and exceedingly important, obvious (and therefore missed) truth. When a person really (sic) understands it and all it implies, then he can say he understands general semantics. Now if you are warming to the game and are tempted to ask "What is truth?" I shall reply with the question, "Which 'is' are you talking about?" There are at least four of them. But the discussion of "is" immediately brings us to the problem of existence—what do you mean by that term? The meaning of existence cannot be considered apart from the meanings of meaning. So we are back full circle.

If you are tempted to give up at this point and write me off as a hopelessly befuddled writer (which may be true) on a preposterously confused subject, let me say that there has been some method to this madness. I am trying to make the point that talking about talking, language about language, involves a level of complexity not found in talking about things. There is not just a quantitative difference but a qualitative one as well, involving circular, causal, and feedback mechanisms. Consequently, a simple, serial, logical, progressive presentation will not work as it does, for example, in a textbook on physics, chemistry, and to a lesser degree, biology. In these, one fact, one theory after another can be studied until the student has a good picture of the entire field.

But in discussions of the problems of communication and language structure, the meanings of each technical term can be understood only in the context of the whole system and not apart from it. One must know the whole before the meanings and the parts become clear, yet we can learn only one part at a time! Nor is this dilemma peculiar to academic discussion of linguistic matters. It is inherent in practically all human interaction and communication and is one of the factors which makes the discussion of even simple daily life problems quite complicated. Listen closely to a group discussion, for example, at a PTA meeting, a faculty conference, a meeting of the board, or a club meeting of any kind, even one where most of the members are fairly homogeneous in interests, and you will be amazed at the amount of time that seems wasted discussing matters that are beside the point, illogically and emotionally presented, and factually untrue. It seems so difficult for one person to see another's point of view even on simple matters, and it is tempting to ascribe this to the natural stupidity, ignorance, and general recalcitrance of the participants.

But I believe this is only part of the case. To "see" another person's point and to know how he feels about it, one must have his point of view, that is, we must see it in the context of his life experience and his psychophysiological state at the moment. Only by knowing this whole (and this is impossible) can we understand the meaning to him of the part under discussion. So when the discussion wanders and repeats and drags out, we ought not to consider this a complete waste of time and energy. These meanderings help give us the context, the background against which the participants evaluate the situation. The situation is not too far removed from what happens on the psychoanalyst's couch. Although "obvious" points may be simply stated, their meanings on many levels are not as easily comprehended. In a way, we can say that the psychotherapist is engaged in getting his patients to see the significance of the obvious.

Thus, when we have an over-simple picture of the processes of communication, we tend to become impatient in discussions and place the blame for slowness of progress wholly upon the inherent orneriness of the others instead of upon the process itself. Most of us have been educated to "get the facts," with little attention paid to the equally important problem of transmitting them to others and the even more important and much more difficult task of trying to discover what they mean to others and to ourselves. The person who believes in letting the facts speak for themselves is speaking only to himself. A firm belief in a spurious simplicity is a frequent cause of self-duplicity.

If we seem to have wandered from the point under discussion, we have and we have not. We have if we are looking for a serial presentation of facts and theories; we haven't if we seek a view of the whole by which to gain insight into the significance of the parts. In any event, this is the method by which we shall try to solve or reduce the dilemma previously mentioned, a dilemma presented by the fact that two kinds of learning have to take place before "full" comprehension is possible—a learning of the parts, mostly by association and contiguity, and a learning of the relationship of the parts to the whole and of a new relationship, the significance of the whole as a whole, through the sudden insight we call Gestalt learning.

Since, as we have stated, we cannot wait for Gestalt learning to take place at the end of a long line of serial learning as we can in physics and chemistry, and since we have to have both operating almost simultaneously, our method will be to present one or a few facts or theories or bits of speculation, giving as precise a definition as we can at the moment, and then try to relate it to the whole, knowing full well that the significance of this will not come at the moment, yet hoping that it will give hints and hunches as to what will later be understood more clearly. This means that we will be making many references, using many terms which will be only briefly explained at the moment, with the understanding that they will be studied in greater detail later on. Thus we shall be weaving a complex tapestry; a thread, then a tracing of the thread through a design yet to be woven and only vaguely understood, with the hope that the tenuous understanding thus acquired will reach back and aid the placing of the thread and increase the knowledge of the part it will play in the completed work.

Inevitably, whenever we act as human beings and cease copying animals in the use of our nervous systems, we have to indulge in self-levitation. We shall be talking about the defects in the structure of the language we use in daily life and how this literally warps the functioning of our nervous system; yet to do this we shall have to use both this defective language and a nervous system already damaged by it. We shall attempt to show, for example, that whenever mis-understanding of almost any kind occurs between people, if we examine the structure of the talking that takes place, we shall find certain patterns of misevaluation present. And we shall find these same patterns of misevaluation when we examine the way we talk to ourselves as well as in the talking of the neurotic and the psychotic. We do, in part, talk our way into insanity. Note that I am not saying that this is *the* cause of psychotic, neurotic, or foolish behavior. It is one factor, and one largely disregarded by most psychiatrists and psychologists. Most of us know that the way we think helps determine the way we talk; not too many are aware that the reverse also takes place.

Having provided myself with what I consider a well-designed rationalization for any and all looseness of structure and fuzziness of thought to be found in these pages, I would like to take advantage of it right now to wander up another alley and attempt to answer briefly here, and in much greater detail later, some of the questions which have been raised concerning the usefulness and applicability of general semantics.

Quite often it is stated that much in general semantics is childishly simple and obvious and has been said before in many ways and in many places. It is interesting to know, in this connection, that Korzybski himself was fond of repeating again and again, "This is baby stuff." Now, if it is so simple, why make so much of a fuss over it; why build a complex system and wind up with such trivia? Primarily, because, though much of this has been said before in many philosophies, religions, and ethical and psychological systems, its usefulness has been largely vitiated by being surrounded by and embedded in a good deal of nonsense in the form of unsupported inferences, false facts, authoritarian dogma, contradictory theories, and invalid reasoning. Thus the "good" is difficult to distinguish from the "bad," and as a consequence both have been rejected. Stated another way, this wisdom of the ages and the sages is rejected either because it is derived from a doctrine whose basic assumptions are unacceptable or because it is rendered innocuous by being offered as *ad hoc* advice, largely useless because it is not part of an integrated system within whose framework it becomes meaningful on all levels of abstraction, i.e., on the non-verbal levels of feeling and emotion and the verbal levels of factual knowledge, inference, and theory. The general semanticist likes to think that because he offers these obvious simplicities as part of a comprehensive methodology, they become more acceptable and usable.

There is, however, a more serious problem related to this cry of "obvious." Everyone knows it is silly to worry over problems about which we can do nothing, that it is childish to lose one's temper over trivialities, that unreasoning hatred destroys us; yet we find it exceedingly difficult to act as if we know it. It is simple knowledge, it is obvious, it is great wisdom, and it's old stuff. Only recently have we begun to understand the great part that unconscious, irrational processes play in inhibiting our free and rational use of this simple and profound wisdom. Consequently, many psychiatrists claim that all such books variously titled, "How to Stop Worrying," "The Power of Affirmative Cogitation," "Pray Your Way to Peace," "How to Think Straight," and the like, have very limited usefulness. In short, they believe that the average person cannot, without professional help, use a direct rational approach to control irrational processes.

Is general semantics simply another such rational methodology sharing all the weaknesses of these self-help systems? This entire book is, in a way, an attempt to give a qualified and partial "no" to this question. General semantics is a rational methodology to be used by the individual himself and consequently has some of the limitations of all rational systems for controlling the irrational. However, there are, I believe, a number of important differences. First, general semantics is a very broad methodology containing much more than directions for controlling worry, hate, feelings of inferiority, etc. It covers the whole range of human evaluation, and the prescriptions offered for control of such unwanted feelings or emotions are derivable from, but not inherent in, its basic assumptions and general theoretical foundations. Thus, these prescriptions for control of the non-verbal level are not *ad hoc* admonitions as they are in most of the above books but are part of a methodology for rational control of all problems of proper evaluation in any area whatsoever. They are linked both to an explicitly stated ethical system which is not in contradiction to anything known in science today and to an explicitly stated program for proper evaluation which is firmly rooted in the psychoneurological structure of man as known to date.

Secondly, it seems to me that most self-help books are largely self-defeating. What they prescribe is admirable, but often the attempts to use these prescriptions can lead to an exacerbation of that which they seek to ameliorate. A person who directly attempts to cut down on his worry may start to worry about his failure to do so. In general semantics terminology, this may produce vicious second-order effects—worry about worry, fear of fear. It is my opinion that the relatively indirect, long-range approach of general semantics is more likely to succeed. By "relatively indirect," as we shall see in much detail later, we mean that the problem of controlling the non-verbal levels of evaluation is just one aspect of an overall pattern of proper evaluation on all levels of abstraction. By attacking on all levels, we are less apt to provoke the anxiety that a specific back-groundless attack would do. Stating it in very simple terms, we can rarely say, "Stomach, stop churning! Butterflies, go away! Tensions, relax!" and have it happen. You can do it if you are a yogi or if you have mastered a system of direct relaxation such as Jacobson's. But relaxation is only part of the problem, a method of relieving symptoms without getting at the causes.

Now if I were to claim that general semantics helps get at the causes of neurotic symptoms, I would bring down on my head both the general semanticists and their violent critics among psychiatrists. The latter claim that general semantics, being "purely" (often equated with "merely") a rational system, cannot get at *the* causes of neurosis but can deal only with superficial, intellectual aspects of mental diseases. The reply to this is yes and no. Yes, general semantics cannot get at *all* of the causes; other techniques are also needed—no one system yet devised is a cure-all. No, general semantics is not, therefore, completely useless. It will help with those causes of neurotic behavior which stem from misevaluations produced by the structure of the language we use in daily life—and this is no small part. More importantly, it is a mistake—one of the patterns of misevaluation— to talk as if "cause" and "symptom" were separable. In the human nervous system "symptoms" feed back to become "causes" and "causes" themselves become "symptoms."

Moreover, since the organism functions as a whole, anything which will reduce a "symptom" inevitably must have some effects on the "causes" producing it. Otherwise we fall into the trap of thinking of human beings as zombies possessed by evil spirits labeled "traumatic childhood experiences" which have almost a separate existence *in* the nervous system affecting all of the person's behavior, without rational, conscious behavior (other than therapy in the form of psychoanalysis, or its variations) having an effect upon it. We shall worry this point later.

But, above all, as far as mental illness is concerned, the usefulness of general semantics is as a form of preventive medicine. I do not think it can help the severely neurotic person. It is a highly rational approach and the person in the throes of emotional upheavals will find it extremely difficult to apply. The psychotic, of course, cannot use it at all. But one should not therefore infer that it cannot be used by a qualified fairly "normal" person as part of a program for helping sick people; it is simply very unlikely that they can use it themselves.

Since its greatest usefulness is as a preventive therapy, this necessarily means a long-range program starting early in childhood. General semantics can be taught at all levels of complexity from prekindergarten through postgraduate. It is certainly not a hopeless task for the adult beginner; but for the serious novice it will be a long, arduous, yet fascinating, journey of self-discovery, of sudden joyous insights into ancient wisdoms and modern scientific structures. As with all journeys into the unknown, there will be long periods of despair at seeming lack of progress, a great temptation to quit, to write it off as a useless, hopeless task, and to seek an easier, quicker solution in the newest panacea. It is understandable that we should like to have a speedy, simple solution to the most difficult, unique, and important problem in human development, a conscious rational control of the self. But to expect such a solution to be easy contradicts all our past experience. It is the height of foolishness to expect to change easily and quickly after having practiced patterns of misevaluation all our lives.

But even if one resolutely does start learning and practicing his general semantics, this does not mean that he will achieve nirvana—a solution to and end of all problems. General semantics is not a panacea; it will not end all anxieties, alleviate all worries, give *the* answer to the infinite variety of complexities that all of us face. Rather, it is an aid, a potent one, among a host of other tools man has developed for controlling both his external and internal environments. Like any tool, it has its limitations. As far as controlled scientific experiment is concerned its effectiveness is still largely untested. We might add, however, that this is true of all extant psychological systems. Most testimony in its favor is just that—personal testimony of disciples. In fact, it has been used in all kinds of situations and on a variety of problems—in labor-management disputes, as a means of preventing battlefield hysteria and breakdown, as part of a group therapy program, as part of an accident prevention and training program, as a means of increasing objective reporting by policemen, and so forth. All who have reported using general semantics in some part or some way proclaim its usefulness, but there has been no accurate measurement of its effectiveness as yet. There are several reasons for this: the lack of accurate measuring instruments, the relative newness of general semantics and thus the lack of a long enough period of time to test long-range programs, and the small number of qualified practitioners in the field.

In this book, I shall present part of general semantics theory and methodology, together with some of my own thinking about it and the uses to which I have put it. Just why I have chosen to apply it to certain problems and neglected others equally or more important, is something I shall not attempt to justify—probably I couldn't if I wanted to. Undoubtedly, unconscious drives, frustrations, unfulfilled needs play a large part in this choice. I leave to the amateur and professional psychologists among my readers the joy of reading out of it and into it what they will, undoubtedly even without my permission. Enough of these preliminaries.

Some Basic Concepts

IN this chapter, we shall be concerned primarily with two important terms: factual knowledge and inferential knowledge. We shall define them and try to show that knowing the difference between them makes a difference for the better in our behavior. It is important to know that this is the way we shall use these terms, and that it is not the only way they can be and have been defined. All definitions are arbitrary. Their value is determined by the degree to which others will agree with them, by their freedom from contradiction with other terms in the system of which they are a part—their validity, and by their agreement with verified observations if they pertain to the material world—their truthfulness.

A factual statement, as we define it, is one which is made only after observation and which is verifiable by accepted standards. In other words, it is a verifiable descriptive statement. We use the term "observation" here and elsewhere in a very broad sense to include not only visual, but any sensory perception. A factual statement does not go beyond or add to what has been observed. An inferential statement is not limited by observation; it is a statement about that which has not been observed. It may be a guess which takes off from the point where observation ceases or it may be a wild and woolly fabrication in no way related to observation. Thus, if I look out the window, see water falling from the sky, and say, "It is raining," I have made a factual statement (provided someone is not pouring water from a bucket from the window above). If I add that it is raining 1000 miles away or around the corner, I am making an inference.

Factual statements approach certainty; they have a high degree of probability of being verified. Inferential statements have widely varying degrees of probability of being verified. The reason why factual statements only approach certainty, but never reach it, is that they are based upon observation, and there is always an element of uncertainty in any observation. Since no two observations, even by the same person, are ever identical, think of how much greater must be the differences between the observations of the "same" object by two different people. If no two observations are identical, it makes no sense to say that one is true and the others are false. What the scientist does is to make a series of observations under conditions as nearly the same as possible (they are never identical) and to average them out in some statistical fashion.

THE CHOICE OF STANDARDS: HOW LONG IS IT REALLY?

We shall have much more to say about uncertainty in observation when we discuss the abstracting process, so let us turn to the problem of obtaining an acceptable standard. Suppose, as a do-it-yourself aficionado, you decide to build a table 30 inches high. Your measuring instrument will probably be a tape measure or yardstick or folding 6-foot rule. You put one end at the bottom of the leg, the top edge of the table coincides with the 30-inch mark on your rule, and you say, "The table is 30 inches high." Is that a factual statement?

Before we answer, let us pose another situation. A friend of yours drops in while you are measuring your table, and it so happens that he has a pair of giant calipers that will span the height of your table. These calipers are accurate to 1/1000 of an inch. The friend proceeds to measure the table and proudly states, "It is 30.019 inches high." Is that a factual statement? If it is, then is your statement that it is 30 inches high false? Or would you say that since the second measurement is more accurate than the first, it is closer to the "real" height? If it is, then presumably we could get closer and closer to the "real" height of the table by devising more and more accurate instruments.

This sounds logical until we try it. As we refine our measurements we gradually approach the molecular level. The table is a mass of constantly moving atoms and molecules, and when our measurements get close to molecular dimensions, we find that our nice, neat, hard, sharp table edge is in a cloud of dancing molecules—and where is the edge of a shifting cloud?

What, then, is the "real" height of the table? Our answer is that there is no such thing. It is a meaningless question because, as of this date, there is no possible way, actual or imaginable, to arrive at an answer. The table is 30 inches high. The table is 30.019 inches high. Both are correct; both are accurate; both are factual statements. Nor do they contradict, for two different standards are used. For measuring furniture, the accepted standard is the 6-foot rule. If, for some reason, the measurement has to be accurate to 1/1000 of an inch, the calipers are the standard.

The choice of standard is determined by the purpose for which the thing being measured is used. How standards are set up in the first place, and by whom, is a complex problem which shall not concern us here. It is enough to state that it varies, depending upon the thing being standardized. For building furniture, making dresses, laying bricks, etc., the standard is based almost wholly on practical experience with these materials. When we come to such items as standard weights, thermometers, the general run of scientific equipment, theoretical issues also come into play. The important points to remember are that there is always an element of arbitrariness in the selection of all standards and that they are never considered absolutely accurate—there is always a range, plus to minus, within which they are, by definition, and therefore relatively, considered accurate.

Even in such simple activities as sewing and brick laying, theoretical issues may determine the choice of standard, methods of verification, and belief in what is observed. For example, to the eye, railroad tracks converge as they recede. But most of us do not believe they do because we know that a train with rigidly spaced wheels could not run on converging tracks. Thus, theory concerning the operation of trains, in part, causes us to reject the naked eye as a standard and substitute the foot rule.

Again, many of us will watch a magician pull rabbits out of thin air, yet we reject the idea that this is an instance of magic in the supernatural sense. Others who believe in magic will accept it. Do the rabbits "really" come out of thin air? It depends on the standards accepted, and these will depend upon the total orientation of the observer. If he accepts modern science he will say, "It only looked as if the rabbits came out of nowhere, but in the light of theoretical issues, I infer that it could not have happened that way." Thus, we see that observation alone is not enough for determining factuality; both theoretical and observational verification are necessary. Observational verification means verification by others; theoretical verification means consistency with a set of accepted theories. It is a factual statement when we say, "It looks as if the rabbits appeared out of nowhere." To say, "They do not appear out of thin air" is a much more complex problem.

As we have stated, inferences are not directly linked to observation and therefore they have widely varying degrees of probability of being correct. Such statements as, "Tomorrow there will be a high and a low tide at the seashore," and "The sun will rise and set every day next year," are inferences with such a high degree of probability of being correct that they are close to being factual statements. Nevertheless, according to our rules they are still inferences. All statements about the future are inferences, as well as all statements about the past other than those based on actual observation by the speaker or writer.

The Significance of Knowing the Difference: the Lethal "Empty" Gun

What difference does this make to us in everyday life? Consider the "unloaded" guns which kill so many each year and will, I infer, continue to do so. Our hero makes the inference that the gun is empty, but he doesn't know this is inferential knowledge; to him it is factual knowledge and therefore he *does not have to check.* If he had learned the difference, he would have known that his knowledge was only inferential and needed checking, because inferential knowledge is less likely to be correct than factual knowledge.

Take for example, a news item about a truck driver who has run over and killed two children who were in an "empty" box in the middle of the highway. In the past, our truck driver has flattened empty boxes with his truck as a service to motorists. He knew "for sure" this box was empty; he was certain that he had factual information, so why check? Here is another news story about two oil refinery workers who were killed and a third seriously burned when they were showered with a chemical compound. The accident occurred when they went to the top of an 80-foot cracking tower and started to remove a metal disk between a valve and a 3-inch vent line through which pressure normally escaped. "They believed," according to investigators, "that the pressure in the pipe had been turned off. Apparently, it was still on." Again, if they had known that since they had made no observation, any knowledge about pressure in the pipe was only inferential and not factual, they might have checked and been alive today.

In a less serious vein is a Christmas news item about a man who had ordered a load of coal. He heard noise coming from the cellar. The noise ended and the doorbell rang. He went to the door and gave the two men standing there money for the coal. A little later the coal arrived. The money had gone to the ash collectors who undoubtedly were surprised at the size of their "Christmas gift." But if this makes you too cheerful, consider the case of the man who was churned to death in a pulp-mixing vat when a fellow worker turned on the "empty" machine while he was inside cleaning the paddles.

It is most important that we understand that there is nothing wrong with making inferences. We have to much of the time. The misevaluation arises when we *act as if* our inferential knowledge were factual knowledge. Make inferences, but know that they are inferences! This knowledge makes an exceedingly important difference in our behavior in any situation. Our actions, attitudes, expectations will be different—*and they are much more likely to be appropriate for the situation.* We can summarize this as follows. If we know that we are making an inference and not a factual statement, then: (1) We are less sure of what we assert, and therefore are less likely to assert it dogmatically. (2) We are prepared to be proved wrong, and therefore are much less likely to be hurt, physically and emotionally, if we are proved wrong. (3) We expect the unexpected and therefore are more prepared for it.

The big difference, then, is an attitudinal one. If we know our statements in a particular case are inferential and not factual, we do not feel insulted when they turn out to be wrong; but if we thought they were factual, then most likely we would resort to any number of face-saving devices which in the end would only make things worse.

We find this confusion of factual and inferential knowledge in almost all areas of human behavior. There would be no soap operas without it, and what a calamity that would be! The heroine sees her husband getting into a car with a strange woman and knows for sure that he is having an affair. Does she bother to check? Not she—she knows her knowledge is factual and not inferential. Of course, if she did check she would find out immediately it is really her husband's long-lost sister, whom he had never mentioned because she had disgraced the family forty-five years ago. Besides, that would ruin the plot and end it in five minutes instead of dragging it out for eight months before she learns the truth. Watch the "situation comedies" on television and try spotting this misevaluation. It's fun, informative—and nauseating.

But this trouble is not confined to pulp literature. In the very best literature of every nation, the same pattern of misevaluation is to be found again and again. Think of Romeo in the tomb when he sees Juliet stretched out on a slab. "Dead," says he, so he kills himself. She wakes up, really checks, then kills herself. Think of Othello and the inferences he makes about Desdemona, or consider Hamlet when he runs his sword through the curtain. Think of De Maupassant's "The Necklace" or the "Piece of String." Good literature is, to some extent, a mirror of life, and the widespread occurrence of this pattern of misevaluation is evidence that people of all kinds and all levels of intelligence have been victims of it.

Even those of us with some knowledge of general semantics can fall victims to this confusion. I have ridden in the automobile of a man who knows something about general semantics and this business about the difference between factual and inferential knowledge. Intellectually he agrees that knowing the difference makes a difference. But it doesn't seem to change his behavior. He races through a blind intersection where there is no light or stop sign as if he had factual knowledge that another car was not coming down the cross street. It is "pure luck" that keeps him alive and thousands of other drivers like him.

I maintain that no man who has really learned general semantics can drive like this. This does not mean that one must become a "creeper" who would be dangerous in traffic. Rather, it means a little more sense in estimating the degree of reliability of one's knowledge of the traffic situation. Nor does it mean that one should become a back-seat driver; that is not the time to teach or learn these things. Personally, I simply relax and let fate take its course. There is nothing I can do about it except get out and walk. Incidently this professor is an excellent driver, mechanically. His reflexes are fast, he can get out of tight spots without losing his head, he can maneuver quickly. This has been found to be generally typical of the accident-prone driver. He depends on his skill to escape hazardous situations into which he gets when he acts on his wild inferences as if they were factual knowledge.

To repeat: Such people may know intellectually that they have only inferential knowledge about what is going on over the hill or around the curve or what the driver ahead is going to do, yet it makes no significant change in their behavior. Agreed there may be other factors involved, such as a desire to show off or to get a thrill, or the aftermath of an argument with the wife or even Freud's "death wish." No matter! Each of these is a form of infantile semantic reaction to a situation. For example, there is the failure to be able to index "emotionally" as well as "intellectually," between situation 1 (argument with wife at home) and situation 2 (riding in a car without her). No matter that some of the causes of these patterns of behavior may be traced back to childhood! They are still examples of a breakdown in proper abstracting. All of them involve a misguided inference acted upon as factual knowledge. Some might even be quite unconscious: e.g., the inference that driving this way will cause others to applaud one's skill; or the inference that this wild "thrill" driving will solve the inner conflicts, anxieties, boredom—it may, temporarily, but at the risk of life and the ever-recurring need to "up the dosage." All these factors intermix and mutually reinforce each other.

Our contention is that when the habit of recognizing inferences for what they are sinks in deeply enough—and this takes much time and effort—gradually those parts of one's reactions and habits which are caused by the confusion of inferential and factual knowledge will come to be recognized. The thrill driver may learn to ask himself, "Why am I doing this? Am I really getting the results I think I am? Are there better ways of solving my problems?" The angry man may learn to say, "It's no use taking my anger out on the car; it solves no problem. What's a better way?" Just being able to recognize the hidden inferences, or even being able to ask oneself if one is making them, is a big step toward more mature behavior. If one keeps harping on the importance of distinguishing between the two, after a while it may dawn on us that this applies in important areas in our lives and can produce a difference in behavior that makes a difference.

It is quite true that many times we are not in a position to check our inferences. But the general semanticist maintains that just knowing they are inferences will have a beneficial effect upon behavior in terms of expectations, preparation for being proved wrong, etc. We do not claim that the confusion of inferential and factual knowledge is *the* cause of tragedy in life or in literature. There are many other factors. It is our theory, however, that if a person is trained in this knowledge, preferably from childhood, acting upon it will become a habit, a habit that pays off in more mature behavior when the really critical and important situations occur.

Teaching the Difference: Is That "Really" Grandma?

How can the importance of observation and checking be taught to children? They can learn it as part of every subject. I've seen children spot a dozen misevaluations in *Little Red Riding Hood*. *Aesop's Fables* have provided endless sources. Even comic strips can be learning devices. If we cannot keep the children (and adults) from reading them let's put them to use. If you can't beat 'em, join 'em!

History is another fruitful area for finding this and other patterns of misevaluation. How many crucial battles have hinged on a commander's making an inference about the enemy and proceeding to act as if he had factual knowledge, when a little checking—possible in many cases, but not in all—might have changed his orders? Suppose the Trojans had checked that wooden horse? Of course, it is important in using historical material to stress the fact that in many cases it was not possible to check the inferences and that it is very easy for us to have the wisdom that comes with hindsight. But there are many instances where it seems quite probable that if the people involved had been more explicitly aware of the differences between factual and inferential knowledge, they would have acted more appropriately.

One of the saddest things I find in my classes, even at the graduate level, is the reverence students have for the printed page, especially textbooks. If it's in the book it must be true! It comes as a great shock to most of them when they hear that statements such as "Napoleon was defeated at Waterloo," "Caesar crossed the Rubicon," "Washington was the first president of the United States," are not factual statements at all. The only factual statement we can make concerning these occurrences is one such as this: "This book says that Napoleon was defeated at Waterloo." Practically all our historical knowledge is inferential and therefore is neither true nor false.

True and false apply only to factual statements. We can talk about inferences only in terms of degree of probability of being verified.

When the student recovers from this undermining of so much that he once dutifully and unquestioningly accepted as factual, he begins to reacquire those most important qualities which his education has usually managed to strangle quite efficiently—curiosity and the temerity to question authority. Now at least he has a tool for measuring what he receives! Knowing that it all has not been finally and absolutely said, that much of what is in the history books are mere hunches, best guesses (and bad guesses), hearsay evidence, and above all, the product of fallible and human writers who select some material and reject other on the basis, usually, of their own peculiar biases and interests, has a remarkably enlivening effect upon the spirits of the student. Now he becomes a part of the stream of knowledge. To some extent, no matter how small, his evaluation of the evidence the books present, counts. History is no longer a mass of factual data to be dutifully memorized, but a detective story to be unravelled by him if he is interested. A concomitant gain for him is the realization that different history books about the "same" period might not be alike, and it might be interesting to see what different authors have to say. Now the author himself becomes important. *His* history is seen to have an effect on the history he writes. It has been a gratifying experience to me as a teacher to see the amazement of students who for the first time read a British history of the American Revolution or a Southerner's history of the Civil War (pardon me—the War Between the States). Then the questions which arise are not "Who is right? Who is wrong? Which is true? Which is false?" but "Which is more likely to be substantiated in the light of other sources, other evidence?" They are no longer shocked when the books disagree. As a result, they come to expect these differences on important issues and suspect the authors of plagiarism (scholarship) when they don't find them. Best of all, history comes alive because it is seen as a product of living people and therefore something that is being constantly rewritten and reëvaluated.

The general semanticist doesn't pretend that this view of history is his own invention. Most competent historians accept it and probably have impressed it upon their students. As evidence we have the famous statement that, "Caesar crosses a different Rubicon every year." But sometimes, at least in my classes, such ideas seem totally new to most of the students. Obvious though this knowledge may be, it never seems to have dawned upon them, and it strikes many as most peculiar that they learn it, not in the history class, but in one that is focused upon linguistic structure.

THE LAWS OF NATURE:
ARE THEY DISCOVERED OR CREATED BY MAN?

It is no secret, of course, that even in the so-called exact sciences, exactness is relative because of the effect of the observer upon the observed. The laws of nature are more man's than they are nature's. How do we get them? Are they discovered or invented? Like most either-or questions about the material world, the split is only a verbal one. They are both discovered and invented. By using many controlled observations and experiments, scientists note certain recurring similarities in a series of events and when these are quantified through the use of mathematics, we get "a law of nature." The meaning of these similarities is given to us by theory which in part guided the observations and in part is derived from them. But in noting the similarities, differences which are considered not to make a difference are neglected in order to make the law precise.

As an example take the law of gravitation. What is it? It is a statement, a factual statement, based upon many verified observations and an inference that what has happened in the past will continue to happen in the future. We have no way of knowing or proving that it will. If we write it out in mathematical form, $D = \frac{1}{2}gt^2$, the formula tells us how far any object will fall in a given time under given conditions. The conditions are remarkable because they do not exist and have never been observed to exist. They are so-called "ideal conditions." The object must fall in a perfect vacuum and must not be influenced by any force other than gravitation. Since these conditions are never found, the law is a generalization which never applies exactly in any particular situation. If you want to know where and how far this book will fall when dropped from the window at this moment, you have to put away your pencil and paper and get over to the window and look. Otherwise you can make no factual statements, only informed guesses, inferences based upon the law.

This state of affairs does not bother the physical scientist. He knows that his theories are "as if" affairs—complex inferential structures. Even though he has never seen an individual atom, he builds models of atomic structures. How, for example, can he account for the chemical activity of various elements? In effect—and this is a tremendous oversimplification—he says, "Let us suppose that an atom of chlorine is composed of a nucleus with a certain number of positive and negative charges, and let us suppose that there are planetary electrons arranged in such and such a way. Now, if it has this structure, and if I do this with it, then such and such should happen." So he performs his experiment and his prediction comes true. He then repeats his experiments, proposes that others test the theory, and finally says, "Yes, the atom of chlorine has such a structure." But this is purely inferential knowledge, and he never claims that it is factual. It may have a very high degree of probability of being correct, but it is still an inference.

THE SCIENTIST "VERSUS" THE LAYMAN: MAPS THAT FIT THE TERRITORY

The scientist, when he acts as a scientist, does two things a layman often fails to do. First, he knows that he is making inferences, not factual statements, and proceeds to check them. The layman often confuses the two, and neither bothers to check nor sees the necessity for doing so. Secondly, the scientist is not personally insulted if his inferences turn out to be wrong. In fact, he deliberately tries to prove himself wrong by devising experiments which, if successful, would destroy his theory. How many of us do this in daily life? This does not mean that the scientist is some sort of superman. Quite frequently, as soon as he leaves his laboratory, he acts as much like a fool as the rest of us. Just why there is so little carry-over from the laboratory to personal affairs is a complex problem we shall touch on later. It is sufficient to say here that one reason seems to be that the nature of his work forces him to use a language whose structure fits that part of reality with which he is dealing. Outside the laboratory he uses the language of the layman, a map whose structure seldom fits the territory. According to Wendell Johnson, what one aims to accomplish through the scientific method can be summarized in one word: prediction. Although the scientist strives to accumulate factual knowledge, his chief reason for doing so is to enable him to build theories with a high degree of predictability. In this way we gain control over our environment. In similar fashion, the general semanticist aims at using a language whose structure enables him to make statements with a high degree of probability of being verified, provided this is his intent in a given case. Note that it is not the general semanticist's desire to make *every* statement verifiable, as we shall see in our discussion of phatic communion.

This is one of the meanings of the term "language structure."

The general semanticist is not so much interested in the grammatical structure of the language as he is in its implicatory structure. If we make a statement about persons, things, or events, what does it imply that we will find out about their structure if we go out and look at them? Note that he does not ask what a thing *is,* but rather how it is being used: not what *is* he, but what does he say? If we say he *is* a Communist, the language implies a simplicity not to be found when we go look at him. It implies that we have a nice, neat, sharp, definition of Communist which will fit all to whom the label is applied. It implies that he will act the way we say Communists act in all situations and at all times, and it implies that our definition of Communist is the only possible valid one. There are apparently many people who use this simple verbal map which fits no known territory when we try to check it. The structure of the language is not similar to the structure of the situation.

When our maps do not fit the territory, when we act as if our inferences are factual knowledge, we prepare ourselves for a world that isn't there. If this happens often enough, the inevitable result is frustration and an ever-increasing tendency to warp the territory to fit our maps. We see what we want to see, and the more we see it, the more likely we are to reinforce this distorted perception, in the familiar circular and spiral feedback pattern.

Much of the time, we are not aware of the implications of the structure in the language we use daily. Thus if I say, "It is raining in Philadelphia," there is nothing in the grammatical structure of the sentence to indicate whether this is an inferential or a factual statement. The implication is that there is no difference. Grammatically, the sentence is classed as a declarative statement which is either true or false, with the implication that it must be one or the other. However, if it is an inference true and false do not apply and we should not attempt to apply them. How many of our most heated arguments, both personal and political, involve an attempt to apply these terms to inferential statements because we have never learned the futility of such an attempt!

A Look Ahead

In later chapters we shall talk about the elementalistic structure of the language we use in daily life, its polar structure, and its static structure. The first means that we split verbally that which cannot be split non-verbally; the implication is that because it can be done verbally it must be so on the non-verbal level. For example, we argue about heredity versus environment and physical versus mental. Verbally, we can discuss heredity as if it existed apart from the environment and the physical body as if it existed apart from the mind. But when we make observations, nowhere do we find an organism without an environment or a mind without a body; rather, we discover all these factors inextricably interwoven and interconnected. We shall make a map much closer to the territory if we ask, "To what degree do psychological factors play a part in this illness?" instead of, "Is it mental or physical?" But because we can split them verbally, the implication of the language is such that we think we will find these splits in nature. So we look for them, and not finding them, warp our findings to fit our maps instead of changing the maps to fit the findings.

By the polar, two-valued structure of our language, we mean, in part, that as commonly used, language is heavily loaded with polar terms such as good-bad, black-white, beautiful-ugly. Such terms imply a simplicity not found in reality. Most of us know that we seldom find these extremes. It is a cliché to state that there is good and bad in everyone or that we are a complex mixture of all these qualities. The problem is that too often we act as if we do not know these things and categorically label one side all good and the other all bad. "You are either for us or against us," we cry in international affairs. Maybe it is not as simple as that. At least India claims this. The more we proclaim this dichotomy, the more natural and logical it seems and the more "right" it feels.

The static implications of our language are almost self-evident. He *is* an X; she *is* a Y; once a Z, *always* a Z. No indication of the process of change here. If you swallowed the Party line in 1935, no matter if you and times have changed; everyone knows, "Once a Z, always a Z." The general semanticist recognizes that there are many reasons for clinging to absurd positions other than the structure of the language in which they are expressed. But he maintains that if people were explicitly trained over the years to be aware of process and complexity and to reflect this in their talking, then, as with the explicit recognition of the differences between factual and inferential knowledge, they would be less likely to fall into this pattern of misevaluation.

Let us take an extreme case—the man who feels that people are always talking about him, plotting against him, hating him. He *knows* this is true. To him it is factual knowledge and needs no check-ing. He twists the meaning of any utterance to confirm these infer-ences; he warps the territory to fit the map. This is the classical pic-ture of the paranoid. How did he get that way? There are many factors, and treating and curing him is a long, difficult, tedious, and often unsuccessful job for a skilled psychotherapist. It it most in-teresting to note that if he finally is cured, the cure, in effect, means getting him to "see" that he has been confusing inferential and factual knowledge. Is it not probable that *one* of the factors that contributed to his becoming a "mental case" was his unawareness of the differ-ences between the two and his consequent constant confusion of them? We shall try to present some evidence for this in other chapters. Only when language and thought are elementalistically split, can the idea of the mutual interconnection and interdependence of the two be discounted.

SUMMARY

A factual statement can be defined as a descriptive statement made after observation (which includes any sensory perception) and verifiable by accepted standards. The methods of verification and the standards used are determined by the purposes of the experiment or operation in the context in which the statement is made and by past experiences with similar cases. Theoretical issues also play a part in the setting up and selection of standards. Thus for weighing sugar in a grocery store a scale accurate to ⅛ of an ounce is the accepted standard. Past experience and pragmatic issues are almost the sole dictators, in this case, of the standards chosen. When we desire to weigh the amount of sugar in the bloodstream, the standards and methods used are chosen on the basis of past experience and also on theoretical issues, such as the presence of biological factors which interfere with extraction of the sugar, pH of the bloodstream, and rate of metabolism.

Factual statements approach, but never reach, certainty. Two factors are involved. First, all observation is relative to the structure and state of the organs of observation and these change continuously. Second, events never repeat exactly. Verification, by definition, requires at the minimum, two observations of the "same" event. But the "same" event never occurs again. So we have a changing organism reacting to a changing event. Absolute certainty, then, is an impossibility.

Inferential statements go beyond a description of what has been observed. They have widely varying degrees of probability of being correct because they are not linked directly to observation but represent a jump into the unknown which may or may not take off from verified observation. Some inferential statements, such as "The sun will rise tomorrow," have such a high degree of probability of being correct, that they can for most purposes be acted upon as if they were factual statements. But they are still inference, as are all statements about the future or that part of the past not directly observed by the maker of the statement.

There is nothing wrong with making inferences; we have to most of the time. The chief function of science is to produce theories—complexes of inferences—having a high degree of predictability. The misevaluation arises when we act as if our inferential knowledge were factual knowledge. If we know we are making an inference, we are less likely to assert it dogmatically; we will, if possible, check it before acting; and we will be prepared for the unexpected. If we are making factual statements, we can be reasonably certain we are correct and, therefore, do not expect the unexpected to happen.

The confusion of inferential and factual knowledge is a causative factor in many accidents, needless quarrels, and misunderstandings ranging from the comic to the tragic. It is found in practically all forms of literature where plot is an important element in the story and, in a sense, is an indication that this pattern of misevaluation has always been with us. Finally, we find it present in the language and thought of the neurotic and psychotic.

By "structure of the language" we mean, among other things, its implicatory structure. Language serves to predict that the referent, upon observation, will have a certain structure. If this prediction is verified, we say that the map fits the territory. When our language makes no clear distinctions between inferential and factual knowledge, there is the implication that no such distinction is needed and hence nothing is lost by identifying, that is, confusing them.

The thesis of the chapter is this: Knowing the differences between inferential and factual knowledge will help keep us from making as much of a fool of ourselves as we usually do.

❀ 3 ❀

Some Limitations of Language

IRVING J. LEE often likened language to a tool, perhaps man's most important one, more useful than fire, the wheel, or atomic energy. It is most likely that none of these, most certainly not the latter, could ever have been put to use by a non-symbol-using creature. But, like any tool, language has its limitations. There are certain things we cannot do with it, and the attempt to make it do what it cannot do often leads to trouble.

In expanding upon this, Lee compared language with a fish net. The very small fish escape from the web; the very large ones cannot be encircled. In the case of language, the small fry are the infinite details of the material world; no matter how fine we weave the mesh, an infinity escape. We can never describe completely even the simplest bit of matter. We can never exhaust what could be said about a single grain of sand. For convenience, and by utter necessity, we concentrate on a large number (though relatively few) of the characteristics of grains of sand, noting those similarities important to us at the moment and neglecting differences which seem to make no difference for our generalizations. In this way we come to talk about "properties" of sand. These are the fish—descriptions and inferences—for which the net of language is most suited.

But there is something very peculiar about the catch: it is non-existent. It is as though the fish had slipped from their skins and what we have left is lifeless and unchanging, a dull and hazy replica of the ones that got away. For words are *about things;* they are *not* the things themselves. The world of things is constantly changing; it"is" bright, hard, soft, green, rosy, acrid, black, burnt, rubbery, loud, sharp, velvety, bitter, hot, freezing, silent, flowing, massive, ephemeral, wispy, granitic. Or rather, these are the names we use for the way it seems to us. Above all, it appears "real"; it is not words. Whatever we call a thing, whatever we say it is, it is not. For whatever we *say* is words, and words are words and not things. The words are maps, and the map is not the territory. The map is static; the territory constantly flows. Words are always about the past or the unborn future, never about the living present. The present is ever too quick for them; by the time the words are out, it is gone. When we forget this, we tend to act as if words were things, and because they are so much more easily manipulated and molded to our desires, there is the danger of building maps that fit no known territory and the greater danger of not caring whether or not they do. We then tend more and more to live in the past and the future and we lose the present, the sense of nowness, the feeling of the immediacy, mystery, and flow of the sensory world; we drift into the gray, dead world of words.

THE QUEERNESS OF THINGNESS:
WHAT IS RED LIKE, "REALLY"?

The non-verbal quality of the sensory world—the world of thingness—is the large fish which escapes the net of language. If you were asked to decribe the color "red" to a man blind from birth, you would very quickly discover that this is an absolute impossibility. No matter what you said, you could never convey to him the sensation you experience when you see a color called red. The same observation applies to smells, tastes, sounds—any sensory perceptions. They are literally unspeakable, as are all feelings and emotions. During his lectures, Alfred Korzybski would ask the members of the audience to pinch themselves, to concentrate on the feeling, and then try to describe the pain. It does no good to say sharp, dull, or prickly, for then you have to describe these words, *ad infinitum.* Incidentally, it might interest the reader to know that it is quite difficult to get some people, especially the more sophisticated intellectuals, to perform this little experiment. It is silly, childish, and obvious. They "know" words are not things. But to really know it on all levels of abstraction, one must actually do and experience this non-verbal act. If not, then one is acting as if his words were the actual sensations.

All that words—descriptions and labels—can do is evoke sensations and feelings which the reader or listener has already experienced. They can never transmit new experience. If one has never experienced what is described, one is absolutely incapable of experiencing it through description alone. No woman can make me feel what it is like to give birth to a child. I may infer it is similar to a bad case of cramps, but I will never know, no matter what she says. Since I know that a toothache differs in "quality" from a headache, and that a burn does not feel like bruised skin, it is a reasonable inference on my part that birth pains are different in some respects from anything I have ever experienced or ever will.

This poses an interesting question. If you feel a pain in your jaw and say, "I have a toothache," have you made an inferential or factual statement? Certainly it has been made after observation, but what about verification by accepted standards? What is the accepted standard for sensations, feelings, emotions? It can only be the person experiencing them. Only you can feel your pain and the experience itself represents the verification. Your statement is a factual one for you and inferential for everyone else. We can only guess that you are reporting the "truth" about your feelings.

The limitations of language go even further. I have no way of knowing what "red" looks like even to another sighted person. He cannot tell me; I cannot check. I can only infer that what he experiences is similar to what I experience. It cannot be identical because our nervous systems are different, and an experience is a product of both what is "out there" and the way the organism reacts to it. But in order to get on with the business of living together and reaching some kind of agreement, we are forced to assume a similarity in response. The danger lies in our forgetting that this similarity is only a convenient inference. There may be important differences in what different people perceive in the "same" situation or in what one individual perceives at different moments. Hundreds of experiments designed by psychologists, physiologists, and others demonstrate this dependence of perception upon both the structure of the stimulus and the structure and state of the responding organ.

Let us take a simple example. Eat a lump of sugar and concentrate on the taste. Then take another and another. After a few lumps, the sweetness changes. It may become cloying or its sweetness may be diminished. What has happened? Has the sugar changed its taste? If you say no, you have become satiated, but the sweetness of the sugar is the same, why do you assume that the first taste of sugar is the "real" taste, and that after six lumps it is less "real"?

Or place a piece of red paper on a gray background. Place another piece of the same paper on a bright green background. Compare the two and you will find that the pieces of red paper look different. Which is the "real" color? It won't do to say that the real color is that of the red paper by itself. It is never by itself; there is always a background. Which is the right background? One is as arbitrary as the other.

We could go on and on with this. How about the color-blind man who presumably sees only a shade of gray when he looks at your red sheet? Who is seeing the correct, the "real" color? If you say you are because your range of color perception is greater than his, consider these facts: The majority of people cannot see ultraviolet light. If we filter out light in the range of the visible spectrum, red to violet, in an ultraviolet lamp, the average person would see nothing and would say that the lamp is not lit. However, it has been discovered that a few people do see a fraction of the ultraviolet range. This means that they see a color they cannot describe to us if we are one of the majority who cannot see ultraviolet light, and we cannot imagine what the color is like. It is no good to say it is like violet; that would be like saying green must be like yellow because it follows it in the spectrum. If you have seen yellow but never green, you cannot imagine, on the basis of yellow, what green is like.

Now, since there is, normally, ultraviolet light in daylight, it will be reflected from the "red" sheet of paper, so that the person who can see ultraviolet light will see a different shade of "red," that is, red and ultraviolet. Which is the "real" color of "red," his or ours?

We met this problem before when we tried to find the "real" height of the table, which upon analysis we found to be a meaningless, unanswerable question. A similar solution can be found in this case by tracing the sequence of events. Light waves (shower of particles?), reflected from the paper to our eyes, are electromagnetic waves and have no color. These waves hit our eyes and give rise to a series of complex psychophysical responses, resulting in the sensation red, gray, or some other color. Two things should be noted here. First, the electromagnetic (light) waves have no qualities (no color, sounds, smells) and their existence is inferred. Second, when a response is aroused in an organism, that response is in terms of some sensation like red, gray, etc. The particular quality of the response depends upon the structure and condition of the organ and the organism. Given a different organism, a different sensation arises in response to the "same" electromagnetic waves. Thus, the light *waves* produce this sensation of *light* in the organism, but one is not the other

Incidentally, by distinguishing between sound waves and sound, we can speedily dispatch that old riddle concerning the tree that falls in the forest when no one is about. Does it make a sound? The answer is no! We infer that the tree produces sound waves, a reasonable inference based on past factual data on falling objects. But sound is sensation produced in and by an organism as a result of being stimulated by sound waves (which are not sound) and until such an organism is present, the tree makes no sound. If a man is present when the tree falls, it is a factual statement for him to say, "I hear a sound," provided he is not deaf. But any statement I make about his hearing it is purely inferential.

WHAT IS A QUALITY?: TO-ME-NESS

In asking what is the "real" color of a piece of paper, we imply that color is *in* the paper, that it exists independently of the responding organism. But since the color, or any quality for that matter, is a product of both the observer and the observed, in order to make language fit these facts as discovered by science, we must change the question to, "What color does it appear to me at this moment?" In this way, the structure of the language fits the structure of reality. By adding "to me at this time," we imply in our language a universe characterized by constant change, one whose qualities are given it, projected upon it, by a responding organism. By omitting these words, we imply a simple, absolute, static world where the organism is simply a mirror, largely a distorting one, of an ideal world whose qualities are independent of and unchanged by the observer.

This may not matter much when talking about color, taste, or sound, but when we are evaluating the realm of the social, it makes quite a difference whether one says "Johnny is bad" or "Johnny appears bad to me now." If he *is* bad, he has badness in him; it is a part of him, and he is always bad in everything he does and will appear that way to every "normal" observer. When we add "to me, now," we imply there is a possibility that he may not appear that way to everyone else. We are more prepared to consider other evaluations of his behavior, on the possibility that they may be more accurate than our own. Actually, if I tell you Johnny is bad, I tell you very little about him other than that I probably dislike him if I dislike those I label bad. If I say that he appears bad to me, I invite the obvious questions, "What kind of behavior do you call bad? What did Johnny do?" If I then describe what he did, we might discover that you do not consider such behavior bad; rather, to you, it may show that Johnny is independent and self-reliant. To Mr. X, this behavior may mean Johnny is trying to hide his insecurity and lack of parental affection. Who is right? All may be partly right and partly wrong, but at least the situation can be discussed on a much more objective, descriptive level. The probability of agreement and of more appropriate behavior with respect to Johnny is much greater. When we say *and mean,* "It appears this way to me," we invite checking, discussion, reëvaluation. When we say, "It is," we cut off further investigation. It is the contention of the general semanticist that the constant, conscious use of the "to me" will help make proper evaluation more likely, for language structure influences thought, behavior, and feelings. Constant talking in absolute terms produces a feeling of the "rightness" of such patterns of evaluation, and this emotional barrier is most difficult to crack in attempting to change behavior. It stifles questioning the appropriateness of patterns of evaluation and talking both by the speaker himself and by others, and is one of the foundation stones in man's grimmest prison—prejudice.

CRACKING THE LANGUAGE BARRIER: PHATIC COMMUNION

Because feelings, sensations, and emotions cannot be transmitted by language, but only evoked in the listener, and because of our great need to find out how others feel and to communicate our own feelings to them, we spend much time trying to crack this sound barrier. A writer uses hundreds of examples, descriptions, image-evoking words, hoping they will be similar enough to past experiences of the reader to provoke his memory and recreate a similar non-verbal reaction in him. For this reason it may take an entire novel or play to make a simple point. One of the themes of the play, *Death Takes a Holiday,* is that love is stronger than the fear of death. Why doesn't the author simply make the statement and call it quits? Obviously because it doesn't work; we don't "feel" this by reading one sentence. It takes the writer with his shotgun loaded with pellets of description to wing the emotions of the reader.

Another technique we use in our attempt to overcome this lingustic barrier, interestingly enough, involves the use of non-symbolic language, the language of sound as such. This is the language of lovers and infants and animals, and we all use it in addition to symbolic language. Bronislaw Malinowski called it "phatic communion."

When Fido growls and bares his teeth, he is letting us and other animals know that he is angry. When the baby howls and bares his gums, he communicates to us his unhappiness. And Fido and the baby are equally adept at reading our feelings by the tone of our voice totally apart from the verbal meanings of the words used. All of us gather our impressions of a person's sincerity, for example, by the inflections of his voice, not by any protestation by him.

Not only do sounds serve to convey expressions of feelings, but also the general musculature of the body plays a part in this type of communication. The good poker player "reads" the faces (the tiny movements of the muscles around the eyes and mouth) of the other players to see if they are bluffing or suppressing excitement. Indeed, there is evidence to suggest that the very young infant is frighteningly adept at picking up the "true" feelings of his mother toward him, which she herself may have repressed. Thus, if she unconsciously rejects him and, feeling guilty, talks fondly or rather, uses fond language, he will feel this rejection by "reading" the inflections in her voice and the tensions in her muscles.

WHEN SENSE IS NONSENSE

Much social talk is in the same category. It is our attempt to escape the desperate loneliness that is, in a sense, our lot. No one can know how we feel, what we see; nor we, they. Each is a solitude. No logic or analysis or theorizing is nearly as effective in softening this aloneness as phatic communion. Misevaluation enters when we expect them to. It has been stated that a bore is a man who, when you greet him with, "How are you?" tells you. You are not really asking about his health but saying, "Let's be friends." If you are fixing a flat tire on a hot day and a passerby asks, "Got a flat?," he is asking you to be friendly. If you take his words literally, you are likely to become angry and say, "Any damn fool can see I have."

It is often a temptation to snicker or feel very superior to the logically absurd "itsy bitsy boo" talk of lovers. But if we remember that it is the sound, not the literal meaning that conveys the affection in this case, then any attempt to talk "sense" in this kind of situation is itself a form of nonsense. Consequently the general semanticist does not demand that we talk sense all the time. All he asks is that we distinguish between situations that call for big talk and those that do better with small talk, and not confuse the two or try to pass off one as the other. Small talk is the oil in social machinery. Big talk—logic, theorizing, factual statements—will help solve the problems; small talk eases the way.

Most commonly both types of communication occur simultaneously and in varying degrees, which serves to complicate mutual understanding and gives the lie to the assertion that facts speak for themselves. Meaning occurs on all levels of abstraction, and differs in character at each level. At the feeling level it is a diffuse, deep, primitive, alogical meaning expressed in the scream of anguish, the coo of affection, the snarl of hatred, the *tra la la* of the poet.

SIGNAL "VERSUS" SYMBOL REACTIONS:
DELAYED REACTIONS

Subverbal responses, called signs by some writers and signal reactions by Alfred Korzybski, must be distinguished from verbal or symbol responses or reactions. When you hit your thumb and howl with pain, the howl is a sign of the pain, an undelayed signal reaction. When the lookout crow gives a danger "caw" at the approach of the farmer, it is a sign that he senses danger. In these cases the distinguishing characteristic is that the vocal or other signal response is undelayed. The feeling and sign of it are almost synchronous.

Symbol reactions, on the other hand, are delayed responses. "It hurts" are words *about* feelings or a painful occurrence and are of a higher order of abstraction than the undelayed howl. They require some "thinking." An infant jabbed with a pin will scream—a signal reaction; the scream is a sign of his pain. It does not take long, however, before he learns to howl deliberately to attract attention; the scream is now a symbol response. Just where the dividing line is we cannot say. There is probably a continuum from the undelayed signal response to the delayed symbol reaction which may even involve a delay of years. For example, a student may feel that he is unjustly treated by a teacher. But he delays his response until he graduates and then goes back to give the teacher a piece of his mind.

One of the aims of general semantics training is the development of the habit of delaying responses, thus increasing the chances that our responses will be more appropriate for the situation. The delay does not have to be more than a fraction of a second in many cases, just enough to pass from the unmediated signal reaction to the modified, thought-out symbol behavior. This may mean the difference between acting like an animal and behaving like a man. The man who "blows his top" at the drop of a hat, who gets fighting mad at the mention of a word like yellow, chicken, or Communist, never gives the higher orders of abstraction a chance to operate, so his responses are less likely to fit the occasion. He is at the mercy of his feelings and may soon regret his actions. Of course, there are some occasions where "instantaneous" response is most appropriate. When a brick is falling from a building and you are under it, if someone yells, "Look out!" there doesn't seem to be much time for evaluating the situation. Yet even here a quick glance might tell you which way to jump or you might jump under the brick.

SOME DEVICES FOR DELAYING RESPONSES: THE INDEX, THE DATE, THE ETC.

The general semanticist contends that too often signal responses are made where symbol reactions would be more appropriate. Learning a general pattern of delaying response is more likely to produce proper evaluation. Three semantic devices for achieving this end are the date, the index, and the *etc.* Korzybski was fond of repeating that if one could just learn to use these three in all situations, he could forget all of general semantics theory and still have the most important part of the system. *Theoretically,* if we could learn to introduce these devices into all our evaluations and have the habit sink down to the feeling level, we could never become neurotic or psychotic; we would never indulge in the wrong kind of worry. We shall have much to say about this later, but one example, which we shall bring up again, will suffice at this point. This is the classical case of the young man who comes to the psychiatrist because, among other things, he hates women. After some probing, the psychiatrist discovers that his trouble began in childhood when his mother maltreated and rejected him. He soon both hated her and felt guilty about it. This hatred was soon generalized to all women. After perhaps a year of treatment, or two or three, after much difficult and trying work on the part of both patient and therapist, he is "cured." In effect, he is "cured" when he can apply the three devices to his illness. As a result of therapy he learns to index his hatred. On the insight, feeling level, he "sees" that woman 1, his mother, is not woman 2, 3, 4. He then learns to put a date on his hatred. It was proper to hate his mother as a child; twenty years later, both he, she, and times have changed. Finally he learns to add the *etc.* to his evaluation of her actions; that is, he learns there is more to be said about the situation. Maybe she couldn't help what she did, or she didn't realize the significance of her actions, or maybe he was expecting too much of her or maybe . . . .

The general semanticist does not maintain that merely by saying "person 1 isn't person 2, time 1 isn't time 2, and there is more to be said," this young man could cure himself. But we do think that if over a long period of time, preferably from childhood, we are trained to talk this way, there is more chance that we will not wind up on the psychiatrist's couch. The time to make the use of these devices habitual is not when the pinch is on, but over the long run of relatively unstressed situations.

These devices make the structure of the language fit the structure of reality. As far as proper evaluation is concerned, the three basic characteristics of the world around us are that events are infinitely complex, they are changing all the time, and no two are identical. If this is so, then dating statements implies a constantly changing in-process reality. Indexing referents implies non-identity of events. The addition of an *etc.* to statements indicates that in the face of the complexity of things and the limitations of our knowledge, there is always more to be said. This practice cannot help but have some inhibiting effect upon the tendency in all of us to be dogmatic and absolutistic. The constant use of these devices makes it "feel right" and obvious to do so; this in turn increases the chances of our using them and producing maps that fit the territory.

When we fail to use these semantic devices we fall into the "all-ness" pattern of evaluation characterized by statements such as, "Everyone knows Negroes are inferior people," "You can't tell me anything about Mexicans. I was brought up among them," "Once a criminal, always a criminal."

Consider the difference it would have made if Senator McCarthy had been taught to use these devices so that he and others of his ilk could have been able to say, "The fact that this man joined the Communist Party in 1934 does not necessarily mean he is a Communist today." Or, "Not all of those who joined movements to the left of my political position are necessarily Communist Party members." Or, perhaps best of all, "Perhaps my definition of a Communist is not the only possible valid and useful one." Now it is quite possible that a man who joined the Party in 1934 is still a member today and just as possible that many liberals are being deceived by Communist front organizations. But we can't be sure until we do some careful checking. If we are victims of the "allness pattern," verification and the more mature pattern of behavior will be automatically and effectively short-circuited. Our language patterns then do the thinking for us.

Reports of marriage counselors are filled with remarks flung at one another by couples whose marriages are on the rocks: "You always burn the toast," "You always make a fool of yourself at parties," "You never think about what I want," "You never really loved me," "Your mother always tries to get me," "All men are alike; you can't trust them." Granted such statements may be motivated by factors other than conscious evaluation of the marital situation. They may reflect unconscious hatreds, projections, etc., but it would be much more difficult for a person to speak this way if he had consciously acquired the habit of indexing and dating his statements.

Constant failure to use these semantic devices invites further use of the "allness pattern" and reinforces the unconscious drives which help sustain it. We shall have more to say about the mutual inter-action of conscious and unconscious factors in later chapters. We shall conclude this chapter by repeating something we have already empha-sized and shall continue to emphasize throughout this book: Although everyone knows this stuff, all of us at one time or another act as if we don't. Nobody really believes that words are things, that things never change. Still, in hundreds of ways we act as if we do. Read the letters sent to the editors of newspapers and magazines or to "advice to the lovelorn" columnists, for example, and note how frequently are found the words "never," "all," "everyone knows," "they say." Such letters imply a simplicity not to be found in the people and situations they presume to describe. Nor is this failing limited to the few who write letters. The editors and columnists themselves are frequently as guilty as their correspondents—often, I presume, deliberately and with malice aforethought. We are surrounded by tabloids, digests, sum-maries, condensations of all types which presume to give "all" the "really important" news that is fit (and fitted) to print.

The complexity and variety of daily events does necessitate some selection and condensation. Nevertheless an awareness on our part that something important probably has been left out, that distortion and bias most likely are present, can, perhaps, diminish the chances of a misevaluation of important events. The deliberate and constant use of semantic devices helps to provoke and maintain the vitally important awareness of the dangers of oversimplification, dogmatism, and static-mindedness, and aids in the development of that sophisticated innocence which enables us to look with a fresh and inquiring eye upon the world around us.

❊❊ 4 ❊❊

The Abstracting Process

WE have discussed in some detail, and in various ways, the notion of linguistic structure. Structure of any kind involves an ordering of parts and relationships among these parts, between the parts and the whole, between the parts and the environment, and between the whole and the environment. In living organisms these relationships can be described in terms of function. The four multiordinal inter-related terms—order, function, relation, structure—are basic to general semantics. Any situation, object, event, or occurrence can be better understood when it is analyzed in terms of structure and function, rather than in the static Aristotelian system of essential properties.

In this chapter we shall try to draw together some of the diverse elements we have discussed, give them some kind of order, and try to show some of the relationships among them. I shall also present, in modified form, a model or diagram created by Korzybski which he called the "Structural Differential." It is, in a way, a map of the whole of general semantics. As its name implies, it sets out the structure of general semantics and at the same time differentiates the substructures or orders of abstraction that make it up, as well as the orders of these orders, by assigning relative values to them in terms of their importance to us.

THE EVENT LEVEL: NO THINGNESS

According to modern science, everything in the universe is composed of atomic structures of various complexities interrelated in some fashion with a variety of electromagnetic waves or energy manifestations. Our concepts of these relationships are changing almost daily and need not concern us here except in a general way. The important point for the general semanticist is that without atoms and electromagnetic waves there would be no universe as we know it. This atomic level of events is therefore most important.

Korzybski called this basic level the "event level"; goings-on are "events." All of us are familiar with pictures of this level: there are billions of atoms in a pinhead of matter; they are moving at tremendous speeds and in all directions. Each kind of atom has its own peculiar structure or specific variations of it (isotopes). The electromagnetic spectrum runs from the very short waves such as cosmic rays to increasingly longer waves such as x-rays, gamma rays, ultraviolet light, visible light, infrared waves, heat waves, to very long radio waves. If we had to characterize this level of events we would use three terms: infinite complexity, constant change, non-identity of events. No two events are identical and there can never be any repetition of a given state of affairs because all measurements take place at a given time and, by definition, time moves on.

It is useless to say, "Maybe events do duplicate, do repeat," for the simple reason that there is no known or, at the moment, even imaginable way of determining whether they do or not. We could find out only by running an experiment which takes place at a given time. The next experiment to determine duplication takes place at another time and, according to Einsteinian physics, the time of any occurrence is one of its characteristics. Here again we see one of the faults in our linguistic structure. Verbally, we can talk as if space and matter and time existed independently, but any examination of the world around us shows that all matter exists at a time in some space. Consequently a better verbal map would be "matter-space-time."

If all of this seems queer, consider that all our knowledge of atomic structures and electromagnetic vibrations is purely inferential. We cannot see, smell, or touch individual atoms. We cannot see light waves vibrating at billions of vibrations per second, travelling at 186,000 miles per second. One of the best analogies to describe this state of affairs is the example of the unopenable watch. Suppose a little green creature from Planet X drops out of his flying saucer into our laboratory. He sees a watch, but it is sealed and he has no way of opening it. He can see the hands moving at certain speeds, and he can hear ticking. He would like to know how it works, so after a lot of pondering, he draws a diagram of a certain arrangement of wheels, gears and springs, and says that if the watch had that internal structure its hands would move the way they do. Then he builds a model and lo! The hands do move like the watch's. So, says he, "That is the structure of it." But we know that we can have a number of watch mechanisms producing these "same" results. If he could build several models representing different mechanisms and they all produced the "same" results, he would have no way of choosing between them, no way of saying, "This one is it really."

In practice, the scientist keeps producing newer and newer models, each a little better than its predecessors. It is judged better because it accounts more simply for more facts observed in experiment, and gives a wider range of predictability as to what will happen if we perform other experiments. But we can never be certain that our models are correct, because we can never make direct observation. Events (goings-on on the atomic level), we would say, have inferential existence.

Now we move to the next higher level of existence. All living organisms are irritable, that is, they respond in certain ways to stimuli from their environment, both internal and external. The simple amoeba can respond in a gross way to strong light; it moves away from it. But since it has no eyes, it is most probable that it forms no images. It cannot see as do higher organisms such as dogs, cows, and men. Nor can it hear the way we can for it has no ears, though it probably, again in a gross way, responds to intense vibrations. As we move up the evolutionary scale, we find animals with specialized organs such as eyes and ears for responding to stimuli. But the numbers and kinds of these organs are very limited. We, along with all other creatures, miss most of what is going on—as inferred by science.

Korzybski called this responding to the environment "the process of abstraction." We abstract—pick out, respond to, are sensitive to, pay attention to—certain stimuli and miss or cannot abstract the rest. We have no organs to detect x-rays, cosmic rays, or radio waves. What we abstract is always in terms of feelings and sensations of some kind. Electromagnetic waves of certain wave lengths hit our eyes and through a complex process, about which very little is known, we get the sensation of light, color, shape. Through an equally mysterious process, we project this image and see things as being "out there" instead of in the head. Below and above certain wave lengths in the spectrum most of us see nothing; we cannot see ultraviolet light or infrared. It is thought that bees can see ultraviolet light, but we cannot imagine what it looks like to them.

What one will abstract—perceive—at any given moment depends on many factors. Some of them are: (1) Our position in space; we cannot see all sides of an object at once. (2) The structure of the perceiving organ. (3) The psychophysiological condition of the organ and the entire organism in which it is functioning. Fatigue, disease, accommodation, and adaptation change responses to stimuli. Motivation is very important; we tend to see, hear, taste, what we want and expect, with past experience, language patterns, and emotional factors playing a large part in what is finally abstracted.

SEMANTIC REACTIONS

There have been numerous experiments performed to show the parts the above factors play in perception such as the Ames experiment with distorted rooms and the influence of labels upon what is abstracted. If a man is told he is eating rat meat, what he tastes, sees, smells, and feels will be quite different from what he would abstract if the meat had been labeled pork. A rose by any other name would definitely not smell as sweet. Perfume manufacturers know this when they give exotic names to their products. Prejudice, bias, unconscious factors all play their parts. It is an extremely complex, dynamic affair and all these factors interact to produce in response to a given stimulus, a certain complexity of feelings and sensations. This total dynamic response of the organism to words and other stimuli in connection with their meanings on all levels of abstraction is called a "semantic reaction."

What we abstract, then, is never a mirror image of "reality," but an interpretation of the interaction between the atomic goings-on and our psychophysiological responses to them. During the process of abstraction, much "information" is lost due to our lack of receptors for many kinds of information (ultraviolet light, cosmic rays, and so on), and also much "misinformation" or "noise" or "distortion" is introduced into our interpretation by the very activity of the nervous system itself.

THE ABSTRACTING PROCESS AND AMPLIFIER THEORY

Recent developments in feedback and information theory have contributed much to our understanding of the abstracting process. John R. Platt has introduced a rather novel concept which he calls "amplifier theory." It is based upon "the parallels between biological responses in all living systems and electronic amplification processes." He writes:

The general principles of amplification are shown in the operation of many familiar devices. A radio or television set amplifies radio waves and transforms them into sound or visual patterns. A photoelectric cell or photomultiplier tube amplifies faint light signals of a certain kind to which the amplifier responds. For the radio and the photocell, and for the eye, the least detectable signal might be a single photon or quantum of radiant energy, but usually it will include several photons, enough to produce a response above the background noise level. The sense of smell requires chemical amplifiers whose input signal consists of a few molecules of certain particular chemicals that come in and react and initiate a chemical and electrical neural pulse.

The amplifier uses the energy of the selected input signal to trigger a much larger release of output energy. These two energies may have any ratio, provided the output is strong enough to be relatively immune to statistical fluctuation. For a photomultiplier tube the energy amplification factor within the tube may be measured in millions, and the current released may then move a relay to control thousands or millions of times more energy still. In the biological amplifiers of the retina, the energy of the elementary light signal may be multiplied thousands of time in producing a single neural spike; and such a spike may operate a kind of biological relay and be multiplied thousands of times more in the energy of a gross motor response.[1]

Platt finds that certain features are common to all amplifiers, whether biological or man-made. For example, the structure of the sensory organ in the living organism or the "sensing" mechanism—the transducer—in the machine determines the kind of signal detected.

Man-made amplifiers, with electronic amplification, and sensory nerve endings, with chemical and electrical amplification, must transduce their input signals into electrical or chemical terms before the signals can be amplified. In a photomultiplier the input transducer is the photocathode which converts photons of incident light into emitted electrons. In a radio, it is the antenna. In the eye, it must be a retinal pigment molecule

[1] John R. Platt, "Amplification Aspects of Biological Response and Mental Activity," *American Scientist*, vol. 44, no. 2 (April, 1956), pp. 180–183.

capable of photochemical change. What each amplifier responds to depends entirely on the nature of its transducer.

After noting many other similarities between biological and man-made amplifiers, Platt draws these conclusions:

1) *Amplification requires selection.* Even with the same kind of input transducer, a separation of two amplifiers in space implies a separation and selection in inputs. This is what makes direction vision possible.

The input transducer is functionally selective as well as spatially selective. An indiscriminate amplifier that responded equally to every kind of input, that is, to every fluctuation in its environment, would be useless physically and biologically. It would not be an amplifier at all but only a site of continuous power dissipation.

2) *The dimensionality of the output is always less than the dimensionality of the potential input field.* For each sensory amplifier, the field of all possible inputs is, of course, inferred and not observed. But it is at least as manifold as the realm of known physical variables which we know from observing other amplifiers having other input transducers and having apparently independent response patterns. This potential information is thrown away by each particular amplifier. It cannot enter into information theory which only deals with sensory amplifier *output* information—for this is the code translating the raw stimulus field into the language of the information network.

My radio set is useful because it gives such a highly limited response to its environments. It ignores wind velocity and bacterial population. Even among radio waves, it ignores in its own dimension, alas, those signals too weak or rapid for a faithful response. But in other dimensions, happily, it omits the whole multiply-infinite electro-magnetic spectrum of communication it is not tuned to.

3) *Information is always lost in an amplifier.* Here I speak of the potential information leaving the input transducer. The amplifier adds noise and distortion and transformations, such as changing the signal from radio to audio frequency or cropping it to produce a pulse in its *own* dimension; the output does not represent all the input information.

4) *All that an observer on the output side knows about the input is the one output variable.* This is all a single amplifier can tell us about what

it "saw." All that we can respond to is the output, for our response is but a further amplification.

Thus we see that although information is lost and distorted in the abstracting process, this factor is vitally important to the functioning of the organism. If we responded to every stimulus we could not function. Choice and selectivity are inherent in living at every biological level. Similarly, although the amplification introduces new "information" which is not present in the incoming signals and distorts that which is received, without this amplification we could not react to them.

THE OBJECT LEVEL: WHATEVER YOU SAY IT IS, IT IS NOT

Let us return to our discussion of the Structural Differential. On my desk is an object labeled "pen." The scientists tell me it is composed of atoms and reflects and gives off various energy manifestations. It reflects light waves which produce the sensations in my eye called "green and gold." Its atoms are formed into certain molecular structures to which my nose is sensitive. I label the smell "inky." The molecular structures labeled "styrene polymer" I cannot detect at all. By inference, according to the manufacturer, they are there. I do not, cannot, abstract any odor from the metal clip, though any broken-down mutt could. He could pick out this pen by smell from a dozen others. He can abstract what I cannot. I touch the barrel and get a sensation I label "smooth," though if I looked at it under a microscope I could see hills and valleys in it. Presumably, to a microscopic animal crawling over it, it would be rough. In my childhood, I was frightened by a gross of pens; whenever I see one my stomach flip-flops. Joe, here, when a child, fell into water but saved himself from drowning by hanging on to a case of pens floating by. He gets all warm and glowy when he sees one. These feelings affect what we abstract. To him it means friend and the colors are warm; to me it means foe and it looks cold and repulsive.

Now for the difficult part. This object I label pen—what is it "really"? It is the mass of sensations aroused in me by the goings-on on the atomic level. This sentence is the right answer and it is completely false to fact, because the sentence is verbal and the sensations are not. In response to the question, I should stick the pen in my mouth, sniff it, look at it, feel it, *and not say a word*. What my senses "tell" me, that's what it "is."

At this level of abstraction, language can communicate nothing. On the contrary, the attempt to use it can hinder non-verbal communication; it can block what the senses have to "tell" us. It is true that how we label an object will modify what we abstract, what we perceive, what our semantic reactions will be. Naming a flower helps us to recognize it. By placing it in a botanical category we, in effect, say, "Look for the pointed leaves, the five petals, the elongated pistil, the bulbous base, and other characteristics of this *species*." But, at the same time, such categorization can cause us to neglect characteristics that are peculiar to this particular flower. In other words, categorizing and naming an object tend to call attention to similarities between the object and the class to which it is assigned, and to neglect individual differences. And the differences are often more important than the similarities, especially when dealing with people. This tendency is carried to an extreme in prejudiced behavior where the label we applied to a person almost completely replaces looking at him as a unique individual who is not a Catholic or Jew or Negro or anything else we may call him. What is he "really?" Look at him, listen to him, and stop labeling him! Theories about the influence of his race, culture, or religion, on his character may help you to understand why he acts as you think he does, or it may not, but whatever you say he is, he is not. Your saying is words and most certainly those words, though they help determine how you perceive him, are not the man.

The point is this: If we stop talking about the object, our senses communicate to us a different message. This is not necessarily a better message, though it may be. The important thing is that we learn something about the object that is hidden when we talk. The words get in our eyes. One of the most frequent complaints of those who produce abstract art is that people will not or cannot look at the work simply as a structure of shapes, forms, colors, and shadows to be enjoyed on a purely sensual level. They have to know what it *is,* what it is called, what it represents. When the artist replies, "Look, what you see is what it is," he is apt to be called a faker—which he may be, but not because his work is non-representational. As long as people insist on being told what it is or what it represents, they will never find out.

The basis of this insistence on naming is the assumption, largely unquestioned, that a thing is static and unchanging, having an essence or set of qualities in it independent of the observer. If this were the case, then giving it a name would help us pin it down. But when its qualities—shape, size, color—are a function of the abstracting nervous system and, therefore, are different for every observer and from moment to moment, then giving it a fixed name used by all and at all times can never tell what it "is."

TECHNIQUES OF SILENCE

A number of techniques have been devised by general semanticists for learning silence on the non-verbal level. One, suggested by Wendell Johnson in his *People in Quandaries,* is a sort of game you play with yourself. Seat yourself at a desk or table in a quiet room. Pick up an object and feel its texture, look at it from various angles, smell it, and say nothing to yourself. Concentrate on the sensations. The moment you find yourself saying, "It is a pencil, it is red, it is smooth," drop it. The object of the game is to see how long you can stay on the non-verbal level and keep from moving to the verbal level of abstraction. At first it may appear impossible to keep from talking. If you persist, however, after a few weeks you may be able to up your time from a few seconds to minutes.

Another technique is even simpler. Start feeling things, closing your eyes to concentrate as much as possible on the varieties of textures your fingers will communicate to you when you stop verbalizing. Or concentrate on the taste of some food. You may have been eating it for years yet never really savored the multitude of textures, odors, and tastes because you have been so busy talking and thinking while eating. Try being a gourmet a few minutes each day. Try listening to instrumental music, closing your eyes and concentrating on the flow of pattern and sound without trying to verbalize its significance and meaning.

It is useless to think about performing these experiments, talk about their usefulness or absurdity, or theorize about their significance. All of this is verbalization and can tell you nothing about what you will experience if you actually perform them. If you do work at them faithfully a few minutes or more a day, you will begin to discover a world you never knew existed—or at best only hazily. Literally, a new world is discovered, a new set of semantic reactions becomes possible. There is nothing magical about this, though sometimes the results seem to be; it's not hypnosis or hallucination or anything abnormal. Rather, it is the discovery of powers of abstraction only dimly experienced previously because they had been buried under a smothering blanket of words. This is the world of the artist and poet, the portal to mystic experience and transcendental vision which great works of art, literature, and music can evoke. This is the level of abstraction on which we live our most intimate and personal life. It is the most important level of experience, for it is the level of feeling and sensation and emotion.

The verbal level, with its plotting, planning, theorizing, predicting, operates in the final analysis for the sake of the non-verbal and not *vice versa*. This is one reason the general semanticist assigns more

value to this level than to the verbal level. This is not to say that
the verbal level is valueless—far from it. It is extremely important,
a level of abstraction achieved only by man. It is his unique and
distinguishing characteristic, and the foundation of civilization. In
the evolutionary scene, it has come last and serves to increase man's
chances of survival because it gives him greater control over his environment than any other creature. But we are jumping the gun
again; we haven't come to the verbal level yet, so we will save
further discussion of what is meant by the relative importance of the
various levels of abstraction for later chapters.

'Twixt Empiricist and Skeptic: Is the Desk Still There When I Leave the Room?

One of the most difficult things to understand about the abstracting process is that the event level has no characteristics. Atoms and
electromagnetic vibrations have no color, no size, no shape, no taste.
Literally they are no-thing. "Thingness" arises as a result of their
impinging upon a nervous system capable of responding to them.
However, we cannot imagine nothingness. All experience and im-
aginings are in terms of sensory experiences, so talk and thought
about atoms and atomic structures must be in terms of size, shape,
structure. No harm or falsification arises as long as we realize that
we are projecting our sensory experiences onto the non-sensory level
of events. Trouble comes when we forget or do not realize this, and
begin to talk about the qualities of atoms as if they existed independently of an abstracting organism.

When we remember that we are dealing with two different levels of
abstraction we are no longer caught on the horns of the dilemma
which have impaled extreme empiricists like Locke and extreme
skeptics like Berkeley and Hume.

We can explain this statement best through an example. Suppose
you and I are in a room. We see before us a desk which appears to

have color, texture, shape. I leave the room. Question: Is the desk still there? The empiricist says yes, the skeptic no. The argument of the skeptic can be summarized in Berkeley's words, "To exist is to be perceived." All we can know about the world is what our senses give us. This is the only reality we can know and since our sensations, and therefore the qualities of any object, exist only in our minds, then everything is "internal" and there can be no "outside world."

The general semanticist would answer the question by examining it more closely. The word producing the dilemma is "the." It implies that there is one desk, the same to all observers. Actually, the question should be reworded to read, "Is *my* desk still there?" Any desk, any object, is *my* object. It is what my nervous system creates out of the mass of stimuli from the atomic level. When you respond to these "atomic" stimuli, you create your desk, your complex of semantic reactions. *We create the world as we perceive it.* When I leave the room, what remains, I infer, are the atomic phenomena, and this is not a desk. But *the* (my) desk, which is my response to the atomic phenomena and in me, disappears. If you remain in the room your desk remains with you and your desk is always different from mine because your nervous system is different from mine. So, once more, we see that the dilemma has been created by a semantic confusion of two different levels of abstraction. The structure of the language used did not conform to the structure of reality as given us by Science, 1959.

Note that we have not proved that anything exists outside our minds. This cannot be done. But Berkeley's conclusion that everything exists inside the mind is just as incapable of proof. General semanticists would say that the existence of atomic phenomena, the event level of abstraction, is inferential. Why make these inferences if they cannot be proved to be a fact? Because by making them we gain control of the environment. By acting as if they existed we build drugs, metals, radio sets, and hydrogen bombs. We believe in atoms because in the final analysis, it works. Actually we have no alternative but to act as if we believed in an external world; otherwise we would never plan for the next meal or the next task or the next moment. The most extreme skeptic would quickly die of starvation or wind up in an insane asylum if he followed his beliefs to their logical conclusion.

THE VERBAL LEVEL: WHAT DO WE CALL IT?

All animals cease abstracting at the non-verbal level, the object level. Only man has the ability, presumably based upon the development of his cortex, to move to the next level of abstraction—the verbal. The higher apes show rudimentary symbol-using activity, but so little as compared with man's that for all practical purposes we can say that man alone has a symbol-using capacity. Not only does he abstract on the object level but he can talk about what he abstracts and can represent it in symbols of various kinds.

THE LOWER ORDERS: DESCRIPTIONS AND NAMES

The verbal level can be subdivided into the lower orders of description and naming of individual objects and the higher orders of inference, generalizations, and class terms. We know relatively little about the neurological centers which may be involved in the different levels of activity, but there is some evidence, largely of a negative kind, based upon the study of brain-damaged individuals such as aphasics, that the ability to handle inferences, generalizations, and class terms depends upon the use of cortical areas not needed for the lower verbal level. When these higher centers are damaged, the person loses the ability to use and comprehend class terms and abstract ideas, just as young children cannot understand them until these cortical areas mature. I doubt whether the distinction between the two is as sharp as I imply in my description of them, but for convenience we shall assume it. We shall have much more to say about the significance of this qualitative difference between the two verbal orders in subsequent chapters.

Here on my desk is an object whose qualities I have formed by abstracting from (reacting to) the event level. The object is not words, but I can talk about it. I can label it "pen$_1$", the subscript indicating that this is my name for the particular object before me. What does pen$_1$ mean to me at this moment? It means, roughly, an object about 5 inches long, smooth, green and gold body with a clip, ballpoint with blue ink in it. These are the characteristics in the object, pen$_1$, which I abstract. The scratches on the barrel and the taste of the ink and plastic are not included in my meaning-at-the-moment of the word pen$_1$. To a manufacturer of these pens, the smell of the plastic, the springiness of the clip, the tightness of the fit of the parts are important and would form a part of his meaning of the term. In other words, what I abstract from the object level is different from what he abstracts to form the meanings of the label pen$_1$. In both cases, each of us neglects to abstract many characteristics we could discover in the object upon close observation.

Thus, past experience with similar objects, purposes of the moment, context in which the word is used, motivation, and many other conscious and unconscious factors help determine which characteristics of an object will be abstracted at any given moment to form the verbal meaning of the name. Just as the object has fewer characteristics than the event, so the name refers to fewer characteristics than can actually be discovered in the object. As we proceed to higher orders of abstraction, we leave out more and more characteristics.

THE HIGHER ORDERS: INFERENCES AND CLASS TERMS

Abstracting does not stop at this first verbal level. The next level consists of class terms, generalizations, and inferences. I can talk about the class "pens" or "pens-in-general." Class terms refer to fictional entities. The label pen$_1$ refers to a specific object. "Pens-in-general" or the class "pens" refers to no particular existing thing. The class "pens" has no objective existence. If I asked you to show me "pens" you could not do so. You might show me pen₁, pen₂, pen₃, but these would be individual objects, each differing from the other, and the word "pens" as a class term refers to no one specific pen you could point out. Like the tree and the forest, all you can discover on looking are individual trees. By neglecting the characteristics peculiar to any particular tree, we can move to the next order of abstraction and talk about the forest, which has no objective existence. By knowing only a few similarities and neglecting most of the differences we form the class term, "forest." What exists on the object level are individual trees, all different from each other. By abstracting only the similar characteristics we build in our minds a very convenient fiction—the forest. It is a fiction because the term refers to no discoverable object; all you can discover—see—are the individual trees.

Perhaps it might be more clear if we use the word, "triangle." We can have triangles of all shapes, each an individual, triangle₁, triangle₂, triangle₃. A higher order of abstraction refers to triangularity, which is characteristic of triangles-in-general. Triangularity is not a quality or characteristic of any particular triangle, but arises as a result of comparing individual triangles. The construct triangularity arises as a *result* of the comparison and is not discovered in any one triangle. You cannot point to triangularity in any individual triangle.

The Process of Classification:
That Peculiar Average Man

Class terms and classes, then, are at least one step removed from the non-verbal level, as opposed to individual names for objects which are on the first verbal level (or order) of abstraction. Classes of anything are man-made and do not exist in the same sense that objects exist. Their existence is a product of our ability to produce higher-order abstractions. An excellent example is the "average man." He has no objective existence; he can be found nowhere. Because he has no objective existence, he has characteristics not to be found in any particular man. For example, he can have 3.2 children, a feat impossible for even the most unaverage male. He is a most valuable creation because he enables us, for example, to manufacture suits by the millions. The only trouble is they fit him much more precisely than they do any living man. This does not matter much with suits, but when we begin to talk about his ideals, his tastes, his habits, we are on much more dangerous ground. Forgetting that he is a fiction we may try to force living people to fit the fiction, rather than readjust the fiction when we apply it to any particular man. The "average man" is so much more tractable, uniform, and convenient to handle than his lower-order counterparts that frequently we ostracize or even imprison or execute people for not conforming with the ideal Marxist man, True American, Good Neighbor, Executive Type, Typical Worker, True Believer, Our Kind of People, or Them.

As stated earlier, these higher-order abstractions are valuable in that they enable us to deal efficiently with large numbers of items. The "average man" may represent eighty million individual men. On a statistical basis, what we say about him may have a high degree of probability of being correct—for example, an insurance chart of life expectancy. But it must be remembered that this chart holds good *only for the group as a whole.* It tells very little about how long any one particular man will live. Now the "group as a whole" is a high-order abstraction and does not have objective existence, as an individual man exists on the object level; therefore, the life expectancy chart is good only for this higher-order abstraction and not for the lower-order abstraction, the individual. Therefore the insurance company is not especially perturbed when one of its clients departs this best of all possible worlds at age 30 instead of 65. He will be balanced out by the thousands who will linger well into the 60's.

Classes, such as plants, animals, men, women, mammals, do not exist in nature. These are all higher-order abstractions created by us because it is convenient to do so. As stated before, we create these classes by noting similarities and disregarding differences. Which similarities we note depends upon all those factors which influence abstracting at any level.

Take our little green creature from the flying saucer. He breeds vegetatively. There are no sexes among his kind. When he first encounters what we call men and women, he won't see males and females, for sex is meaningless to him, and the anatomical differences in the sexual organs will not be a basis for classification. However, let us say that his source of food and energy is the blood of animals which he obtains by biting into the neck of his victim like a vampire bat. But, unlike the bat, this blood goes directly into his blood stream and its type must therefore be the same as his own. Consequently he classifies earthlings by blood type and not by sex. Incidentally, we do the same thing in blood transfusion; sex never enters the picture.

BUT WHAT IS IT, "REALLY"?

Thus we see that we can put an individual thing, animate or inanimate, into as many categories as we choose and we fall into a familiar pattern of misevaluation when we say one is more real than another. I am sitting on something most people call a chair. But suppose I do not use it to sit on but to prop open a door? Is it a chair or a doorstop? Or if I burn it in a stove, is it a chair or firewood? Or if a child turns it upside down and crawls under it, is it a chair or a castle or a tunnel or a refuge or a dog house? If we persist in classifying it as a chair, we are, in effect, saying that its classification is independent of us, that it has the qualities of "chairness" in it. Actually, we call it a chair because, presumably, it was manufactured for sitting purposes, and we assume that most people would use it for that purpose—unless, of course, they are savages who never saw or use chairs, and they don't count anyway. Thus the purpose for which it was originally designed determines its classification. Is it not reasonable, then, to say that if its uses change, so does the classification? Most of us, I presume, are familiar with droodles. We see a conglomeration of lines and ask, "What is it?" Until the man who drew it tells us, it can be any of a dozen or more things. It is interesting to note that as soon as it is named (classified) it suddenly takes on a recognizable shape. If it is called something else, the same lines take on a different shape. What is it "really"? Since it is a set of symbols and not a thing, it is whatever we are told it is. If it were an object then of course one answer is simply to wave the hand, and another is to rephrase the question to "What do you call it?," the implication being that you can call it anything you please depending on your purpose of the moment.

The difficulty many people have in accepting and understanding the idea that categories, classes, laws of nature, etc., are higher-order abstractions and do not exist "out there" can be traced to the fact that their education has been largely along Aristotelian lines. Bruner put it this way:

> To one raised in western culture, things that are treated as if they were equivalent seem not like man-made classes but like the products of nature . . . .
> Our intellectual history is marked by a heritage of naive realism. For Newton science was a voyage of discovery on an uncharted sea. The objective of the voyage was to discover the islands of truth. The truth existed in nature. Contemporary science has been hard put to shake the

yoke of this dogma. Science and common sense inquiry alike do not discover the ways in which events are grouped in the world; they invent ways of grouping. The test of the invention is the predictive benefits that result from the use of invented categories . . . . Do such categories as tomatoes, lions, snobs, atoms and mammalia exist? Insofar as they have been invented and found applicable to instances of nature, they do. They exist as inventions, not as discoveries.[2]

THE SOCIAL LAWS: OF TIDES AND TRENDS

When we recognize that classes and classifications are man-made we gain tremendous flexibility in evaluation. Seeing them as man-made we feel free to change them. We become their masters instead of their slaves. Thus higher-order abstractions such as "the law of supply and demand" or any other so-called economic laws, are seen simply as rough predictions as to how a given group of people in a given culture at a given time will react under a given set of economic conditions. By selecting the conditions, the culture, the time, we can create as many laws as we wish; change the variables and the law changes. How good these laws are depends upon their predictability, simplicity, and range of application. If the predictability is low, as it is with most economic laws, the law in question is not very good. It does no good to say that, "other things being equal, in an ideal society where there is perfectly free competition, with no cartels, price fixing, etc., where people are not guided or misguided by irrational, emotional, moral, or religious factors and customs, the law of supply and demand holds and therefore, there is such a law and we must conform to it." If the conditions under which it is said to operate have never been observed and only very roughly approximated, then it is not enough to say that because it seems logical it should work. There must be verified observation

[2] J. S. Bruner, J. J. Goodnow, and G. A. Austin, *A Study of Thinking*, New York, John Wiley and Sons, 1956, p. 7.

before any factual statement can be made. Logic alone is not sufficient, for it is only verbal, and proof requires non-verbal as well as verbal confirmation.

As much as one may have disliked Franklin D. Roosevelt and his policies, we must at least give him credit for recognizing that economic laws are man-made statements about the ways of men and can be changed by changing the conditions under which they are supposed to operate. He refused to be bound by the "boom or bust" cycle which many businessmen and economists claimed governed capitalistic society. Stuart Chase in his book, *The Proper Study of Mankind,* quotes one Congressman who, in 1929, said that he would no more question the law of supply and demand than he would the movements of the tides. Roosevelt did question this and other economic "laws," did interfere with the business cycle, and the sky did not fall in.

I do not wish to imply that economics or any other social science is useless. Rather, I feel that not enough reliable data have been gathered upon which to build these laws. They were built too soon, by men who had an oversimple view of man and society. They are maps that do not fit any recognizable territory. Our job is to assemble the data, run the experiments, and then build more reliable laws. This is much more complex and difficult than deriving laws in the physical sciences for at least two reasons: first, the difficulty of manipulating people; second, the running of the experiment itself changes the conditions of the experiment. Dropping a ball from a given height to determine how fast it will fall does not make the ball change its speed. But when you experiment on people, the knowledge that they are being used as guinea pigs changes the results. I must also add at this point that in this respect general semantics is in the same boat as the other social sciences, for much of it is based on these sciences and therefore its "laws" are also open to questioning.

ORDER₁, ORDER₂: DOES THE BARBER SHAVE HIMSELF?

An interesting example of the difficulties we get into when we do not realize that classifications are arbitrary affairs is the following familiar paradox: In a certain town there is a barber who shaves every man who does not shave himself. Does the barber shave himself? The paradox is unsolvable as long as one assumes that a man *is* a barber and this can be his only classification. The paradox dissolves when we realize that a man is classified as a barber only when he is barbering other people and that as soon as he barbers himself he is no longer a barber but is now to be classified as a man who shaves himself. If we leave out the category "barber" and just say, "There is a man in town who shaves everyone who does not shave himself," we still are acting as if the classification is rigid and not man-made. When the man is shaving other people his classification becomes "man who shaves other people." When he shaves himself, he belongs to another category, "man who shaves himself." And we also have to fix a date to our statements. We must remember that all these classifications are arbitrary and man-made and should be changed when the thing classified or its use changes.

Theoretically, we can proceed indefinitely to higher and higher orders of abstraction. From "pens-in-general" we can move to the higher level "writing instruments" which would include pencils and typewriters as well as pens. Note that writing instruments refers to fewer characteristics actually to be found in the object "pen" than those terms lower in the abstracting sequence such as "pen₁" though it brings in other characteristics (of the typewriter and pencil) not to be found in the original pen. That is, as we move to higher and higher levels of abstraction, we abstract fewer and fewer characteristics discoverable on the object level.

Similarly, beginning on the first verbal level of description and factual statements, we can move up to the next level of inferences, then proceed to make inferences about our inferences, or build theories upon these inferences onward and upward indefinitely. As we move up away from the object level, our chances of obtaining reliable knowledge about any *specific* object or situation become less and less. Thus, using the law of gravity, I may be able to predict whether an object will hit the ground if thrown horizontally with a given force under given conditions without ever looking at any specific object. But our prediction about whether it will hit the ground will never be as accurate as our actual observation of the object when it hits, because there are so many variables about which we do not have enough knowledge to make accurate predictions such as wind velocity, air density, or even little Joe who might run out and catch it before it hits the ground. Consequently a value judgment is placed on the different levels of abstraction. Lower-order abstractions are of more value than higher-order abstractions in proportion to their closeness to the object level as far as reliable knowledge of *specific* objects, occurrences, and situations is concerned, *but only in this respect.* In certain other respects higher-order abstractions are more valuable than lower, such as in making statements of predictions about larger classes of objects, occurrences, events, viz., the natural laws.

Bruner and his colleagues consider this categorizing ability the very heart of thinking, if we may mix a metaphor. They discern five achievements of categorizing:

1. [It] reduces the complexity of the environment.
2. [It is a] means by which objects of the world about us are identified. . . . When an event cannot be . . . categorized and identified, we experience terror in the face of the uncanny. And indeed, "the uncanny" is itself a category, if only a residual one.
3. [It] reduces the necessity of constant learning. For the abstraction of defining properties makes possible future acts of categorizing without benefit of further learning. We do not have to be taught *de novo* at each encounter that the object before us is or is not a tree.

4. [It provides] direction . . . for instrumental activity. To know . . . that a substance is "poison" is to know *in advance* about appropriate and inappropriate actions to be taken.

5. [It] allows for ordering and relating classes of events.[3]

However, because in our culture we tend so much toward the use of higher-order abstractions and the neglect of the dangers inherent in using generalizations, the general semanticist is forced to concentrate on emphasizing the necessity for moving down toward the descriptive and object levels for verification when generalizations are applied to an individual person or object.

We might, for example, make the generalization that, based on their history, Germans are a martial people. If we have had no personal contact with any Germans, if the only opportunity we have had to learn about them is from some history books, and if we are in a situation where some statement about Germans and martial tendencies is required of us, then making the generalization is the best we can do. If this is just chatter, we can leave it at that. But if this generalization is a poor one and if making it can do harm (and such generalizations usually do), it is important that we have more reliable knowledge, and so then we had better start checking through cross-references and through a series of observations. It must be emphasized that the statement, "Germans are martial," tells practically nothing about the individual Hans Schmidt. A generalization is never 100 percent true for every member of a class except in certain highly technical, never social, situations. And we can never be sure that this Hans Schmidt is not one of the most pacific individuals extant. If you let the generalizations get in your eyes, you won't be able to see him.

THE STRUCTURAL DIFFERENTIAL

The Structural Differential is a schematic representation of the

[3] *Ibid.*, pp. 12, 13.

abstracting process.[4] Occurrences on the atomic level are called events. They are infinitely complex, changing all the time, and no two are identical. This is represented by the mass of dots at the top of the diagram. Each dot represents one "characteristic" of the event, some atomic relationship or energy manifestation whose existence we infer. We have made this mass of dots shapeless to indicate, first, that it is indefinitely large and, second, that on this level there are no qualities such as color, size, shape, or taste. However, in order to think about this level and to make models, we project our sensations of qualities upon it and act as if atomic phenomena have at least size and shape. Note how the language forces misrepresentation. I am forced to use the term, "characteristic of the event," yet the event can have no characteristics, meaning shape, color, and the like.

A living organism which is affected by and capable of reacting to some of these atomic phenomena, will react to occurrences such as light waves, heat waves, molecular patterns, or atomic vibrations, to produce in his nervous system qualities he has labeled "color," "taste," "smell," "solidity." These form the object he abstracts from the event. Each circle in the diagram represents one of the "characteristics" abstracted. There is a large but finite number of these circles, indicating that he has not and cannot abstract all the characteristics of the event. Incidentally, the term "characteristic" should not really be applied to the event level, since it implies it has qualities such as the object has. But because any word would imply this anthropomorphism we put quotes around the word when it is used in connection with the event level.

The object, then, is the recognizable part of the event. The inner sphere represents those internal conditions of the organism which

---

[4] The diagram used here is a modification of Alfred Korzybski's Structural Differential as it appears in his *Science and Sanity,* by permission of Charlotte Schurchardt Read, Literary Executor of the Alfred Habdank Korzybski Estate.

A SCHEMATIC REPRESENTATION OF THE ABSTRACTING PROCESS

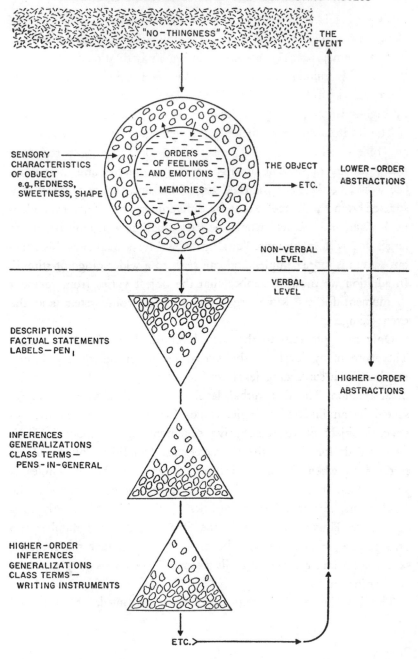

modify what is abstracted by the sensory organs at the moment of abstraction such as fatigue, memories, motivation, drives, needs, feelings, and emotions. The arrows pointing in both directions indicate that there is mutual interaction; how we feel modifies what we abstract and vice versa. We will leave for later discussion what is meant by high-order and low-order feelings and emotions.

The horizontal arrow labeled ETC. indicates that there should be an "object" drawn for every abstracting organism that reacts to this particular event. The arrangement of the circles and their number would be different for each organism, since no two objects abstracted from the "same" event by different organisms are ever identical. Thus, the "object" would be very small for an amoeba, much larger and with many more "quality circles" for a man since his nervous system is more complex and can react to a wider range of stimuli. In addition we must remember that the object varies from moment to moment for the same organism as its nervous system and the event change.

Only man proceeds to the next level of abstraction, the verbal. There are many levels to the verbal level—in theory, an infinite number. Each succeeding level represents a higher and higher order of abstraction. The first verbal level or order of abstraction, represented by an inverted triangle, stands for the name given the abstracted object or for descriptive statements made about it. Each circle stands for one of the characteristics (qualities) of the object referred to when the name is applied. The number of circles is smaller than those in the object because at any given moment the label refers, not to all characteristics of the object, but only to a certain set. Thus each time the label is used a different number and arrangement of circles would be drawn, showing that the meaning of the term and the corresponding semantic reactions vary with the context in which it is used.

The first line of circles represents those undefined, structure- and function-implying terms associated with the object such as "before," "behind," "on top of," "later," "sooner." These terms cannot be defined by other words. Their meaning is "felt," that is, it can be indicated non-verbally by pointing, waving of the hands, or other gestures, though the words themselves are spoken. They are the connecting links between the non-verbal and verbal levels.

Moving to the higher levels of abstraction, we find ourselves in the realm of class terms and inferences. The triangles indicate that these class terms refer to still fewer characteristics of the particular abstracted object which *might* have stimulated their use. As we move to the bottom of the triangle, more circles appear and these stand for those characteristics belonging to other members of the class but not to the abstracted object. And, of course, it is on this second verbal level that inferences begin. ETC. at the bottom of the diagram indicates that these abstractions can proceed indefinitely and the long arrow from the inference level to the event serves to emphasize that our knowledge of the event is purly inferential and that there is a circularity to the abstracting process.

One of the great values of the Structural Differential is its usefulness as a training device. By looking at it and by pointing to it as we talk, we can see that the object is not the event, that words are not the things they represent, that inferences are not factual statements. We see that class terms and inferences are at least a step removed from the non-verbal level, the level on which observations are made, and therefore are less likely to be correct than specific labels and descriptive statements.

Learning this "is not" pattern of evaluation is most important; using the eyes to see it and the arms to indicate it, as well as saying it, helps make this knowledge "sink down" to the feeling levels, where it can begin modifying behavior. Consequently, the Structural Differential is an important training device in centers where general semantics is taught.

One of the aims of learning general semantics is to make us conscious of the abstracting process. This consciousness makes it easier to avoid confusing and identifying (acting as if one level were the same as another) different levels of abstraction, for as we have previously stated, all patterns of misevaluation, from the most trivial to the most serious, can be described in terms of the confusion and identification of different levels.

Another source of misevaluation, a variation of the above, is the reversal of the abstracting process. Ideally the process should move from the non-verbal to the verbal levels and then back. An observation may be instigated or guided by higher-order abstractions such as theories and expectations, but these should only be aids and modifiers. They should not distort what is being observed. When such distortion becomes very great we say a person has hallucinations. If, for example, he develops a fanatical belief in the existence of ghosts (higher-order abstractions), he may suddenly start "seeing" them. Thus instead of observation giving rise to theories about what is seen, the theories produce sensations. If we give more value to higher-order abstractions than to lower-order observations, we are likely to distort what we see to make it fit the theories; we warp the territory to fit the map. This is a reversal of the natural, evolutionally evolved order of abstraction.

❋❋ 5 ❋❋

Some Consequences of Process Thinking

The Quick and the Dead

AS we move from the object level to the higher verbal levels, there is a gradual change in the psychological quality of the abstractions which can be recognized by introspection. Lower-order abstractions such as feelings and sensations are constantly changing, since they are the direct result of contact with the external world which itself is in constant change. If we assume that we are a product of evolutionary adaptation to the environment, this offers, perhaps, indirect verification of our assumption of the process character of the atomic level.

As we move away from the object level, the abstractions become more and more static and independent of the immediate environment. Descriptive and factual statements are intermediate. Based on direct observation, they must be changed as what they describe changes. But, since they are verbal and can be written, they are static as long as we care to keep them. However, in order to be adequate maps, they must be dated to indicate that the territory they describe has changed, even if they themselves have not.

Higher-order abstractions such as classifications are static. A tomato "is" a vegetable as long as we care to keep it in this category for the simple reason that we classified it as such in the first place. If, for some reason, we decide to call it a fruit (as per a

77

superior court decision earlier in this century—or maybe it was vice versa) then it becomes a fruit. Since a classification is a manipulation of symbols and not objects, it remains "put" until we decide to change it. This is not quite completely true because the meaning of the classification changes each time we use it, but compared to the constantly shifting nature of the lower-order abstractions, it can be considered so for practical purposes.

If these classifications purport to reflect some features of the non-verbal world, then as our knowledge of this world changes, the classifications should be changed, because they by themselves will not. Because they are a number of steps removed from the non-verbal level, there is a timeless quality to them. The law of gravitation has no date attached to it when it is used in the calculation of the movements of objects.

ALL ABOUT NOTHING: VALIDITY AND TRUTH

We can remove ourselves almost completely from the non-verbal world by manipulating symbols which have no non-verbal referent. Pure mathematics and pure logic are systems of symbol usage which have structure but no content. They consist of sets of rules for manipulating the symbols, but the symbols do not stand for any thing. As a consequence, they are completely timeless. In arithmetic, $1 + 1$ always equals 2 exactly—by definition. Note that we can make allness statements on these higher levels of abstraction because the non-verbal world does not intrude. However, the moment we make our $1 + 1$ stand for something on the object level, such as, say, a quart of water, then our map no longer fits the territory exactly.

In a pure mathematical system, true and false do not apply, only valid and invalid. True and false belong to the level of description and factual statement. They can be determined only after observation and, of course, are never completely certain. Valid and invalid apply to sets of relationships and are a measure of the consistency of a symbolic system. In mathematics, equations are solved by following the rules laid down for the system. When the rules are broken, the solution is invalid; if the system contains contradictory rules, it is destroyed. True and false are matters of degree and vary with the standards chosen. Valid and invalid are absolute terms, and there can be no in-betweens or varying degrees of validity, unless, of course, this is built into the symbolic system as part of the rules. But a rule must never be broken.

NON-ADDITIVITY: WHEN 1 + 1 NEVER EQUALS 2

On the non-verbal level, 1 + 1 never equals 2 exactly. If we actually add 1 cubic inch of water to another, we do not get exactly 2 cubic inches. There is always a loss of material involved in any transfer. Also, although the final volume may be very close to 2, the surface area has changed radically. The ratio of surface to volume in each cube is 8:1. When combined, this ratio is less, roughly 13.5:2 instead of 16:2.

Perhaps this doesn't matter very much when we add 2 pints of milk to a cake mix, but it is of extreme importance in living processes. Protoplasm is a colloidal system. Colloids are suspensions of very finely divided material in some medium. The ratio of surface area to the actual volume of suspended material is enormous. For example, milk is a colloidal suspension of casein in water, along with other dissolved and suspended substances such as sugar and fat. The casein particles are so small that 1 cubic inch of them has a surface area measured in hundreds of square feet. Since the ratio of surface area to total volume is so great, the electrostatic charges which accumulate on the surface of each particle play a great part in the stability of the system. A very small amount of acid will neutralize the charges which keep the particles from combining and as a result coagulation occurs. The particles of casein "add up" and the milk curdles. Cheese is proof that in the realm of things $1 + 1$ never exactly equals 2.

Protoplasm is even more sensitive to electrostatic charges and this accounts, in part, for its irritability—its "life." Neutralize the charges and it coagulates; the cell is dead. One small electrical charge or change in acidity may cause a cell to contract. Add "just one more" drop or charge and a vast change may take place, out of all proportion to the size of the increase; the cell may die. Although we add the charges arithmetically, the results are non-additive and it is the results that are of interest to us. In part, lightning results because the tiny particles of water suspended in a cloud have an electrical charge on their surfaces. When these particles coalesce, although the volume-to-volume ratio may be relatively the same, the ratio of surface area to volume decreases and there is not enough surface to "hold" the electrical charges; the surplus is discharged as lightning.

Perhaps the most dramatic example of this principle of non-additivity on the non-verbal level is the atomic bomb. Two "identical" subcritical masses of U-235 when kept separate can be melted, drilled, pounded, shot at and nothing much will happen. But when one is placed on the other—add them—an atomic explosion occurs.

In social affairs the failure to be aware of the non-additive nature of things can be disastrous. The driver who has "just one more for the road" is drinking and thinking additively, but the effect of that fourth drink is not just 25 percent more; it may be the difference between life and death, for the effects of alcohol do not mount in a straight line as the driver's language implies. One child plus one child makes two in a family. But think of the complications in human relationships it produces; it is not "just one more" mouth to feed.

In a way, this is recognized in the saying, "Two is company, three's a crowd," and in the other direction, "Two can live as cheaply as one." The trouble with the latter statement is its allness implications, which may serve to deceive the poor naïve young man contemplating marriage. It may be true for rent and, to some degree, for food, but for a host of other factors such as feeding and clothing children and the responsibilities and problems of living together in general, it is an understatement of monstrous proportions.

In other words, additive thinking and talking about the non-verbal world is another map which does not fit the territory. The structure of the language used implies a static, simple world that isn't there and the use of such a language prepares the user for a reality he will never find. The general semanticist holds that by making ourselves explicitly aware of the non-additive character of the universe, we will be more likely to use a language whose structure implies it, and therefore we will be less likely to deceive ourselves because of the language we use to describe it.

The Realm of Is: Aristotelian Logic

We can see this deception at its peak in Aristotelian logic. It stems from an assumption about the nature of the universe opposite to that of the modern scientist and philosopher. For Plato the "real world" was not the one given by the senses; all we see and touch are distorted images of reality. His "real world" was occupied by things which were static, their essences (real qualities) in them by virtue of their nature. This idea is reflected both in Aristotle's biology and in his logic. His biology is simply a classification of things. They are given names and a place in the scheme of things. *By knowing their names you know what they "are."* The name determines what it is, a neat reversal of the abstracting process.

Nowhere is the idea of process introduced. It is a dead world, with things in their proper place eternally. Observation shows that even on the gross level of the naked eye constant change is the basic fact of life. Classifications, we have seen, are higher-order abstractions and as such are static. Aristotle's basic error lay in his not knowing that classifications are man-made. He assumed that classes exist in nature independent of the classifier. Consequently, he reversed the natural order of abstraction and gave more value to the higher-order abstractions, classifications, than to the lower-order non-verbal level. Observable change and process in things became a distortion of the "real" order of things as represented by the higher-order abstractions instead of the static higher-order classifications being understood as special cases, convenient limitations and distortions, as-if-at-a-date-models of the non-verbal world.

This becomes quite clear when we examine his logic. His "laws of thought" can be stated in the following fashion:

1. A is A—the law of identity.
2. Anything is either A or not-A—the law of the excluded middle.
3. Something cannot be both A and not-A—the law of non-identity.

Now, strictly as a logical system, this is completely valid and if used as such, no misevaluation arises. The trouble comes when we fix the variable A by letting it stand for something non-verbal. Obviously, in a world of process, A is never A. It is constantly changing, but "A is" implies that it remains the same in essence. By the time one finishes saying, "This pencil is this pencil," it has changed. One might object and ask, "Can't we assume that the pencil, for purposes of discussion, hasn't changed enough from moment$_1$ to moment$_2$ to make a difference?" The answer is, "We can." But in that case the law should read, "A may be assumed to remain constant for the sake of discussion." This is a totally different kind of statement from "A is A." It recognizes the process nature of the non-verbal level, distinguishes between the verbal and non-verbal levels, and introduces the observer into the picture. Indeed, for the sake of analysis we have to do this. We have to "stop the clock" because higher-order abstractions are unavoidably static. But we are not permitted to project this characteristic upon the lower-order abstractions on penalty of serious confusion and distortion of the abstracting process.

We can deal with the two other laws in a similar way. We can take the curse off the law of the excluded middle by making the "is" mean "may be classified as." By this substitution we recognize, first, that *we* are doing the classifying and, second, that "anything" may be classified in a myriad of other ways depending on our purpose. The law of non-identity is made acceptable by changing it to read, "Something should not be classified both as *A* and not-*A* at the same time in the same context." For analytical purposes we can decide to label a man who acts in a stated fashion a Communist. Then, in the given context of the discussion, we are not allowed to change the definition or have it mean two different things at the same time; he cannot be both a Communist and not a Communist. But again, the implication behind this linguistic pattern is that *we* make the classification and can, in another context, change it and that someone else might make a different, but equally valid, classification.

THE REALM OF THE POLAR: THE TWO-VALUED ORIENTATION

It is obvious that Aristotelian logic is strictly two-valued, and, as general semanticists are fond of pointing out, so is a large part of our thinking. We tend to talk in polar terms—the villains are all bad, the heroes all good; you are either for us or against us; you are either black or white. The allness pattern is quite apparent in the two-valued orientation. The general semanticist advocates the multivalued orientation, the introduction of degree thinking. How bad, how good, what degree of guilt, how dark, what shade of gray, how slow, how much for me, how much against me?

The counter-argument to advocacy of the multivalued orientation can be stated simply: Either you get on the train or you don't. If you do it halfway, you drag along the tracks. The counter-

counter-argument runs like this: There are many alternatives, not just two. You may get on the train or take a bus or walk or run or stay home. One could, of course, include all the alternatives in the category "not getting on the train."

When we examine these arguments it becomes apparent that part of the confusion is due to our equating arguments having different logical forms. A polar argument—he is either good or bad; for us or against us; if one is true, the other must be false—can be considered a set of contrary statements. But if one is false, it does not necessarily follow that the other is true; both can be false—he may be neither for us nor against us. The other type of argument involves a set of contradictory statements—he is either guilty or not-guilty, either for us or not-for us, either white or not-white. In this case, if the first statement is true, the second is false and if the second is true, the first must be false; both cannot be true or false.

The contradictory form of the two-valued logic seems airtight and inevitable. It is quite true that if we have defined "getting on the train" as "stepping into the train when it is at rest at a station and depositing the body wholly within its confines," then either you get on the train or you don't. There is no middle ground, no degrees of on or off.

Where, then, does the multivalued orientation come in? It enters where we set up our alternatives. The man with the two-valued orientation is prone to polar, contrary thinking. He argues that you are either all good or all bad and that no other alternatives are possible. He argues that you are either all for me or all against me or, if he uses the contradictory form, you are either for me or not-for me, and will insist that these are the only possible alternatives.

The man with the multivalued orientation will not use the polar or contrary argument; instead he will use the contradictory form. But before he sets it up he will examine as many alternatives as possible. Thus, if the question of Communist or non-Communist arises, he will examine many definitions and descriptions of so-called Communist activity and after evaluating them to the best of his ability within the time limits imposed, will state as clearly as possible *his* definition of what constitutes Communistic behavior. All other behavior then becomes non-Communist. He admits that other definitions of Communistic behavior are possible and examines conflicting definitions. But after all this is done, he comes to a decision *and then acts in a strictly two-valued manner.*

It is most important that we fully understand the latter statement, for it is a key to much confusion among some general semanticists and Aristotelian philosophers. At the biological level we seem to be designed to function in a strictly two-valued way. A nerve either fires or it does not; there are no degrees of discharge. When action is required, it is most efficient, most effective, and most satisfying when it is the resultant of a clear-cut, non-equivocal, polar decision. Equivocal decisions produce anxiety.

We frequently try to twist our equivocal decisions into polar ones, as when we choose a car principally by the color. In other cases we keep needling ourselves on to a choice by saying, "It is better to do something than to do nothing; . . ."

The present point of view suggests that anxiety occurs when a polar decision cannot be produced from vital information. The anxiety may appear unreasonable to other men. Or it may be a learned lesson that saves the anxious men from an easy decision and a worse fate. Until it is resolved, an equivocal decision uses up network time that could be used for other decisions, and perhaps distorts what other decisions are made.[1]

If we are faced with a non-trivial problem, its resolution will be the result of a decision leading to an action. If we use the multi-valued approach, we will evaluate as many aspects of the problem

[1] John R. Platt, "Amplification Aspects of Biological Response and Mental Activity," *American Scientist,* vol. 44 (April, 1956), p. 192.

as possible in the allotted time, examine all the alternatives we can discover, and admit that different definitions and solutions are possible. But at the moment of decision we will select what we consider to be the best set of contradictory alternatives and stick to it until new data arrive which indicate a change is needed. Suppose that as a result of previous decisions I decide to go to the mountains for a vacation, having eliminated the seashore and other alternatives. I then have to choose a method of transportation and I look over the alternatives—bus, train, car, plane, boat, scooter, bicycle, hitchhike. After much deliberation I come to a decision, the train, and to avoid equivocation I put it into the contradictory form: either I take the train or I don't. If I put it into the contrary form—either I take the train or the boat—no action is possible. My choice may narrow down to the two but in the end this must be converted into "train or no-train," "no-train," then including taking the boat, car, plane, etc. And unless I discover new data different from that which dictated my choice, I stick to my decision. This is equivalent to refusing to change an agreed-upon definition of terms within a given context of a given argument at a given date. Any other course leads to irrational, indecisive, non-problem-solving behavior.

S. I. Hayakawa writes the following concerning the relationship of the two-valued to the multivalued orientation:

In spite of all that has been said to recommend multi- and infinite-valued orientiation, it must not be overlooked that in the *expression of feelings,* the two-valued orientation is almost unavoidable. There is a profound "emotional" truth in the two-valued orientation that accounts for its adoption in strong expressions of feeling, especially those that call for sympathy, pity, or help in a struggle. "Fight polio!" "Down with slums and up with better housing!" "Throw out the crooks! Vote the Reform ticket!" The more spirited the expression, the more sharply will things be dichotomized into the "good" and the "bad."

As an expression of feeling and therefore as an affective element in speaking and writing, the two-valued orientation almost always appears.

It is hardly possible to express strong feelings or to arouse the interest of an apathetic listener without conveying to some extent this sense of conflict. Everyone who is trying to promote a cause, therefore, shows the two-valued orientation somewhere in the course of his writing. It will be found, however, that the two-valued orientation is *qualified* in all conscientious attempts at presenting what is believed to be truth—qualified sometimes, in the ways explained above, by pointing out what can be said against the "good" and what can be said for the "bad"—qualified at other times by the introduction, elsewhere in the text, of a multi-valued approach to the problems.

The two-valued orientation, in short, can be compared to a paddle, which performs the functions, in primitive methods of navigation, both of starter and steering apparatus. In civilized life the two-valued orientation may be the starter, since it arouses interest with its affective power, but the multi-valued or infinite-valued orientation is our steering apparatus that directs us to our destination.[2]

I think that we must add that not only is the two-valued approach the starter, but it is also the end product of decision. Thus we come to the rather interesting conclusion that the debate concerning the two-valued versus the multivalued orientation is itself the product of a two-valued orientation. It is not a question of either one or the other; we have to use both. Each is most appropriate at a different level of abstraction. At the non-verbal level, the two-valued orientation is appropriate for arousing our feelings and motivating us. At the verbal level of problem-solving, symbol-using activity, the multi-valued orientation is most valuable. Then, when decision is reached, it is phrased in a two-valued fashion so that it can direct non-verbal action, the doing of which is not-words, even if it means a decision to talk. Once again we see how apparently irreconcilable positions can be resolved by not confusing the levels of abstraction.

Incidentally, Platt makes the provocative suggestion that, "It seems almost necessary that a network (neural) selected by evolution to

[2] S. I. Hayakawa, *Language in Thought and Action,* New York, Harcourt, Brace and Company, 1949, pp. 235–236.

operate with polar option should feel compelled to base its 'laws of thought' on two-valued logic. It is 'self-evident,' 'innate'—born in us—to give an evolutionary twist to Plato and Kant; not something learned, except as survival is learning."

ALL MEN ARE MORTAL: THE SYLLOGISM AND HUMAN AFFAIRS

Aristotle is recognized as the creator of a formal system of deductive reasoning. The syllogistic form, derived from his three laws of thought, necessarily involves allness statements which inevitably are distortions of reality. For example, we can reason, "All Socialists believe in public ownership of industry, he is a Socialist, therefore he believes in public ownership of industry." Such a syllogism is perfectly valid but it tells us nothing as to whether it is true or false. True and false do not apply to deductive reasoning, only valid and invalid. It is perfectly good syllogistic reasoning to state, "All men are made of cheese, he is a man, therefore he is made of cheese." It is the structure of the reasoning that counts, not its content. To determine whether or not the major premise, and therefore the conclusion, are true, we have to make series of observations and from them build a generalization or conclusion. This is called inductive reasoning. Since we cannot examine all men, we use statistical methods and our answers will naturally be inferences about the whole class of men and have a degree of probability of being correct that is a function of the sampling method used.

Consequently, when it comes to dealing with live and important issues in human affairs, syllogistic reasoning, while not entirely useless, is a snare for the unwary and a cause of much violent and unproductive argument. First, it deludes the user by implying a simplicity not to be found in the actual problem. All Socialists do not think alike or to the same degree about any given issue; there are varying degrees and kinds of Socialistic thought. Second, because most major premises in debated real-life problems are necessarily inferential, any conclusion drawn must be tentative and not as final as the neat "therefore" in the conclusion. Third, a study of debated issues will show, I believe, that most of the time people do not bother to, or do not realize the necessity for, examining their major premises. They take for granted that, "All Socialists believe . . ." They assume that only one major premise, theirs, is true and all the rest false.

Syllogistic reasoning is useful after the major premise is accepted by all parties to the dispute, because it shows whether or not conclusions drawn from it are valid. However, it cannot be used to determine whether or not the conclusion is true even if the major premise is accepted as true, because the major premise is a generalization, perhaps true of the class as a whole, but not necessarily true of any one member of the class to which it is applied. This latter can be determined only by observation of the individual case, whether it be a man or a clam. The neatness and finality of the syllogistic form often deludes the user into thinking it gives him factual knowledge when it is really inferential, and thus prevents him from making actual observation of the case under discussion.

Aristotle, a very wise and observant man, realized that in the market place and the forum men dealt not with certainties but with probabilities, with limited, not with complete knowledge, and therefore premises had to incorporate such modifying terms as "many," "sometimes," "more," "less." Aware that this vitiated syllogistic thought, he invented what he called the enthymeme, which was supposed to enable us to deal with probabilities as the syllogism could not. However, he never did work out a system of enthymematic reasoning comparable to the syllogistic. Instead, when we read his *Rhetoric* we find a list of things to do in a debate in order to win it, and lists of what kinds of things, thoughts, situations, are likely or not likely to occur or probably be true under given conditions. The *Rhetoric* is a shrewd practical manual, but an *ad hoc* affair and not a derived system of thought. It is tempting to speculate as to why Aristotle never developed a logic of probabilities. One reason, I would guess, is that his first love was for Plato's static world of essences and certainties and that he considered the world of men, politics, and probabilities a corruption and distortion of it.

I think what I am trying to say is this: Deductive, that is, syllogistic reasoning starts with a generalization, a high-order inference about a class, and ends with a statement about a member of the class. The structure of the conclusion is deceptive. Even in the hypothetical syllogism (if all men are mortal and if he is a man then he is mortal) it is easy to be deceived into thinking that it is a factual statement. Actually, it is an inferential statement of lower order than the major premise. Note that it moves from a higher level of abstraction to a lower, whereas a factual statement involves first observation (low-order abstraction) and then the making of the statement, a higher-order abstraction.

The observation upon which the factual statement is based may be guided by an inference reached deductively. Thus if I reach the conclusion, syllogistically, that an individual is in favor of socialized medicine, it can guide me to an observation of him to see if this conclusion really is true. Until I do, I can make no factual statement about his belief. Thus, inductive and deductive reasoning work hand in hand and both are needed and used in the solution of problems. Deductive reasoning used alone gives a false security about one's knowledge of one member of a class; inductive reasoning alone results in a generalization which produces a false certainty about each individual member of the class. The product in either case is an inference which should be checked by observation.

If I make a series of observations of some Socialists concerning their opinions about socialized medicine, I can proceed to make a generalization (induction) about all Socialists based on my survey. Using this as a major premise, I can deduce a conclusion about one particular member of the group. Or I may simply start with a major premise and come to a conclusion about one member of the group involved. There is a greater probability of my being correct in the former case than in the latter because of the observation involved.

WORDS AND THINGS: VARIETIES OF REALITY

A moving picture analogy is useful in making clear the differences between lower-order and higher-order abstractions. If we project a moving picture of an arrow in flight, the smooth flowing motion corresponds to our lower-order abstractions. It looks "real"; this is what we actually see when we watch an arrow in flight. But if we stop the projector and examine the film strip we see discrete, static pictures lacking the "reality" of the moving picture. These would correspond to our higher-order abstractions such as theories about the infinity of points through which an arrow would have to move going from A to B. They do not change until we decide to change them and though they do not have the "realness" of the lower-order sensory impressions, they have their own values which the lower-order abstractions do not have. They can be manipulated at will, while the lower-order abstraction are largely beyond direct voluntary control. We cannot will to see and hear what we wish—indeed, when we can, it is usually an indication of something seriously wrong psychologically, with the exception, perhaps, of sensory stimulation produced by auto-hypnosis and related mechanisms. In any case, a reversal of the abstracting process occurs and is dangerous unless carefully managed.

The human nervous system, then, has two ways (at least) of reacting to its environment, internal and external. The sensory level gives us a world of motion, solidity, brightness; it is "real" and it is not words. The verbal levels which have no sensory quality, seem much less "real," yet have their own set of "qualities" and their own kind of "reality." Verbal existence is of a different kind than non-verbal existence. We can say that a set of statements has logical existence if they are not self-contradictory. Numbers, mathematical systems, scientific theories, have this kind of logical existence. Higher-order abstractions, even the average man, exist, but it is a verbal existence.

Is sensory existence more "real" than verbal? It is if we are talking about existence in terms of qualities such as hardness or color. It is not if we mean that both lower-order and higher-order abstractions are products of neural functioning. The higher-order abstractions probably involve, to some degree, different and/or different kinds of brain circuits, cells, and other psychophysiological mechanisms than lower-order, so the products are different. But one is just as real a neural product as the other.

Since the organism operates as a whole, misevaluation arises either when we confuse the different levels of abstraction or neglect one level and overstress another. Extreme materialists overemphasize the importance of the non-verbal level; extreme idealists, the verbal level. Aristotelian thought not only gave more value to higher-order abstractions than to lower, but confused the two levels, projected the static absolutistic characteristics of the verbal level upon the non-verbal, and produced linguistic patterns which do not match the structure of the world given by our senses.

All Cretans Are Liars: Paradox Lost

It can be demonstrated that all the Greek paradoxes result from some type of identification of the levels of abstraction. Here are a few examples:

PLATO.   Socrates is about to tell a lie.
SOCRATES.   Plato has spoken the truth.

This remains a paradox only if both statements are considered to be on the descriptive level where true and false apply. When we realize that Plato's statement is on the inference level and that therefore, true and false do not apply, only degrees of probability of being correct, the paradox disintegrates. No matter whether Socrates' statement is true or false, Plato's cannot conflict with it. Only when both statements are capable of being either true or false, i.e., on the same level of abstraction, can contradiction and paradox arise.

The situation is a little more complex when we substitute "Socrates is a liar" for Plato's statement, but if we analyze this statement we see that it is actually a combination of a factual and an inferential statement. In the past, all Socrates' statements have been lies—that is the factual part. To this is added the implication that all his future statements will be lies. If we consider only the factual part, there can be no paradox because Socrates' statement, "Plato has spoken the truth," is outside of the totality of all his past lying statements. It is a statement about these former statements and, since it is on another level of abstraction, cannot be in contradiction with them. If we consider the inferential part of Plato's statement then we return to the category occupied by the statement, "Socrates is about to tell a lie."

There is a Spanish version of this paradox. A hangman and a gallows stand on a bridge between two cities. The hangman has the peculiar ability to tell whether or not a person crossing the bridge speaks the truth when talking to him. If he tells the truth, he is allowed to pass. If he lies, the hangman hangs him. One fine day a young man approaches and says, "You are going to hang me." What does the hangman do? Only if the statement, "You are going to hang me," is mistakenly considered to be on the descriptive level is the hangman in a quandary. He has no directives for dealing with statements which are neither true nor false, so he just ignores our traveler.

SUMMARY OF CHAPTERS 4 AND 5

1. The nervous system is stratified in its structure and function.

2. Although all levels are interconnected and mutually influence one another, the product at each level is unique and differs from all the others. Thus, words are not things. They are on the next level of abstraction and most probably involve neural structures not required for feelings and sensations.

3. The object "is" the mass of sensations (color, smell, taste, etc.) which are produced within us by the reaction of our nervous system to stimuli from the submicroscopic level—the event. We project our auditory and visual sensations "out there."

4. The object is not words. Whatever you say a thing "is," it is not. For all saying is the saying of words which are *about* the object; they are not the bundle of sensations which constitute the object. If I pick up an object which we *call* (classify as) a pen and you ask me what it "really is," my only legitimate answer would be to pick it up, wave it in front of you, and put it down. Only if by "What is it really?" you mean, "What do we call it?" can I answer, "It is a pen."

5. At the atomic level, there are no qualities, no things. Atoms have no color, taste, shape, etc. These qualities—thingness—are our reactions to the submicroscopic stimuli. However, since we can visualize only in terms of sensory experiences, we construct models of atomic structure and act as if they have this structure. This is a great aid to us in gaining control of our environment through the production of predictions of high probability, and as long as we realize the as-if nature of our constructs no misevaluation occurs.

6. The verbal level itself stratifies into higher and lower levels or orders. The lowest verbal level is that of description, factual statement, and naming; inferences, generalizations, class terms are on the higher levels. This ordering into levels is not mere verbal quibbling; it is as much "built in" by the structure of the nervous system as are the differences between the verbal and non-verbal levels.

7. Although the nature and the "feel" of each level of abstraction is different from the others, the organism responds to any kind of stimulus as a whole and on all levels, no matter what kind of stimulus it may be. The meaning of the response—the semantic reaction of the total organism—varies with the level. At the non-verbal level the meaning is in terms of sensations and feelings, and at the verbal level in terms of descriptions, inferences, and other constructs.

8. Because of this total reaction of the nervous system at all levels to any kind of stimulus, the patterns of linguistic usage can have a profoundly disturbing effect upon it if they cause us to confuse the different levels of abstraction, as when we act as if inferential knowledge were factual knowledge or as if words were things.

✸✸ 6 ✸✸

Consciousness of Abstracting

The Possibility of Rational Control of the Irrational

THE abstracting process is characteristic of all protoplasm and reaches its peak among the higher animals. Only man can become conscious of the fact that he does abstract. We can reasonably infer that animals are conscious, that they are aware of their environment, but only man is aware that he is aware, can be conscious of his consciousness. Consciousness of the abstracting process is, for the general semanticist, the key to proper evaluation; for the individual, its fullest development is the goal of living.

There are, and can be, an infinity of life goals. They can range from making a fortune to creating an immortal poem. A general semanticist may cherish these dreams as much as any man, yet they are considered subsidiary products of a richly developed total personality, the prime objective.

But this is a highly intellectual approach to the vast problems of mental health and personality development and therefore quite suspect today. The old, grand, rationalist dream of the completely rational man deliberately ordering and controlling his inner life was struck a deadly blow by Freud and other psychologists. The uncovering of the great influence of the unconscious with its primitive, irrational lusts and hatreds, its blind, desolating, labyrinthian fears, its waves of unbearable, naked anxiety upon conscious thought and behavior, has led many to assert that any completely rational attempt by the individual himself to promote his mental health or to help alleviate his anxieties can lead only to superficial and very temporary changes and often do more harm than good.

It is our contention that, important as these unconscious factors are in shaping our character and behavior, they are not quite as monolithic and unassailable by the individual himself as some would lead us to believe. We base this upon a prior assumption, namely, that the organism works as a whole and changes in one part of it almost inevitably will lead to changes in others, although often this may take a long time. Our problem, then, in the remainder of this book, will be to show how "rational" thought, which we shall call consciousness of abstracting, can produce desired changes in our "emotional" life. Incidentally, we have put "rational" and "emotional" in quotes to indicate that in everyday parlance they tend to imply sharply independent entities, an elementalistic separation that we do not find in the living organism. For us, they will refer to the non-verbal level (emotional) and the verbal levels (rational), as processes which mutually and cyclically affect each other at all times.

I must hasten to repeat again that this control of the rational over irrational processes is an ideal to be reached for, with very little expectation by most of us of achieving anything near 100 percent effectiveness. Again we face our old problem of self-levitation. To the degree that the irrational processes have paralyzed our effective use of the rational, to that degree will we be unable to reverse the process. Our hope is based on the fact that most people still have a high enough percentage of intact "intellect" to get the process under way and start pushing back "the forces of darkness." As we have stated a number of times, the system we offer probably cannot be used by the highly neurotic and certainly not by the psychotic. Its greatest use, I believe, is as a preventive therapy in a lifelong educational program.

Whether you, dear reader, can use it at this sad point of your life, I cannot say. I can affirm, however, that if you have not reached the state where you are in immediate and dire need of a psychiatrist, studying and practicing general semantics can do no harm and most probably will do some good. But it is a long and difficult journey, for the old habits are hard to break. It takes a certain amount of dogged faith that it will work to keep trying in the face of setbacks and long plateaus of apparent non-improvement that are inevitable in any attempt to produce so great a change in behavior.

It is hoped that the structure of the system, the broadness of its foundations, and the range of its application to so many areas of endeavor will provide that degree of inspiration and faith which this so pedantic presentation so ably kills. That is, I hope that it will be seen that this system has greater chances of working than the usual self-help courses because it is not an *ad hoc* conglomeration of precepts for avoiding anxiety or worry, but is applicable to the total evaluative process and based upon the operation of the nervous system on all levels of abstraction and, therefore, of use in every situation and field of endeavor, not just in the area of disturbed mental health.

THE MULTIORDINALITY OF TERMS:
FIRST- AND SECOND-ORDER FEELINGS

We have shown what happens when we confuse the different levels of abstraction and reverse the natural order. Let us now pursue this concept from a slightly different angle: the values to be gained by deliberately selecting the level of abstraction on which to operate in a given situation. We can begin by turning to another of Korzybski's concepts, the multiordinality of many of our most important terms. Take the word "love." I can love a steak, a building, a woman, a painting, a theory, a horse, a bloody fight. All these loves are on the same level of abstraction. But love can also move to other levels.

Thus, I can love my love of a woman, a horse, a theory, etc. This is a second-order love and differs from a first-order love in an extremely important way, namely, that because it is on another level of abstraction, it involves, apparently, different and/or additional psycho-neurological processes.

Perhaps some examples will help clarify this concept. Let us switch to "hate" for the moment and see what happens when we move to the next level of abstraction. Suppose I have been brought up in a family in a town where there is prejudice against Mexicans. I learn to hate them, a blind, unreasoning, and unreasoned hatred. Then suppose that I am sent away to another part of the country and receive a more sensible education. I learn about Mexicans—about their culture and about the nature and causes of prejudice. And suppose some of this "sinks in" and I begin to realize that my hatred of Mexicans is both foolish and harmful, not only to the Mexicans, but, even more, to myself. So I begin to hate my hatred of them.

Two things should be noticed at this point. First, my second-order hate tends to reverse my feelings about Mexicans; it implies a liking for them or at least a desire to like them. This second-order hatred is thus the opposite of the first-order; my second-order feeling of hatred produces a liking for the object of my first-order hatred. It might appear that we have here the ambivalence of feeling that has been noted by psychiatrists in many of their patients and presumably is present in all of us. However, and this brings us to our second point, it is not a true ambivalence because the feelings are on different levels of abstraction and therefore are not true opposites.

These second-order feelings are different in both genesis and character from the first-order. First, they are the product of conscious evaluation and education. Second, because they are a product of higher-order abstractions, they "feel" different from the first-order feeling. They are not as "blind" or "deep" or "powerful," in the sense that first-order feelings are. This difference in feeling is undefinable and can be discovered only by introspection, but I feel quite certain that all of us "know" this difference even though we can't "say" it, for reasons we have discussed throughout this book. The important point is that these higher-order feelings can be deliberately and consciously chosen, generated, cultivated.

While these second-order feelings are not as powerful as their first-order counterparts, still they do have some effect upon them. It takes time and persistence before a noticeable change takes place, but it will happen in any person not pronouncedly neurotic. Indeed, if it did not happen, most of our formal training and education in ethical and moral behavior would be useless. It should not be too surprising that this occurs, considering that the organism acts as a whole and changes in one part inevitably affect the rest to varying degrees.

It takes time and pondering until these second-order feelings can be generated. "Intellectual" at first and then, quite suddenly, the insight occurs and sinks down to the feeling level. The insight is in the form of a powerful feeling of conviction of the rightness and truth of the second-order feeling and this conviction, which is a first-order feeling, can change behavior, that is, the conflicting first-order feelings. We cannot "will" the feeling, the conviction, directly; but we can "will" the second-order feelings. And the will to will this has come from the acceptance of it as a good idea, and the acceptance of it as a good idea is a product of "rational" processes, i.e., conscious high-order abstractions.

These are all cyclical affairs. For example, it is relatively easy to accept the concept of the great value of being an efficient time-binder because of its high level of abstraction. It generates a higher-order feeling. But to translate it to the lower level of feelings is much more difficult. The lower-order feelings are not directly produced by conscious evaluation. A lower-order conviction is deep, satisfying, and difficult to change. We cannot get at it directly; the greatest chance of changing it is by the indirect path through the use of second-order mechanisms. It is of no use to say that convictions are bad. They are a fact of human existence. Rather, let us make use of this phenomenon by deciding to get the proper convictions, among them the conviction that irrationally arrived-at convictions which lead to misevaluation are bad.

One virtue of attempting to "get at" unwanted first-order feelings and emotions by way of second-order ones is that this indirect approach keeps us from stirring up guilt, anxiety, and the defense reactions associated with the first-order emotions. Those of the second order are usually free of anxiety and guilt because they are the products of higher-order abstracting consciously employed and therefore are much more easily changed for the same reason.

Here we have an opening wedge in undertaking a greater conscious control of our "inner life." We can *choose* the level of abstraction upon which we shall operate in a given situation. This theme will be developed in greater detail as we go on.

SECOND-ORDER FEELINGS AND THE ALGEBRAIC LAW OF SIGNS

Returning to the theme of first-order versus second-order feelings, we find, for example, that second-order love, instead of reversing first-order love, as occurs with hatred, tends to reinforce it. If I love Mexicans and love my love of them, there is an increase in my love of them. On the other hand, if I love them and hate my love of them, the tendency is toward a reversal of the first-order love. But if I hate them and love my hatred, the first-order hatred is reinforced. I think it is most interesting that these orders of emotion seem to follow the algebraic law for the multiplication of signs: if we consider love a "positive" emotion and hate a "negative" one, then love of a love (plus times plus) gives a plus, a reinforcement of the first-order emotion. Love of a hate (plus times minus) reinforces the first-order hate, a negative emotion, because plus times a minus gives a minus. A hatred of a love reduces the first-order love because a hatred (minus) of a love (plus) gives a minus, a hatred or reversal of the love. Finally, a hatred (minus) of a hatred (minus) tends to reverse first-order hate because minus times a minus gives a plus (love).

I do not know whether this similarity to the algebraic law of signs is mere coincidence or indicates something of importance about the operation of the nervous system, but it does make for mighty interesting speculation. It should be noted, however, that not all emotions show this characteristic—fear and worry, for instance.

We can, then, choose our second-order feelings. Or we may choose not to use them because some are destructive. For instance, the fear of fear can quickly lead to breakdown, as can worry about worry and anxiety about anxiety. We shall spend some time with these a little later. There are others that lead in very interesting directions: doubt of doubt, the time of times, selfishness of selfishness or, rather, the unselfishness of selfishness, the courage to have courage, the freedom to destroy freedom, an attitude toward attitudes, the good of goodness, faith in faith, the will to will, the security of insecurity, curiosity about curiosity, knowing about knowing, Paul Tillich's acceptance of acceptance, Anatole Rapoport's concept of a culture-studying culture.

As Korzybski pointed out, unless we know the relative order of abstraction on which the multiordinal term is being used, any discussion will be fruitless. To talk of hate in general can lead only to confusion, considering that a second-order hatred can be the reverse of a first-order. Only through consciousness of the abstracting process can we avoid the misevaluations from this type of identification of different levels of abstraction.

FREE WILL VERSUS DETERMINISM

One of the time-worn dilemmas or dichotomies is the free-will-determinism controversy. We must consider it at this point before we can take up the processes of "self-therapy," because many of these processes hinge on its solution or resolution.

With the possible exception of the Heisenberg Principle of Indeterminacy, all modern science seems to be based upon a strict determinism—every event has a cause or causes. Things don't "just happen," Topsy can't "just grow." Question: What is a cause, "really"? Like all the other "really" questions we have asked thus far, this turns out to be a pseudoquestion, a meaningless one, if we mean by it, "Does a cause exist in the same sense that a rock or man exists; does it have objective, non-verbal existence?"

A few years ago, in a large northern industrial city in the United States, there was a race riot. It began on a bus crowded with Negro and white passengers. A white man jostled a Negro, there was a flare of temper, then angry words, then a fight. The passengers spewed out of the bus in a fighting mass and this soon spread to the entire neighborhood. An uneasy peace was finally restored after eighteen hours of vicious fighting, and then only after the National Guard intervened. A number of people were killed, many injured and the resulting increase in interracial hatred set the stage for an even more terrible conflict shortly after. What was the cause of the riot?

WHAT "IS" A CAUSE?

It is obvious that there is no such thing as "the" cause; there are causes, many causes. The question is how many. Perhaps one way of getting an answer would be to break them down into immediate and more remote causes. An immediate cause of the riot would be the jostling of one man by the other. But wait! Would the shoving have taken place if the bus were not crowded? So the crowded bus was the cause, but is it more or less immediate than the jostling? Or perhaps the angry state of mind of both men was a more immediate cause, for without it the shove might have been shrugged off. We can introduce causes indefinitely and it soon becomes apparent that the division into immediate and secondary or remote causes is an arbitrary and quite useless procedure. How about including the education in prejudice which helped produce their state of mind at the moment of fighting? Would you count as a cause the heat and humidity of the muggy summer day? Certainly it helped produce the short tempers. Or, perhaps, the lack of adequate local police who, if there had been enough, could have confined the fight to the bus? Could we call Henry Ford a cause? If he hadn't started the automobile industry, there would have been no crowded buses. If this seems far-fetched, how about considering the parents of the two men a primary cause? After all, if they hadn't produced them, they wouldn't have been there to fight! Let's push it a little further. If these two men had not boarded the same bus, there would have been no fight; therefore, the whole chain of events in the universe from the moment it was "created" which led to these two being at that precise spot, thinking precisely those thoughts, at that precise moment is a cause. In short, everything is causally related to everything else: this is the assumption upon which all modern science is founded.

It is apparent that even though this assumption is accepted, we cannot pragmatically base our actions upon it. In order to act, we are forced to consider some causes more important than others and minimize or neglect the influence of the rest. Which do we select and upon what basis? Anatole Rapoport, in his book, *Operational Philosophy,* suggests that we consider as causes those factors over which we have some control. We can increase the police force, we can reduce crowding of buses, we can clean up slums, we can initiate educational programs to lessen prejudice. Therefore we say that these are the causes of race riots. We cannot do anything about these two particular people being on the same bus at the same time, or their being born, nor can we change the flow of events such as the evolutionary development of man—no evolution, no man, no fight—

so we do not consider these as causes, though actually they are as necessary to the occurrence of the event as any others.

Of course, which factors we think we can, or could have, controlled, are determined by those interested in the situation. The police captain says that the stinginess of the city council in not increasing his budget to allow for more patrolmen is an important cause, but he would dismiss the idea, and perhaps be shocked, if a Margaret Sanger insisted that lack of information and education in birth control among the poorer classes was the most important factor. Cut down on the birth rate among the poor slum dwellers, she would argue, their standard of living would go up, and the slums would diminish as breeding grounds for ignorance, crime, and race prejudice.

When we observe phenomena over whose variables we have no apparent control, we usually select as causes those factors which appear closest to the occurrence in time and/or space. For example, we say that thunder is caused by a flash of lightning, usually because of the close temporal connection, and because the flash is so much more apparent than any other factor. Again, our past experience and purposes of the moment will help determine our selection. A meteorologist might claim that the sudden expansion of the air heated by the lightning bolt is "the cause," while a physicist might argue that the primary cause is the build-up of an electrostatic potential between cloud and earth. Others might focus on the propagation of the sound waves from sky to listener.

No matter which factors we choose as causes, the important point to remember is that *we* do the choosing. We are forced to abstract because we cannot deal with the tremendous numbers of factors involved in even the simplest phenomenon. The vital question in any instant is: Does this particular selection of causes enable me to function effectively in this situation? And effectiveness will be measured by such matters as predictability, simplicity, ease of decision-making, verifiability, relief of tensions, and the like, depending on the problem-solving situation.

Another factor, a semantic one, enters and further complicates the situation. I hold a pencil over my desk; I release it; it falls to the desk. What causes it to fall? One of the causes, we would say, is the pull of gravity. Yet no one has ever seen gravity or felt it or smelled or heard it. It is not a thing; it has only inferential existence. It "really" is only a word, a name for subatomic phenomena whose existence we infer because it provides an explanation for what happened. All we can observe is the falling pen and the sound it makes when it hits.

When we say *A* causes *B*, factually it can only mean that *A* precedes *B*. Yet *A* precedes *B* many times when we say it is not a cause of *B*, that its precedence is only coincidental with *C*, which also preceded *B*, and which is really the cause. For example, every president of the United States who held office in the years 1840, 1860, 1880, 1900, 1920, 1940, died in office. Despite this regular twenty-year interval occurring six times in a row (the odds against its being a chance ocurrence are phenomenal) we are forced to say that it is purely coincidental, because no causal connection can be established between the dates and the deaths of the presidents in office. This is one of the rules which must be followed in debate, otherwise we run into contradiction and useless controversy. If we break it, we commit the fallacy of *ad hoc, ergo propter hoc*—after this, therefore because of this; the Korean War came after President Truman took office, therefore, he caused it; the prosperity of the country increased after he took office, therefore, President Eisenhower caused it. The foolishness of this kind of argument becomes more evident if we say that the Stockholm sank the Andrea Doria after Eisenhower became president, therefore, he was the cause of it.

Yet if everything is causally interconnected, if the flow of events moves forward, as is assumed, then Eisenhower's presidency is part of this flow, has had an effect upon it, and therefore has been a factor, perhaps exceedingly small, but still a factor in the sinking of the Andrea Doria. An exceptionally violent Democrat might argue that if the President had insisted upon certain additional safety regulations in marine shipping, and if he had pressured Italy, Sweden, and other countries to adopt them, the collision would not have occurred. Of course, there is no way of proving him right or wrong.

Still, most people, I think, would rule out Eisenhower's presidency as a cause and would say it was coincidental. Why? Again, because it is *inferred* that he could not have done anything about preventing the accident; we disregard as a cause that which we think we cannot change. Let us take another example, a disease, say typhoid fever. Most people would say that it is caused by the typhoid bacillus, because if it is not present in a person's body, he does not get typhoid fever. The trouble with this reasoning is that the germs can be present and still a person will not contract the disease, e.g., carriers like Typhoid Mary. We say they have a high resistance to the disease. There is evidence to show that all of us, healthy as well as sick, have many disease-producing germs in our bodies all the time. We get sick only when that factor conveniently labeled "resistance" drops. What causes the disease, the germs or the lowered resistance?

If we argue that the presence of the germs is a necessary but not a sufficient factor, then the floodgates open. Necessary, but not sufficient factors include the meeting of germ and victim, all the factors under the catchall label of lowered resistance such as psychological stress, hormonal stress, poor nutrition, atmospheric conditions, etc., etc. Therefore, to keep out of this morass, we concentrate on those "causes" we can control and know most about—presence of germs in the body, carriers of the disease, and sanitary conditions which allow the germs to propagate. We call these the causes. We do not know, or care enough, about nutritional factors or atmospheric conditions in relation to disease, and we cannot change the person's being alive to contract the disease, nor his parents begetting him, nor the effect of his daughter's broken marriage on his state of health, so we say these are not causes. The history of medicine furnishes many examples of changing causes of disease, i.e., what we consider to be causes. Even when we say that the typhoid bacillus causes typhoid fever, actually we mean the toxin it produces and not the bacillus itself. All of the toxin? Maybe only certain parts of this complex molecule.

So we see that what we consider to be the causes of a phenomenon are arbitrarily decided upon. However, such a decision is not completely arbitrary. The rules by which we select the causes are fixed. If we wish to be correct in our thinking, the laws of logic and of scientific procedure govern the selection. These rules have been worked out over the years because it has been found that, on a statistical basis, we seem to gain control over our environment by following them. We predict that if in a community where typhoid epidemics are frequent, we institute certain sanitary procedures and give anti-typhoid injections, the incidence of the fever will drop to a low level. We do and our prediction is verified. So we say we have eliminated and verified the causes of the disease. These procedures were discovered by a long process of trial and error, inference, experiment, theorizing, carried out according to rules laid down by logicians and scientists. But in all cases results are true only on a statistical basis and are never exactly duplicated. Because our predictions are verified, we infer that what we call the causes of an event are the important ones for us, the ones we need to be concerned with if we are to control our environment to a practical degree. We can never prove that these are the only causes without knowing all there is to know about any given phenomenon, and since we cannot know all, we are forced to infer that if we did we would get the predicted result. According to Platt, the amplification processes involved in perception forever rule out the strict determinism postulated by Laplace.

We see that no man can ever even in principle achieve Laplace's program, to "know the positions and velocities of all the particles in the universe," which classically was supposed to permit prediction of the future motion of every particle. There would have to be more amplifiers than particles, with the amplifiers outside the universe. The number of independently knowable particles must always be orders of magnitude less than the number of particles in the amplifiers.

Laplace's determinism, which was the 19th Century determinism, was only tenable for the kinds of experiments he specialized in with a few "particles" and many amplifiers—a few planets and the human eye. But the motions of the millions of molecules in even a microscopic gas bubble are unknowable even in principle, and therefore to us inconsequential, because the amplifiers are impossible to field.

The least amplifier is bigger than the particle or, more precisely, bigger and with more parts than the least input transducer. How much bigger still must be the man who makes it! Here is a regress of another few orders of magnitude. To build the smallest physically operable macroscopic secondary amplifier takes primary amplifiers—eyes and brain, or the automatic machinery they can construct—whose parts must be still more numerous and occupy a still larger volume of space or time. For it takes many sense buds and many decisions and many motor operations in the primary amplifier system to extract from the universe and to shape a single component of the secondary amplifier and to assemble it into the proper place among the other components. (Can we regress one more step? The eyes and brain had to be made in turn by the zero-order amplifier, evolution, using and wasting still more parts and taking an even greater stretch of time. This leads to the amusing thought that there may be an order-of-magnitude connection between the age of the universe and the number of fundamental particles a scientist can detect in any one interval.)

Bigger than the least amplifier also must be the information-handling network that collates the output of many amplifiers and makes polar decisions. It must have more parts or must take a longer time to do its work than the amplifiers, or both.[1]

STRICT DETERMINISM AND THE STATISTICAL NATURE OF CAUSALITY

This inability to know everything introduces another complicating factor. We have said that by inferring the causal interdependence of all phenomena, science gets its work done. But this interdependence cannot be proved because of the very nature of scientific experiment, which is based upon the duplication of conditions and results; verification means duplication. Yet under the postulate of an infinitely complex, ever-changing universe, exact duplication of conditions is impossible. We can keep conditions only relatively the same, and only by ignoring differences *which we infer* are unimportant. Then we do a peculiar thing. When we re-run an experiment and do not get exactly the same results—and we never do—we infer that if we had exactly duplicated conditions we would get exactly the same results. But we have no way of proving this! We simply assume it and we have made much scientific progress on the basis of this inference. But it might be that the differences we get in re-running an experiment are due not only to differences in the conditions of the experiment but also because the same conditions do not always produce the same results.

When we run any kind of experiment, 99 percent of the time we are dealing with people, objects, occurrences which involve billions and billions of atoms. On a statistical basis, relative identity of results might be accounted for by the assumption that differences of reaction among the "same" kinds of atoms cancel out. We do this in our gas laws. The air in this room doesn't rush into one

[1] John R. Platt, "Amplification Aspects of Biological Response and Mental Activity," *American Scientist,* vol. 44 (April, 1956), p. 192.

corner because of the random direction of movement of the air molecules which cancel out to a relatively stable air mass.

THE HEISENBERG PRINCIPLE OF INDETERMINACY

However, we run into trouble when we try to experiment with single atoms, where this statistical canceling out is not involved. We must know the present speed and position of a single atom or subatomic particle in order to predict where it will be at a given moment. But the very act of observation changes the speed and/or the position. We can determine one or the other, but not both. This, put oversimply, is the Heisenberg Principle of Indeterminacy. When dealing with billions of atoms, as with objects, the interference of the instruments of observation is disregarded and is not considered a cause of the phenomenon observed. Yet it is a causative factor. Laws of causation, or causal connection, are based upon predictability. But, if we cannot predict and talk about cause and effect when referring to single atomic phenomena, how can we talk about cause and effect when referring to billions of unpredictable atoms? Does this destroy causality?

Some have rushed forth to proclaim that the Heisenberg Principle does indeed vitiate causal thinking and scientific methodology. Some have even used it as a justification for a return to magical thinking, dressed up in various fancy garbs such as, "Gods Unknowable," "Proof of Man's Limitations," "Realm of the Life Force." This is typical of the two-valued orientation. From a rigid "science will know everything" attitude they swing to the "know-nothing" camp. If it is realized that strict determinism is a useful inference, but *only an inference,* strictly unprovable because we cannot run the universe over its course a number of times to verify our inference, then it does not come as a shock when it is found that this inference may not be useful (though it may turn out to be) with subatomic single phenomena.

EMERGENT PHENOMENA AND NON-ADDITIVITY

The limitations of strict determinism become clearer if we view the problem from another angle, namely, that of "emergent phenomena," or the Korzybskian principle of non-additivity. A basic assumption behind strict determinism is that if we could know all the events preceding a phenomenon we could predict all the characteristics of the phenomenon, and of course this would be verified when it occurred. This is also the assumption behind simple, additive, cause-effect thinking. Thus, if A plus B equals C, if we know all the characteristics of A and B, we will know all those of C. Put another way, C is the sum of A and B, i.e., the whole is equal to the sum of its parts. But note carefully that this has never been observed.

This type of thinking is characteristic of Aristotelian philosophy, which says that qualities or characteristics are *in* things, are their essence—unchangeable and independent of the observer. Non-Aristotelian thinking concentrates not on innate essences, but on structure. All knowledge is knowledge of structure. The chatacteristics of things are a product of their structure and the structure of the observer. As these structures—the relationships of the parts—change so do the characteristics. In additive thinking, C does not contain any characteristics not present in A or B. In non-additive Gestalt thought, C does have characteristics not found in A and B because A and B have formed a new structure, C, which has characteristics of its own different from A or B. The whole is greater than the sum of its parts.

A simple example can be taken from chemistry. Dry metallic sodium is a soft, silvery metal. Dry chlorine is a yellow-green irritating gas. Mix them together in molar proportions and you have, roughly, an additive event. The mixture does not contain any characteristics not found in the separate elements.[2] If we allow a trace

[2] Strictly speaking, this is not true, because of surface adsorption of the gas by the solid, volume changes, etc., but we choose to neglect these in our example since we are interested in chemical and not physical characteristics.

of moisture to enter the mixing chamber, a violent reaction takes place. The resulting product is table salt, which contains characteristics not found in either sodium or chlorine. This non-additive reaction results in a compound, as differentiated from a mixture, which is the result of an additive reaction.

Strict determinism assumes that if you knew all the characteristics of sodium and chlorine you could predict those of sodium chloride. As far as I know, this has never been accomplished. A new plane has never been built which did not have to be test-flown to iron out the bugs—the unpredicted, unpredictable, non-additive characteristics.

Is a watch merely the sum of its wheels, gears and springs? Does not the arrangement of the parts produce characteristics not to be found in a jumbled heap of them? From where do these new characteristics come—the movement of the hands, the ticking noise? They are not found in any of the parts; they come from the structuring of the parts. Or the shape and movement of the fountain? Or living protoplasm? It is a familiar truism that additively thinking an adult man is made up of $1.25 worth of carbon, nitrogen, phosphorous, and other elements. Non-additively his worth is immeasurable.

Now, if no two things, events, situations are identical, and if they are more than the sum of their preceding events and therefore have characteristics not found in the preceding events (their causes), then strict determinism becomes impossible. For example, the chemist predicts that if he adds sodium to chlorine he will get sodium chloride and he can predict the characteristics of the sodium chloride on the basis of his past experience with this experiment. But *this particular batch* of salt will have characteristics different from any other batch. He will neglect them because they are unimportant to him, but nevertheless there is a difference which could not have been predicted, because perfect prediction based on a knowledge of the ingredients alone is impossible in a non-additive reaction, and because he cannot know all the characteristics of all the ingredients in the batch.

The crowning blow to strict determinism is the assumption that no two events, even on the atomic level, are identical. The very fact that two atoms of the same element do not occupy the same position at any given moment makes them different. Add the extra uncertainty of the Heisenberg Principle, and the impossibility of strict determinism becomes self-evident. We no longer say that A is the cause of B with the assurance that the Aristotelian structure of that sentence implies. All we can say is that A is probably one of the causes of B, depending on our purpose and point of view in dealing with A and B. You never know when an unforeseen C might intervene between A and B.

Korzybski suggested that we talk in functional terms in order to break away from oversimple cause-effect thinking. Any event, E, is to be considered a function of numerous factors. Which factors we pay attention to and which we neglect, which we consider important and which unimportant—and we always have to make a choice—depends upon the nature of E and our evaluation of it, e.g., the different causes which the chemist, the policeman, the sociologist, and the psychiatrist, are likely to decide are most important in a race riot.

SUMMARY OF OUR ANALYSIS OF STRICT DETERMINISM

1. Strict determinism is an inference, not an observable fact. To prove that a phenomenon is completely determined by the events that preceded it would require that we re-run the course of evnts, knowing and controlling all the variables and all the factors affecting the outcome.

This is impossible, first, because of the infinite complexity and interaction of events; second, because we can never re-run the experiment exactly for we cannot re-run the flow of events in time.

Everything happens just once and verification requires duplication.

2. Strict determinism is a useful inference which has received statistical verification when dealing with macroscopic phenomena. That is, by neglecting what we consider to be unimportant differences and variations in predicted results and over long runs involving billions of atoms (large numbers cancel out individual variations among them) we achieve a fairly high degree of predictability of events and control over our environment.

No matter how precise we are in our measuring instruments and techniques, we never get the same results twice. For example, in weighing something on an analytical balance we never get two readings exactly the same, so we run a series of weighings and average the results. We explain the discrepancies as inaccuracies in technique, instrument, duplication of conditions, etc., and infer that if we could correct these we would get identical weighings. But this is only an inference based upon circular reasoning. Assuming strict determinism, we infer we would get identical results and, since our results with precise instruments are very close, we give this as evidence for our assumption.

Strict determinism, as of this date, does not seem applicable to single atomic and subatomic phenomena. Consequently, we have no way of determining whether or not one atom of an element is exactly like another, introducing another item of uncertainty into our assumption of strict determinism. Indeed, if spatial and temporal characteristics are considered as part of the qualities of an atom, no two can ever be exactly alike.

3. No one has ever seen a cause. All we can observe is that A precedes B, and then, based on certain rules of reasoning and procedure, we infer that A causes B. This is a useful procedure until we manufacture a higher-order abstraction and say that causes exist and act as if they had low-order non-verbal existence.

4. The non-additivity of reactions of events eliminates the possibility of a strict determinism, because the new characteristics arising from a non-additive reaction—among them the characteristics of the structure-as-a-whole—are unpredictable and strict determinism requires 100 percent predictability.

THE OTHER HORN: FREE WILL

Having discussed half of the free-will-versus-determinism dichotomy, let us turn now to the other pole. Roughly speaking, the argument states that if everything is causally connected and therefore strictly determined, there cannot be any free will. We may think that we are making a free choice in any given situation, but actually what we choose is strictly determined; we cannot break the cause-effect links through choice; we are the slaves of all the preceding events.

Suppose you go into a restaurant with a friend—a strict determinist —and proceed to order from the menu. Let us say that from a list of six desserts on the menu you choose rice pudding. Were you free to choose? Your friend argues that your choice was completely determined by such factors as education, culture, past experience with rice pudding, your psychophysiological condition at the moment, e.g., blood sugar level and strength of contractions of the stomach on reading the menu. All these factors combined at the moment of decision and you could have made no other choice. In fact, you made no choice; it was decided for you.

Now suppose we ask you, "Did *you* choose the pudding?" Your answer is, "Of course I did." "How do you know you chose it?" "I just know." Actually, what you are saying is, "I *felt* free to choose. I *felt* that I was choosing, that nothing was pushing or pulling me." Here, I believe, lies the crux of the argument. *Free will is a feeling,* a feeling that one is doing the choosing himself. Therefore the answer to the question, "Does free will exist?" is a decided "Yes," if by free will is meant the feeling of being the chooser. Since it is a feeling, it is as real and exists as much as any feeling does, as much as any toothache, headache, glow of happiness, nausea, joy, or nostalgia.

But this feeling, *we infer,* is determined by all the multitudinous factors that help determine any other occurrence. It should not be too surprising that such a feeling of being free to choose occurs in an organism which has developed the ability to be aware of itself. To be aware of oneself means that we are aware of at least *some* of the factors which produce a decision. Nor is decision-making any more supernatural or mysterious than any other function of a living organism. No organism can respond equally to all the stimuli provoking it; we must infer that even in the simplest of organisms decision-making, in the sense of selective response to stimuli, occurs. The amoeba, we infer, "chooses" a bit of algae, rejects a sharp grain of sand. We assume it doesn't "know" it is choosing. Chemical stimuli, protoplasmic tensions—who knows what?—propel it, make it "choose." On this level, it might be correct to say its decision is determined. It has no "will" of its own. But a "choice" is made; otherwise the amoeba would die of indecision. But when, in the evolutionary scheme, we reach man, we have an organism capable of being aware of some of the stimuli that propel it toward a decision. This organism is also capable of using symbols, capable of manipulating the environment symbolically, and capable of making inferences (like strict determinism) about the possible consequences of different courses of action. When choosing the rice pudding, you might not be aware of unconscious drives and conflicts, buried memories, and sugar content of the blood, which influence your decision, but you are aware of such factors as weighing the caloric content against total intake for the day if you are on a diet, your memory of delight in eating past puddings, etc. The awareness of these factors and your symbolic weighing of them, together with inferences about possible results, help produce a feeling of being free to choose.

At this point, another factor enters the case. Your feeling of being free to choose helps determine your choice. Or, if you did not feel free to choose, you would not go through any symbolic manipulation of possible consequences of your act. And if you did not, then what you chose would be different. If your determinist friend proceeds to argue that the course and outcome of this symbolic manipulation are determined, we would agree as long as he realizes that *one* of the factors determining the outcome is the feeling of being free to manipulate ideas and that one of the results of this manipulation is the reinforcement of the feeling of being free to continue manipulation. In other words, we have a non-additive reaction. One of the "new" characteristics that arises as a result of a decision-making situation is the feeling of being free to make the decision. The outcome may have been completely determined, but we must recognize that in man one of the determining factors is the feeling of free will, which is both a product of selective response to a stimulus and a cause of it. The feeling of free will is both one of the stimuli for the effect—the decision—and an effect of the decision which thereby becomes a stimulus of it. This feedback, this circularity of action, is characteristic of living organisms possessing a nervous system and is especially prominent in man. Its presence prevents our depicting his operation in additive terms and simple stimulus-response terminology. It also destroys the strict determinist interpretation of his actions, for new characteristics, unpredictable on the basis of input alone, arise each moment as a result of ever-changing structure.

What I am trying to say, is this: In an extremely complicated organism like man, in which one of the most prominent characteristics is the non-additive character of the operation of his nervous system, strict determinism becomes inadmissible. It must not be forgotten that causality of any kind, partial or complete, is an *inference;*

it cannot be proved. The key question, then, as I see it, is this: Shall we make the inference that everything man does is completely determined, that he has no free will, that he can make no conscious and deliberate choices? I believe we should not. Any inference, if it is to be useful, should be founded on some evidence, and I think the available evidence is against it. More important, one of the main tests of any inference is its predictability. What predictions about man can we make if we assume complete determinism and no free will? As far as I can see, there are none which fit what we observe about him. He doesn't act like an automaton and he constantly maintains that he does feel free to choose.

Perhaps the most damaging evidence against the assumption is that even the staunchest determinist does not act as if he believes it. The test of what a man believes is not what he says but what he does. Give a determinist a menu and he will proceed to choose his food; in fact, he will even plan—choose—to write a paper proving he does not choose. The fact is, it would be impossible for a man to live if he acted completely on his belief in complete determinism. He would be the complete fatalist, would make no decisions, would never try to choose, and would quickly die unless completely cared for. And even then, he would have chosen not to choose!

The argument can be summarized as follows: According to strict determinism, any decision a man makes is the only one he can make. In a causally-connected universe the cards are stacked and only one hand, the determined one, is ever dealt. Since he could not have made any other decision than the one he did, he had no choice and therefore no free will.

Our reply to this is that this is an inference, absolutely unverifiable, because we would have to re-run the complete flow of events in the universe to see if the same decision is made. Since this is impossible, a statement of strict determinism becomes meaningless. Not only is it meaningless, it is useless as an inference. Having assumed it, we can make no predictions about the behavior of man which accord with what can be actually observed in his behavior. In fact, it predicts precisely the opposite of what is observed. All men would say they feel they are choosing. They act as if, and must act as if, they do, even the determinist who, while proclaiming strict determinism, chooses his food and decides to write a paper on strict determinism.

The rejection of strict determinism does not mean that all determinism goes out with it. Any behavior, any decision, any choice is determined; this we must assume. But it is not a simple, additive affair. Man can be conscious of abstracting. He has self-awareness. He is aware of manipulating symbols, of inferring what might occur if he follows one course of action or another, and he feels free to do this. All these are factors among a host of others which, we infer, "cause" his decision. After the decision is made, the memory of balancing alternatives and feeling free to do so reinforces his feeling of freedom of choice and decision-making. It feeds back and primes him to use his ability to manipulate symbolically courses of action when the next problem arises.

Thus we see that both free will and strict determinism are limited. We are not free to make any choice whatever. If there are six desserts on the menu, and if we want dessert, we choose one of them. Which we choose is determined, we infer, but our self-awareness and our ability to weigh alternatives and our feeling of being free to choose are factors in the final choice, even though they themselves are caused. With these facts in mind, the free-will-versus-determinism dichotomy can be resolved when we realize that it is due primarily to the confusion of two different levels of abstraction. The feeling of being free to choose is on the non-verbal level. Strict determinism is an inference, a higher-order abstraction. Therefore we cannot pose one against the other, for only abstractions of the same level can be counterposed. The problem, then, must be restated: Given the feeling of free will, what inferences shall we draw about its effects upon decisions that are made in a world which we infer is causally connected? What degree of freedom does a man have in a specific situation, taking into account the self-reflexive nature of the abstracting process?

It is highly probable that many readers will not agree with this analysis, either wholly or in part. No matter. However, there is one element in it I feel must be accepted—that we have to act as if we do choose and that how we choose affects our lives. All of science is predicated on this, otherwise there would be no point to accumulating reliable knowledge. We must act as if reliable knowledge were better than unreliable and, therefore, choose to seek it and use it. The whole system of general semantics is based on the assumption that by becoming conscious of the abstracting process we can choose more mature behavior patterns and more structurally correct linguistic ones. We can choose choice, without having to rule out determinism because, through consciousness of abstracting, we recognize that we are dealing with two different levels of abstraction.

THE PLEASURE PRINCIPLE

The problem of choice leads to another so-called dichotomy which, though not as sharply defined as the free-will-determinism controversy still is to be found, mostly implicitly, in many a philosophical and even psychological debate. It may be posed as the hedonist-rationalist dichotomy, or, in psychology, the existence or non-existence of the so-called "pleasure principle." Philosophically, the problem is often offered as a choice: Shall the goal of life be the attainment of the maximum of pleasure or, and here a number of alternatives are presented, shall the aim be the maximum development of rationality and/or morality? Essentially, the implication of the alternatives is that we do not, or should not, always select that course of action which we presume will give us the greatest pleasure or, put negatively, the least pain. The implication of the hedonist doctrine is that we always should, and have to.

As evidence against the hedonist position are proffered the examples of the martyr who chooses burning at the stake to recantation, or, less dramatically, the man who decides, on his doctor's advice, to undergo an operation which will entail much pain during the post-operative week, even though at the moment his ailment causes him no discomfort. As a final bit of evidence, the psychologists cite the existence of masochistic behavior.

It is our thesis that the pleasure principle holds in every choice we make, that we cannot act otherwise. Consider the man entering the hospital for his painful operation. Why is he doing it? Is he looking forward to the pain and discomfort? Hardly. Rather, he enters because he has made the inference that if he does not have the operation his health will be so affected that he will have years of pain, anxiety, and even early death, all of which he has decided will be more painful *in toto* than the post-operative week in the hospital.

Our toasting martyr has chosen this extremely painful death because he has inferred that if he recanted, his loss of faith would be more painful than his fiery ending. His whole symbolic world would be destroyed. He would be lost, cut off, drifting, open to all the naked horror and anxiety that would result from the destruction of his faith. We devote our lives to, and even give up our lives for, these higher-order abstractions, our faiths, our ethical and moral standards, and the loss of these is judged more painful than any feeling resulting from lower-order physiological disruptions such as toothaches and abdominal incisions and burning at the stake.

Even masochism can be interpreted in this way. If a man receives sexual pleasure from being punished, he feels the pleasure outweighs the pain. Or he may seek punishment because of an unconscious feeling of guilt. Consciously he may not know why, or ever realize, he is seeking punishment or even inviting self-destruction in devious and subtle ways, yet, unconsciously, he is inferring that the punishment will ease the pain of guilt which pervades his every moment and fills him with an unendurable, free-floating, unexplainable anxiety which is more painful than any beating or humiliation to which he may subject himself.

I believe that it is literally impossible not to act in accordance with this pleasure principle. Let us take an extreme and absurd example. Suppose you decide to prove me wrong. You take a hammer and smash your finger to prove you have deliberately chosen pain to no-pain. But do you regularly go around smashing your finger? Rather, so great is your desire and anticipated pleasure in proving me wrong that you infer it will be greater than the painful finger. You may be sorry later, but at the moment it is symbolic triumph you are after.

THE HEDONIST–NON-HEDONIST CONTROVERSY

What, then, is the difference, if any, between the hedonist and the non-hedonist? As far as I can see, it is a matter of degree of emphasis upon the two different levels of abstraction. The hedonist prefers his pleasure now; he gets relatively little from anticipation and fulfillment of higher-order abstractions such as beliefs, loyalties, or moral precepts. He does not care to delay his responses or his pleasures. At the other extreme we have a revolutionist who may spend his life in squalor, misery, and continuous danger in anticipation of one triumphant future day. The religious martyr gambles all present pleasures for the inferred pleasures of the next world. The extreme hedonist claims that only the pleasures resulting from the fulfillment of immediate, non-verbal, lower-order needs, such as those for food, drink, or sexual contact, are important. The extreme

non-hedonist claims that only those pleasures resulting from fulfillment of higher-order abstractions, such as ideals, are of value and
all the lower-order satisfactions merely incidental, unimportant though
necessary for life, even dangerous because they may tempt one to
neglect the higher-order abstractions.

Some people, when they realize the inevitability of our choosing
what we consider the least painful course of action in any situation,
jump to the conclusion that therefore man is inherently selfish and
therefore vile, degraded, and in need of salvation, preferably through
the adoption of their particular road to glory. In one sense, we are
inescapably selfish, if we mean by this that we always choose that
course most likely to be pleasant or less painful, but it seems to me
that since we have no choice in the matter we should not label
it morally good or bad, just as we cannot say that breathing or diges-
tion or sweating are morally good or bad. The moral judgment should
be made only in respect to the kinds of behavior indulged in, and
not on the fact that the least painful solution to a problem is always sought. The hedonist states that pleasure is to be sought mostly
from the satisfaction of the senses and lower-order abstractions and
as soon as possible. The non-hedonist plumps for the pleasure to
be gained from the fulfillment of the higher-order abstractions, and
this may be delayed for years. In both cases the pleasure principle
is at work; how it is employed differentiates the two, and it is about
this "how" that the moral judgment is to be made. That is, we may
say that the hedonist is bad (or good) because he seeks pleasure the
way he does, and the saint is good (or bad) because of the way he
seeks pleasure, but the seeking of it is neither good nor bad. It is as
inevitable as living.

If we do not differentiate between the *seeking* of the least painful
(or most pleasant) alternative in any situation, and the *kinds* of
situations in which it is sought, then we tend to equate the devil
and the saint—they both are selfish because they seek the most

pleasant solution to their problems. In other words, the goal in either case is personal pleasure and no value judgment should be made because no choice is possible. It is on the *methods* used to gain this pleasure that the moral judgment should be based, and to the methods the labels "selfish" or "unselfish" applied.

LOW-ORDER AND HIGH-ORDER SELFISHNESS

Generally speaking, in the Judeo-Christian tradition, "good," "moral," "unselfish," are applied to the pleasures gained through the fulfillment of higher-order abstractions—injunctions to help thy neighbor, love thine enemies, lift up the weak, aid the poor. It is claimed that the pleasure derived from this form of activity is not only "better" but more pleasant and lasting than the hedonist variety. In fact, the Buddhist proclaims that the most pleasant pleasantness is the avoidance of all pleasure and satisfaction of desires, indeed the elimination of all desires. The important point to remember here is that, just as there are differences in feeling between first-order and second-order emotions such as hate and love, so there are different kinds of pleasantness, different orders of pleasantness and feeling, corresponding, perhaps, to the level of abstraction upon which satisfaction is reached. And these differences cannot be defined; they must be experienced.

When we differentiate between these different levels of feelings and the ways in which they are generated, some of the mystery is taken out of seemingly paradoxical statements so common in almost all religious injunctions such as, "The greatest gain is in the giving," "One finds oneself by losing oneself," "Love is found by giving it." The gain, the self, the love that is found, are of a different kind and of a different order than their lower-order counterparts sought by the hedonists. In our next chapter, we shall delve more deeply into this matter of orders of self and orders of feeling and emotion and try to introduce some value judgments concerning them.

CONDITIONED AND CONDITIONAL RESPONSES

The most important difference between man and other forms of life is the degree to which he has developed his symbol-using capacity with language as its most prominent, though not only, characteristic. When talking and thinking about this it is easy to fall into the semantic trap of viewing it additively instead of non-additively. Thus, we talk as if man is "just" an animal *plus* a symbol-using capacity; that because of his animal origin he is merely an animal plus a "brain"; that basically, "really," he *is* an animal. Consequently, if we want to find out how he ticks, we just study the animals and then transfer our findings to man, with a little modification to allow for the changes his symbol-using produces. It isn't at all surprising that we then come to the conclusion that man is just an animal plus more reasoning ability.

There is no denying man's animal origin, nor his similarity to them in many ways. Much has been learned about the structure and functioning of his liver and lungs and heart and kidneys from animal experimentation and study. But when we come to his symbol-using capacity, which, for all practical purposes, does not exist in any animal, it becomes meaningless and sometimes dangerous to make generalizations about him on the basis of animal experimentation.

Most of us are familiar with the work of Pavlov on conditioned responses in dogs. Ring a bell and Fido salivates. Ring a bell and you can get a man to salivate. Therefore man is just another animal. It is true that man can be conditioned in this fashion and part of his behavior is learned through the conditioned-response mechanism. However, this is the lowest level and type of human learning and behavior. It shows his animal origin, and to this degree he resembles the dumb beast. But the conditioned response does not involve the use of his symbol-using capacity, the part if him that makes him human. Yes, man *can* act like an animal, but he need not. He can learn to delay his responses or even prevent them entirely. True, we can condition a man to blink or salivate or jump, but these are the least important kinds of responses man makes as far as psychological and social behavior are concerned.

In man, the conditioned response in learning any behavior pattern of psychosocial significance is the terminal learning method; in the animal it is almost the only one. For example, we can teach an ape and a man to drive a car. But we never give a driver's license to an ape, because in our society the most important part of driving a car is not sheer mechanical skill but the higher-order evaluations necessary for driving in traffic. Most of what we teach the ape we do through the conditioning mechanism. When we teach a man to drive, not only does he have to learn muscular skills (which are almost wholly learned through an animal-like conditioning process), but he also has to learn how to size up and solve complex and constantly novel traffic problems. For this his symbol-using capacities are necessary and cannot be learned solely through the relatively simple stimulus-response method of the conditioning process.

All of this is obvious, yet we have the spectacle of Watson and the early behaviorists becoming so enamoured of the apparently simple stimulus-response mechanism in Pavlov's dogs that they tried to eliminate all symbolic behavior in man. They claimed that reasoning is "just" covert muscle movement. Animals do not use symbols, man is an animal, therefore man does not use symbols. Proof? Watch the dogs learning to salivate on signal. Put in the stimulus, crank the machine, and out comes the response, just like a slot machine. Very convenient, but unfortunately over-simple even for learning in dogs, and preposterous for man. A lovely map resembling no known territory.

In man, practically all behavior, even the instinctual, becomes modified by his symbol reactions. Breathing, the beat of the heart, the movement of the viscera, the dilation of the blood vessels, all can become invested with symbolic significance which changes their behavior and, in turn, modifies the symbol behavior in a most complex and dynamic fashion. The old, additive, stimulus-response, simple cause-effect model of his behavioral mechanism will not work. Man's most significant responses are condition*al,* not conditioned. That is, the conditioned response is no longer automatic as an animal's, but can be delayed and modified through the use of higher-order abstractions.

Consequently, when we run rats through mazes and study how cats team up with mice to operate food chutes, we should not then come forth with "the laws of learning." Rather, they should be labeled "the laws of learning for animals" and we should be wary of applying them to man, the major portion of whose learning involves symbol-using activity which inevitably must change even the simplest learned responses.

I do not wish to give the impression that all psychological experimentation has involved these patterns of misevaluation, but examination of the literature will show that more of it exists than should. The structure of the writing implies that man's nervous system functions in essentially the same way as the animal's in most respects, but this is not at all borne out when we actually observe man in situations he considers of importance to himself. One of the results of such writing is that too many psychology students accept it uncritically as factual and proceed to adopt these patterns of talking about their subject. This in turn subtly influences the nature of the experiments they devise and run and the interpretations of the results they achieve, usually in the direction of confirming the original hypothesis, thus reinforcing the distorted patterns of thought and talk.

In our discussion of second-order love and hatred, we saw how the symbolic processes influence the quality of the feelings they engender. Second-order feelings, or emotions, are less violent, less intense, less "primitive." They tend to take on the characteristics of higher-order abstractions. They are more enduring, more stable, more easily influenced by reason. Some seem to have no easily recognizable lower-order counterparts as love and hatred have. Some are extremely valuable and should be deliberately cultivated; others are an abomination and a curse, to be avoided like the plague. But no matter what their character, the important point is that animals, having no symbol-using capacity, cannot have the second-order feelings and emotions, and no amount of experimentation upon them will tell us anything about ourselves in respect to these second-order effects except in a negative way, i.e., the behavior of organisms without them. The existence and importance of these second-order effects in man are overlooked and, in effect, denied: love is love and hate is hate both in man and beast.

One of the goals of general semantics is the complete integration of the different levels of the nervous system, a mutual interaction of these levels without identification, objectification, or reversal of the natural order of abstraction. Each level would perform its role without warping the activity of the others, the "emotions" not distorting the logic of the higher orders, but rather enlivening their activity, the "reasoning" not cutting itself off from the emotional level, but rather enriching the emotional life. In other words, the lower and higher orders of abstraction should function like the instruments of a symphony orchestra, each playing its proper part, each a part of a whole which would be destroyed if one of them tried to assume the role and character of another.

BEAUTY WITH A CAPITAL B: BEAUTY AND TRUTH

Let us return to our examination of some of the reciprocal effects of the integration, or at least partial integration, and interaction of the higher and lower orders of abstraction. I must remind the reader that the following material in this chapter is purely speculative on my part, has not been verified, and therefore should be treated with even more suspicion than the other parts of this book.

The free-will-determinism dichotomy seems to confound us on the verbal level; it appears most often as a paradox, a problem in logic. An equally hardy philosophic perennial, Beauty, dwells more on the non-verbal levels, or, more precisely, on different orders of the non-verbal level. It is a more mysterious, less tangible, problem. Where free will and determinism stand out clearly and sharply as implacable and irreconcilable opponents, Beauty eludes us. It is not so much a battle as a search. Where is it, in the object or in the eye of the observer? What is it, a sensible quality or an evanescent essence not directly perceived but intuited or revealed?

While opposing camps have many theories as to the nature of the beast, they are rather sharply divided as to its lair. One sees it as a quality *in* things, like color or form or sound. The other, as we have noted, claims it is as much a part of the observer's reaction as is any other quality. Whether my attempt to solve the problem does so or simply adds to the confusion I leave to the reader. Naturally, as a general semanticist, I see the controversy as a confusion of the levels of abstraction.

One of the main objections to the theory that beauty[3] is *in* the object, as are other qualities (we've already been through this business of qualities being in the object—they aren't, but are our internal responses to quality-less atomic phenomena) is the infinite variety of things we find beautiful, ranging from musical compositions to the wailing of a baby, from a steak to rancid butter, from Michaelangelo's Moses to an arrangement of wires, bones, feathers, and bottlecaps labeled "Abstraction No. 24." A bloody battle, a scientific theory, a sunset, a flower, the agonized cry of a tortured man, the smooth hum of a well-tuned motor, the solution to a mathematical problem, the distended lips and ear lobes of a Ubangi woman, the technique of a

[3] It does not make much difference for our purposes here whether we spell it with a small or capital B, so we shall use the small letter unless we wish to wax ecstatic or emphasise or contrast.

surgeon, all these diversities and an infinity of others have been considered beautiful at some time by some men. What single element common to all can be labeled "beauty"?

The problem appears no closer to a solution if we claim that beauty isn't in the object but in the observer. While this would account for the diversity of things found beautiful, there still remains the question of how beauty differs from other qualities. Perhaps, by taking a concrete example, we can find our way to *an* answer. I am writing this seated in a comfortable chair on the porch of our home. I look out over a valley through which the mist is slowly drifting in strangely shaped patches and clumps, now like a procession of sleep-walking ghosts, now floating like prehistoric monsters in a timeless trance. There is a very gentle rain falling; there is no wind. The raindrops drip from leaf to leaf to the roots of the vines that twist about the trellis. The smell of black earth and leaf mold rises from the ground. The trees and bushes and the houses in the distance have the detached, eternal, dreamlike quality of a Japanese landscape. Suddenly I feel a nameless indescribable: What a beautiful scene! It IS beautiful!

Not having the sense to let well enough alone, I proceed to analyze the situation. First, being a general semanticist, I change my language. It *isn't* beautiful; it appears beautiful to me. Why? Well, I enjoyed watching the metamorphic changes of the mist shapes, the sound of the raindrops, the smell of the earth, the timeless quality of the scene. But why were these parts of the scene so pleasant to me? Who knows? Maybe my childhood love of fairy tales had something to do with my seeing and enjoying ghosts and witches in the shrouds of mist. But my "whys" quickly run into a dead end. Why did I like the fairy tales? Why? Why? Why? In the final analysis, the only answer is, "I do because I do." If we cannot say that there is *no* accounting for taste, we can at least state that there is very little.

But where is beauty in all this? I like the shape of the fog, the sounds of rain, the smell of earth, etc. Perhaps there may even have been a hum of a plane overhead or the yell of a neighbor in the distance, which I disliked and unconsciously repressed in order not to spoil the scene, just as there may have been a twinge in my arm or an itch on my leg, which were equally ignored. Each perceived element in the scene produces a pleasant or unpleasant feeling in me to varying degrees. I am conscious of some, unconscious of others.

The abstracting process does not stop at this point. We have seen its integrative, summarizing character come into play as we move up the levels of abstraction. Even at this low-order feeling level, it proceeds to "add up" all these discrete feelings of pleasantness and unpleasantness into one single state or evaluation of the situation-as-a-whole. That is, we find the scene-organism reaction-as-a-whole evaluated as pleasant or unpleasant. And we either like or dislike it *as a whole* to the degree we find it pleasant or unpleasant *as a whole*. This Gestalt-like, structure-forming, summarizing, integrating activity is characteristic of our nervous system in operation and is to be found on all levels of abstraction.

And where is beauty all this time? I believe it is a feeling, a higher-order feeling, a resultant of this summarizing activity. It is a feeling generated by response to the structure as a whole. It is a feeling whose precursor is the feeling of the pleasantness of the whole, or perhaps the latter raised to an intensity which produces a conviction of certainty that sweeps away all doubt about, or notice of, details that might detract its being evaluated as "all pleasant, all beautiful."

If we grant that something like this occurs, why has there been such as air of mystery about beauty which we do not find surrounding other abstractions? I believe that there are two factors involved. First, there is the confusion about its causal precursors. If I see the green "in" the trees, and I find it pleasant, and can connect causally the color and the feeling, I say "The green caused it." The same applies to every other detail in the landscape. I can establish, at least I feel I can, by neglecting unconscious factors, a simple causal connection between each sensory detail and the feeling-response (pleasant or unpleasant) to it. But the feeling of the pleasantness-of-the-whole cannot be traced to any of the individual elements in the scene, for its precursors were the individual pleasant feelings, not the individual sensations which "caused" the individual pleasant feelings.

Now enter the mystery. We argue that since, on analysis, there can be found a response of pleasantness or unpleasantness to every sensory element in the scene—a shape, a color, etc.—therefore there must be some sensory element or quality which "causes" the feeling of the pleasantness of the whole. But because this feeling is not immediately generated by an individual quality in the scene, naturally we do not find it. However, our language structure says it must be there, or somewhere, but it must exist—meaning it must have sensory existence in the sense that individual qualities exist. So instead of changing the map to fit the territory we say, "Yes, there is a quality or structural element—beauty—*in* the object which causes this feeling, but it is mysterious and elusive. You can't just pin it down like a color or sound or shape or observable technique or operation, but it must be there. How else could the feeling of beauty be caused?"

A second factor which contributes to the mystery and confusion is that this is a feeling about the structure-as-a-whole. The structure-as-a-whole has characteristics not found in any of the parts and these non-additive characteristics are perhaps the key ones which "touch off" the feeling of beauty. But these "wholeness" characteristics cannot be pointed to, cannot be directly observed, cannot be discovered by analysis, for analysis, which is a concentration on the elements of a structure, immediately destroys the wholeness characteristics. The perception of structure-as-a-whole is of a higher level of abstraction than is perception of the elements of the structure, and the characteristics of this level, as would be expected, have different characteristics. Being farther removed from the direct sensory level, the "wholeness" characteristics are less concrete, more ineffable, more mysterious.

Perhaps an analogy between the perception of beauty and the concept of triangularity will be helpful. We can point to individual triangles of all shapes, but not to triangularity, which is on the next level of abstraction, a sort of summation or integration of certain characteristics of individual triangles with differences neglected. If you tried to point out triangularity in an individual triangle, you could never find it and might be tempted to talk about the mysterious essence, triangularity, in it. We call this kind of confusion of two levels of abstraction objectification—the projecting of object-like (sensory) characteristics upon a level of abstraction above the object level. Similarly, we objectify beauty when we try to turn a higher-order feeling into a lower-order sensory characteristic. Most sensory abstractions are projected out to the object; we see colors as "out there," while feelings are not projected; we feel them in us. When we try to project the feeling, beautiful, "out there" we compound the mystery. Beauty does not have the concreteness of sensory perceptions. Yet we try to make it so in our attempt at projection.

Note how the language contributes to the confusion! We talk of the *sense* of beauty, the implication being that it can be sensed the way we sense colors or shapes. Talking this way leads to thinking this way and soon to the hopeless quest. We can, if we wish, speak of the sense of structure-as-a-whole, but this is so much more elusive and unanalyzable than lower-order sensing, that it almost inevitably will lead to confusion unless we carefully distinguish between the different levels of abstraction.

I think it is important that we distinguish between the evaluations "pretty" and "beautiful." Both are feelings about the structure as a whole. The difference is one of intensity. When we evaluate something as being pretty we are more or less aware of the abstracting process, of those characteristics of the object which we find unpleasant. However, the pleasant ones outweigh the unpleasant and so produce our feeling of prettiness-as-a-whole, even though we are aware of the unpleasant characteristics. When this feeling reaches a certain intensity or threshhold, all notice of the unpleasant characteristics disappears and the object becomes "all-pretty-without-a-doubt," i.e., beautiful. It is then that beauty becomes truth and truth beauty. One becomes certain that the smallest change in the structure, any rearrangement of a part, will destroy the beauty of the structure-as-a-whole. That and only that arrangement of structural elements could produce this profound and moving feeling of beauty; any other arrangement would be false, would not work, would not seem right, would not be "Truth." For this reason no poem can be translated and remain the same poem. If the translation is a success it is a new poem. "Truth" in this sense is not the scientist's verified public knowledge, but rather the feeling of the rightness or correctness of the structure, a sort of lower-order, verified, private knowledge. Science gives us public truths; art gives us feelings about structure—private Truth.

We can summarize what we have theorized about beauty in the diagram on p. 136.[4]

LOVE WITH A CAPITAL L: A "BECAUSAL" EVALUATION

Moving on from beauty, we shall proceed to a very closely related higher-order feeling or emotion, Love. Here we postulate a similar abstractive structure. As with beauty, there is an evaluation of the structural elements, each giving rise to its particular feeling of pleasantness or unpleasantness in varying degrees, each evaluation a function of a host of conscious and unconscious high- and low-order abstractions. These are summed into one feeling of the pleasantness or unpleasantness of the whole. If concentration is upon the structural elements, there arises the evaluation of pretty or beautiful or their negatives.

[4] The diagram on p. 136 and material on Beauty, Love, and Happiness are adapted from my article, "Some Functional Patterns on the Non-verbal Level," *Etc.: A Review of General Semantics,* vol. IV, no. 3 (Spring, 1947), pp. 196–212.

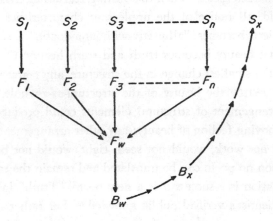

$S_1\ S_2\ S_3\ \cdots\ S_n$ — Sensory perceptions such as color, hardness, taste, etc., or an awareness of any element of a structure at any level of abstraction, such as part of a theory, mathematical proof, etc.

$F_1\ F_2\ F_3\ \cdots\ F_n$ — Feelings of the pleasantness or unpleasantness of $S_1\ S_2\ S_3\ \cdots\ S_n$.

F_w — The feeling of the pleasantness or unpleasantness of the whole structure of what is perceived.

B_w — The feeling of the beauty of the whole, i.e., unqualified certainty of the pleasantness of the whole structure.

B_x — What we say about the cause of F_w (or B_w). We claim it must be due to some mysterious element, S_x, *in* the perceived structure which directly causes F_w, just as $S_1\ S_2\ S_3\ \cdots\ S_n$ directly cause $F_1\ F_2\ F_3\ \cdots\ F_n$, not realizing that F_w is a non-additive summation of $F_1\ F_2\ F_3\ \cdots\ F_n$.

If, however, the concentration is upon a causal relationship between the object and the feeling of pleasantness or unpleasantness, then there arises the feeling-evaluation, like or love. That is, *because* I feel the object or person or theory, has produced this very pleasant or unpleasant feeling, I like or dislike it. If the like passes our postulated intensity threshhold, all doubt and all remembrance or notice of disliked characteristics are forgotten, not noticed, or re-evaluated as nice, and then the like has become love.

The mysteriousness of this sweet mystery of life can be attributed, in part, I think, to our trying to discover *the* element or characteristic or quality *in* the beloved which accounts for this profound feeling; and since, as with beauty, it has as its immediate precursor the feeling of the pleasantness of the whole and not any of the sensory elements, we never find it.

I realize that this is a rather mean, shabby, and, in a way, naïvely simple treatment of so important and complex an emotion. However, only the basic structure is simple; the complexity arises in the dynamic and shifting character of the evaluation of the mass of elements which give rise to this emotion. Happily, elucidation of this mechanism will not dispel the *felt* mystery and majesty of it.

It will be noticed that we have labeled love an emotion and beauty a feeling. Emotions seem to be directed feelings based upon "becausal" evaluations. When we love or hate, we infer that a causal connection exists between the object and our feelings. This varies from the animal-like, infantile, literal identification of stimulus and response, e.g., mother and satisfaction of the infant's needs, to the more sophisticated, complex evaluation of the mature adult.

HAPPINESS WITH A CAPITAL H: A SUMMATIVE EVALUATION

If we draw our model in terms of stimulus and response, bearing in mind what we have previously stated about the oversimplicity of stimulus-response cause-effect terminology, we see that beauty arises primarily from an evaluation of the structure of the stimulus as such, love from a concentration upon the causal connection between stimulus and response. There remains one more possibility, concentration upon the evaluation of the response as such. If the response to the stimulus is of such strength that its pleasantness overbalances all other unpleasantness feelings we have at that moment, we say that it makes us happy. That is, at any given moment all our feelings are summed to produce one feeling of the pleasantness or unpleasantness of the state of our organism-as-a-whole. If this feeling is pleasant we are happy; if it is unpleasant we are unhappy. If the feeling passes the intensity threshhold wherein all the unpleasant feelings of the moment are completely unnoticed, we are in that allness state known as ecstacy; on the negative side our state would be utter despair.

The similarity of structure of these three feelings perhaps accounts for their occurring more frequently as a group or complex of feelings rather than singly. No loving mother ever had a homely child, no lover an ugly mate. And the ecstacy of love and beauty is a poetic commonplace.

These three feelings, which we labeled Truth, together with the feeling of the rightness or correctness of these evaluations, form a constellation which has plagued philosophers and artists from the beginning of recorded history. We have tried to demonstrate that this confusion hinges on a number of misevaluations involving identification of different levels of abstraction, the objectification of higher-order abstractions, and the neglect of the non-additive character of the abstracting process.

We have attempted to show that these higher-order feelings seem mysterious because they are feelings about structure-as-a-whole, the result of synthesizing processes which are automatic and unconscious. The structure-as-a-whole has characteristics not to be found in any of the parts and, most important, these characteristics can never be pointed out, demonstrated, or analyzed. The minute this is attempted, the structure-as-a-whole is no longer perceived, for analysis is a deliberate, conscious concentration upon the parts, a process which is the opposite of synthetic Gestalt activity.

A man in love with a woman may try to analyze his feelings, to find out why he loves her. This analysis, this "cortical" reasoning is conscious, deliberate, and largely on the verbal level. He discovers that he likes her hair, her figure, the way she laughs, the quality of her voice, perhaps, even, her "mind." He may not be aware that she is very much like his mother in certain respects and that this has a potent attraction for him. He knows she is stubborn and this bothers him. She tends to talk too much and this bothers him even more. But these are counterbalanced by her wealth, of which he is conscious, and a host of other factors of which he is not. But in all this analysis he cannot find out why he loves her. Indeed, during the analysis he isn't loving her. Actually, according to our analysis, the only answer to his question is that he loves her because she has produced in him an intense feeling of pleasantness about the whole of her structure, a feeling which is an unconscious, non-deliberate summation of all the individual pleasant and unpleasant feelings the "parts" of her provoke in him. Analysis can uncover only these individual feelings about individual parts and not the higher-order integration which is never discoverable through analysis. Analysis is on the verbal level, synthesis, in this case, on the non-verbal, and the characteristics of the feelings provoked by each process are different.

Of course, this does not mean that analytical activity does not induce higher-order feelings like beauty, love, etc., but that it does so indirectly. For example, a man can listen to a Beethoven symphony and find it beautiful even though he knows nothing of music. If he studies music and the structure of the symphony, his conscious knowledge of the structure can produce pleasant feelings in him and these then become elements in his evaluation of the stimulus-as-a-whole, which leads to a feeling of its beauty even more intense than the previous evaluation. On the other hand, he may concentrate so much on the analysis that the synthesis does not take place. Now he "knows" it is beautiful but no longer feels it, a sorry state that afflicts many "intellectuals," who cannot stop verbalizing and allow the non-verbal activity to operate. The ideal is to be able to function on all levels of abstraction.

OF TIME AND TIMES

Although we most often associate science with verbal-level activity, this does not mean that the non-verbal, aside from the bodily activity of performing an experiment, is not involved. Indeed, the principle of parsimony, Occam's razor, is a direct expression of the influence of the non-verbal level. If we have two theories which account equally well for a set of phenomena and have equal predictive value, we choose the one that is simplest. This choice is not only a desire to save time and effort, but is, I believe, an expression of a feeling about the structure-as-a-whole, a feeling about its beauty. The structure is neat, it has symmetry, it is artistic. If there are two equally valid proofs of, or solutions to, a mathematical problem, the mathematician will select the one which is most "elegant"—a term he cannot define, a characteristic he cannot describe. To him "elegant" is synonymous with "beautiful."

These four feelings are not the only sources of mystery for man. One of the most mysterious is time. What is it? We talk of "time flowing," of "endless time," of "eternity," and of "no time." We distinguish between psychological time and physical time. The science fiction writer reverses time, speeds up time, goes back into time, invents time machines. What is it "really"?

As with most mysteries, analysis here shows a confusion of levels of abstraction. We must carefully distinguish between the "sense" of time and "time." One is a feeling, the other a higher-order abstraction. All of us have a "sense" of duration. It is awareness of awareness, one result of concentrating on our awareness of happenings and our memory of them, an awareness of the repetition of cyclical phenomena. Rhythmic activity is characteristic of all living things and of all their parts. A sense of rhythm is "built in." It cannot be defined; you know what it is when you dance, beat time to music, walk, breathe. When we concentrate on any felt rhythm or repetition of occurrences, a sense of duration arises. It requires a memory of the repeated phenomena; if there is no memory of them there is no sense of duration; the greater the number remembered, the longer the duration sensed. This is called psychological time, which is a higher-order feeling resulting from a summing of awareness of individual occurrences through the deliberate concentration on the memory of them. This may involve, perhaps, an unconscious comparison or matching of the repeated occurrences with rhythmic bodily activity, such as heartbeat and the breathing cycle. I am postulating a process very similar to that which gives rise to the other higher-order feelings already discussed. There is the awareness of individual occurrences; these are timeless. Then, because we are able to be aware of our awareness through deliberate memory and concentration, we get a feeling of the duration of the string of events, a sort of summed-up feeling about the group as a whole.

At this point we can move to the verbal level and talk about this feeling and about the individual occurrences. We can number them. We compare this number with the numbers of other occurrences (times) like the revolution of the hands of a clock or the earth about the sun, the phases of the moon, etc. Then we talk. We say, "time is past," "one hour has gone," "it took two days." What have we actually seen passing? Certainly not time! We saw numbers of events and we had a sense of duration of the compared group as a whole.

Then we ask ourselves, "What 'out there' has caused this feeling of duration?" Answer, "The flow of time." So, like beauty, time becomes a mysterious thing *in* events, or surrounding them, or of them, which causes the feeling of duration. We objectify this feeling and talk of it as having physical properties like sensed objects. It flows, it can be manipulated, it can be measured. Then, because we talk this way, we assume it has physical existence, the existence of sensory objects. The feeling of duration most certainly exists when we are experiencing it, but its immediate precursor is not some property of things "out there," but the result of the integrating activity of the nervous system, i.e., the abstracting process. When we move to the verbal level and try to analyze the feeling of duration and its causes, we always discover, not Time, but times of something occuring somewhere. When we number these elements and compare them with set standards, we get times of times—physical time. Note that these times of something are not felt as duration; that comes when these times are structured into a whole. So we see that, as with beauty, love, or happiness, analysis always destroys what we seek— a higher-order feeling whose fundamental characteristics are produced by the structure-as-a-whole and are not to be found in any of the parts.

We have attempted to indicate or hypothesize the psychoneurological structure of a group of feelings and emotions, concentrating on certain similarities which link them into a complex and which might account for their occurring more often as a group than singly. However, there are important differences and we can group these feelings according to differences as well as similarities. In one group we can put such higher-order feelings as beauty, happiness, truth, despair, awe, wonder, which are characterized by being produced "automatically." We cannot decide deliberately to feel that an object is beautiful or ugly, or to be ecstatic or in despair, much as we would like to. The feeling may come about indirectly, as a result of our desire to see the beauty of an object, but at the moment of the feeling, the process is mostly an unconcious one.

On the other hand, we have higher-order feelings or emotions such as love, hate, fear, worry, anxiety, and doubt. While we cannot deliberately will these to come or go on a first-order level, we can consciously and directly inaugurate a program of thinking which will produce or suppress their second-orders. That is, we can choose to hate our hatred, love our love, or choose not to fear our fear or worry about our worry. I believe this is due to the fact that this latter group is much more cortically mediated and therefore more subject to conscious control.

7

The Value of Values

THE RELATIVIST-ABSOLUTIST CONTROVERSY

THROUGHOUT this book we have stated that choices can be made, or rather, we have to act as if they can, and that this choosing applies not only to objects but also to feelings, attitudes, and values. This brings us to our next important topic: the basis for making ethical and moral value judgments.

We can divide value philosophies into two groups: the absolutistic and the relativistic. Although the proponents in each camp differ among themselves on minor points, we shall arbitrarily ignore these differences as unimportant for our discussion. Charles Frankel, in discussing the philosophy of Jacques Maritain,[1] who typifies the Platonic, absolutistic position, finds the following to be characteristic of the absolutist:

1. Men have to believe that values which sanction or prohibit social action must rest on something outside themselves that is suprahuman, timeless, and unchanging.
2. These fixed absolutes and eternal truths apply to all cultures at all times; they do not vary from age to age.
3. History, the career of mankind, the life of the individual, are meaningless unless judged against these eternal truths.

[1] Charles Frankel, *The Case for Modern Man,* New York, Harper & Brothers, 1955.

144

While some absolutists believe that these truths are God-Given and created, others hold them to be inherent in nature itself. In either case, they are "there," and their authority is not to be questioned.

The relativists maintain that these eternal truths are neither eternal nor inherently true; that they are man-made and subject to change by man, and that their truth is always relative to a given culture at a given date.

The absolutists hold that if we accept the relativist position, we have no way of evaluating one form of action as bad or another as good, except on the basis of personal preference. If theft is not inherently bad then we have no reason for opposing it other than that we just don't like it. If someone does like it, he is free to claim it is good and his judgment is as valid as ours. Or, broadening the base of the argument from personal to group preference, a custom is good if the group or society in which it occurs approves. If a different society evaluates this custom as bad, it is bad; and one judgment is as good and valid as the other. If certain Eskimo tribes seal up the old and ailing in igloos and leave them to die, there is nothing essentially wrong or bad in this procedure. It is right for them although it is wrong for us in our culture.

THE SUPPOSED AMORALITY OF SCIENCE

The relativist's inability to provide a universal standard for making choices stems from his assumption that such a standard, to be valid and useful, would have to have its roots in scientific fact and procedure and this is impossible, he claims, because science is amoral. Science, according to him, cannot tell us what our values should be, only how to achieve our goals once they are chosen.

This view of the amorality of science has come under attack in recent years. Essentially the argument runs as follows: There is a value system in science, but it is implicit rather than explicit, and therefore so obvious as to be totally ignored or taken for granted. Actually, the scientist, when acting as a scientist, is more moral and ethical than any saint. He never lies or distorts the truth as he finds it no matter how personally distasteful to him its implications may be, for this is the cardinal sin in science. He is always searching his soul (his theory) to find its weaknesses, always ready to confess his errors when they are pointed out or when he discovers them himself. His God is Fact and before it he is most humble. No theory, no belief, no matter how beloved, is strong enough to resist the contrary fact.

Of course the scientist, being as human as some of us, often deviates from this ideal. He is tempted to, and often does, cling too long to a theory which he may have built over a lifetime of devoted and dedicated work. Yet even he, though he may not be objective enough to see that his theory is no longer tenable, will subscribe wholeheartedly to the ideal of submission of theory before the court of fact. The map must be made to fit the territory; the territory must never be warped to fit the map.

THE LYSENKO CONTROVERSY

Now these are value judgments and there is no known way of proving scientifically that distorting evidence is inherently bad, that verification of observation is inherently good, or that all men everywhere must subscribe to, or see any value in, these values. An excellent example of this is seen in the Lysenko genetics controversy. Stated roughly and oversimply, Lysenko, a Russian agronomist and horticulturist, asserted that acquired characteristics can be transmitted to offspring. He claimed, for example, that if the seed of winter wheat is treated by certain freezing techniques, it changes to spring wheat, and all the progeny of this treated winter wheat will be of the spring wheat strain. According to Western scientists, and to the majority of Russian geneticists prior to the rise of Lysenko, this meant that freezing changed the genetic makeup of the winter wheat; according to all present theory this is impossible. Lysenko outraged the western scientists even further by his claim that genes did not exist and chromosomes had nothing to do with the inheritance of characteristics. In fact, he discarded the whole of Mendelian genetics and turned back to the discredited Lamarckian theory. In the course of the dispute most of the Russian geneticists who supported the Mendelian position were killed off, disappeared, or were forced to make humiliating recantations. Lysenko was promoted to the top position in the Institute of Genetics. The final blow to classical Mendelian genetics came at the final session of the V. I. Lenin Academy of Agricultural Science on August 7, 1948, when Lysenko dramatically proclaimed that his theories had been approved by the Central Committee of the Communist Party. Amid thunderous applause a science died in Russia.[2]

Of course Marxists and fellow-travelers all over the world supported Lysenko and ground out thousands of articles, pamphlets, papers, and books, "proving" the correctness of his views. It is around that little word "proof" that the crux of the controversy is to be found, not in the specific evidence on each side. As Julian Huxley stated after a careful sifting of claims and counterclaims, "It speedily became clear that the major issue at stake was not the truth or falsity of Lysenko's claims, but the overriding of science by ideological and political authority."[3] All of Lysenko's claims may have been true, yet there still would be as great a controversy, for Lysenko had no use for scientific method. He never ran controlled experi-

[2] Conway Zirkle, *Death of A Science in Russia,* Philadelphia, University of Pennsylvania Press, 1949.

[3] Julian Huxley, *Heredity East and West,* New York, Henry Schuman, 1949, p. ix.

ments; his language was fuzzy and bristled with political dogma and even diatribe and invective when explaining his theories. He neglected contradictory evidence and was not above distorting what evidence he had. But worst of all was his standard of proof—conformity to Marxian doctrine. A theory was true if it was consistent with Marxian ideology, false if it was not. In other words, a theory is tested primarily against another theory and only secondarily against fact. In Western science the opposite is true.

After Stalin died Lysenko, along with many others, fell out of favor and his theories with him. Now the Party faithful are busily engaged in proving that classical Mendelian genetics is supported by Marxian doctrine. It's a mighty flexible doctrine; you can prove anything with it, even contradictory theories. And because it proves everything, it proves nothing.

It is interesting and provoking that neither Lysenko nor the Marxists can "see" that doctrine should conform to fact and not vice versa. It is "obvious" to Western scientists that it should and the opposite is "obvious" to the Marxists. How, cry the absolutists, can you prove one is right, the other wrong, without recourse to some absolute standard which is neither of East nor West, but independent of all culture and all times?

The hidden assumption in this argument is that if one does not have absolute moral and ethical standards he can have none at all. We have met two-valued orientations before and, as with most of them, "it ain't necessarily so." Even if there were absolute, God-given standards, we are still left with our problem; it is simply put off one step farther, for we still have no way of proving that it is moral or immoral, right or wrong, to obey the word of God. It may be expedient because He is omnipotent, but I can imagine a good case being made for disobeying them on the grounds that we have no choice in the matter. The argument of the theologian that we do have choice simply pushes the argument one step farther. As

Frankel states, "There is, in short, no way around the fact that it is human beings who write their own moral tickets, and that we act on our own responsibility when we choose the values on which we stake our lives. The demand for a total justification of our values is only an expression of the human desire, as insistent as it is pathetic, to have the benefits of free choice with none of its troubles and risks. 'It was the woman who made me,' said Adam. 'It was the serpent,' said the woman. 'I am one of God's creatures,' whispers the serpent." [4]

In this chapter, I shall attempt to make explicit some of the values on which the general semanticist, or at least this one, stakes his life. The Aristotelian structure of our language contributes mightily to the confusion found in philosophical discussions of value. We say that something *has* value or it *is* valuable, the implication being that the value exists in the object independent of the valuator, i.e., the object is said to have intrinsic or inherent value. If this is true then it follows that all men must find such an object valuable. This is obviously untrue for observation will show that almost anything deemed valuable by one man or group will be regarded as useless or even a menace by others. If it is argued that the value is there waiting to be discovered and that the fault lies with those who are too ignorant, uncivilized, or bad to appreciate the value, analysis shows that there is no possible way of proving this assertion. Even if it is used as a working hypothesis without attempt at proof, it seems to me to be practically useless in solving such value problems as being able to predict whether or not something deemed valuable by one person will be so judged by another.

A DEFINITION OF "VALUE"

I believe that the more useful, correct, and common sense view is the one we have assumed in regard to the nature of qualities—that

[4] Frankel, *op. cit.,* p. 64.

they are the end results of functional relationships between observer and observed. Let us take, for example, da Vinci's Mona Lisa, which is considered very valuable by many men and for many reasons. Many find it extremely beautiful; it satisfies an esthetic need. Many will say it is valuable because it is rare, and if it is rare, it is wanted, because the possession of a rare object gives some people a feeling of power, or bolsters the ego, or satisfies some complex of unconscious and conscious wants. Carrying this one step farther, this passion for possessing the rare gives the painting a high monetary value. Some will deem it valuable simply because they have been told that it is, and though they derive no esthetic or intellectual enjoyment from it, will assume that if they had it they could sell it and thereby satisfy their desire for money.

In one case we began with the non-verbal level—the process of satisfaction of a need and the resulting pleasant feeling. Then we proceeded to the verbal level and postulated a causal connection between the object and the pleasant feeling. We said, or reasoned, or inferred, that the object caused it, and will continue to do so in the future. On the other hand, we may start with the inference that an object or person or group or process will satisfy a need at some time. In either case, evaluative processes are at work, but because the Aristotelian structure of our language cannot handle processes adequately, it forces us to objectify them. Instead of saying, "The Mona Lisa, under certain conditions, at times satisfies my needs, may do so in the future, or has in the past because of such and such characteristics I abstract from it," we are literally forced to turn away from this process-implying map to a thing-implying one. In effect, we say, "The Mona Lisa *has* value because it satisfies needs," or "It satisfies needs because it *has* value."

In the first case we imply that through the process of satisfying needs the object gains something, a quality we call "value." If the object does not satisfy, it does not gain value, or when it ceases to satisfy the quality disappears. The object no longer "has" value. This is a very peculiar quality indeed. It is not a sensory abstraction such as redness or bitterness, nor is it a feeling abstraction such as pleasant, hateful, beautiful. It has no non-verbal referent. Rather, it is a higher-order abstraction, a shorthand way of saying, "the object satisfies some of my needs." But the Aristotelian structure of the sentence, "It has value," deludes us into thinking and talking as if the object had a quality—value—in the same sense that it "has" sensory qualities or that it names some higher-order feeling like beauty or love produced by our interaction with the object. Since its referent is not a low-order abstraction, a sensation, or feeling of some order, it must, then, refer to a higher-order abstraction which may be either a statement on the same level of abstraction, i.e., another and briefer way of saying something like, "This object satisfies me and therefore I desire it," or it may be a still higher-order abstraction such as, "I classify this object as valuable." Moving toward the lower verbal levels from this meaning of, "It is valuable," we would come to, "A valuable object is one which is desired because it satisfies certain needs at certain times." We could move still lower to the descriptive level by using a specific example of an object being valued, describing as specifically as possible the processes which occur.

Coming to the second alternative, "It satisfies because it has value," the sentence implies that a quality in the object either produces satisfaction by itself or is at least a needed ingredient in addition to other qualities. We have already discussed the peculiar and impossible characteristics of this quality. Consequently I think we are forced to the conclusion that since it has no non-verbal referent it cannot be a quality in the sense we have used this term throughout this book. An object cannot "have" value.

But this does not mean that the term "value" has no value—we shall be using it after we strip away its Aristotelian structural implications. When we say that something is valuable, or has value, we shall mean, "We assign a value to it. We give it value." According to the context in which it is used, "value" may refer primarily to the degree of intensity of the feelings of wanting, expecting, or desiring an object, theory, or person, in comparison with other desires and expectations. Or it may refer to the processes by which we weigh alternatives and make inferences about the possibilities that an object, theory, or person will satisfy certain needs to certain degrees at given times. Or it may refer to higher-order abstractions which name complexes of attitudes and the kinds of behavior and reasoning which accompany them as, for example, when we talk of the importance of certain values such as courage and integrity. But in no case shall value mean a thing or a quality *in* something independent of the valuator. Values are assigned and created; they are never discovered in the sense that we discover an object. When we say that a man discovers a value of, say, education, we mean that he discovers that he can use it, that it will satisfy certain needs, and because it does, he assigns a value to it—he judges it and orders it in the hierarchy of his other values. When we say we value money, for example, the element or process of comparison is always present. Money is useful to a degree compared to other things we have or want; its value rises and falls in comparison to them. To one alone on a desert island it has no value except as kindling; the highest values in that situation are food and water. All of this is obvious and I mention it only to emphasize one very important point: valuing means comparing; to compare requires a standard of comparison.

A RESOLUTION OF THE RELATIVIST-ABSOLUTIST CONTROVERSY

The foregoing remarks on value have been preliminary to the central idea of this chapter: a discussion of some of the values important to the general semanticist, how he arrives at them, and the standards of comparison used. We shall use the terms "ethical" and "moral" interchangeably and inherent in their use will be the idea of a value judgment. To simplify matters in this chapter we shall strike what Wendell Johnson calls the "semantic bargain." For convenience we shall use the old linguistic structure, but mean the new. For example, we will write, "Courage *is* a value or valuable; it *is* part of an ethical and moral code; and we assume that it *is* a good thing to be moral." We shall mean the *process* of being courageous which is a complex of behaviors, judgments, and attitudes.

Our first step will be to offer the general semanticist's position on the absolutist-relativist controversy over ethical standards. Are they, or should they be, absolute, applicable to all men in all cultures at all times, or are they, or should they be, relative only to a given group at a given time? If, as we hold, a value or ethical judgment can be made only in reference to a value or ethical standard, then the question arises as to how we arrive at that standard, i.e., against what standard do we judge? Obviously, we soon fall into an infinite regress unless at some point we set standards which are basic, which have not been derived from a comparison with any others, which must be accepted either on faith or simply as a necessary working hypothesis, as a place to start. In the traditional religions these standards are presumed to be God-given, transmitted to all men or to a select group by spiritual leaders who have received them through revelation. Because they are God-given, they are to be accepted and obeyed without question or dire consequences will follow.

The extreme relativist holds that if we examine many cultures, we will find that many of the basic standards in one culture, presumably God-given, contradict those of another, also presumed to be God-given. They conclude that even though people in a given culture may believe that their basic standards are divinely inspired, actually they are man-made, handed down through generations as part of the culture and enforced by a fear of breaking taboos, which is acquired through the educational process.

This relativist position seems, on the face of it, quite conclusive. The evidence offered is enormous. For example, the devout Moslem may, with the blessing of Allah, kill unbelievers in a holy war. In the Christian religion all killing is a sin. Clearly, if God is One, and if he is omnipotent and omniscient, he would not hand down contradictory edicts. Of course, it is assumed that God has a logical "mind." To further complicate matters, the cultural relativists show that even the people in a given culture hold contradictory basic beliefs, or at least their actions indicate this. In the Judaic-Christian ethical and moral system, one of God's unequivocal commandments is, "Thou shalt not kill." Yet in the many bloody and horrible wars that have occurred throughout history, men of the cloth have blessed each side, assuring them that God was aiding them in their slaughter. American airmen went into battle with the motto, "God is my copilot," and met Japanese fighters who were equally sure that their cause was the blessed one. On our coins we stamp, "In God we trust," and recently the words "under God" were inserted in the Pledge of Allegiance, yet at the same time we build nuclear weapons to blow the atheistic Communists, and probably ourselves, to kingdom come. Obviously, we don't trust God to punish the atheists who say he doesn't exist and presumably break all his Commandments.

The absolutist reply is that the cultural relativists are taking a very shallow and simple view of a very profound and complex problem involving such things as original sin, the existence of the devil, man's limited understanding of how God works, and the problem of the existence of evil in general. We shall not involve ourselves in the debate at this moment except to indicate that it is an intensional argument with no conclusion because it involves a confusion of different levels of abstraction. We shall meet it later.

But there is one counter-argument of the absolutists that is relevant to our discussion at this point. If basic standards are man-made and transmitted by society, why should they be believed or obeyed? Obedience through fear of punishment by the group is not ethical or moral behavior, but simply bowing before superior power. How do we know which standards are good, which bad, which merely devices for keeping the rulers in power? If we obey only through fear and not because the standards are intrinsically good, then it is not immoral to break them as long as we don't get caught. This, say the absolutists, is precisely what has happened in our society. Having lost faith in the absoluteness and divine origin of our basic standards, we have no faith in the inherent goodness of any standards and have become drifting, rootless, unhappy cynics torn by the anxiety of indecision, because we have no way of making the clear-cut decisions which absolute standards allow.

Our position is this: We agree that a cross-cultural set of basic standards is necessary, but they should not have to be supported by appeals to authority or purported to be of divine origin, for this cannot be proved or disproved. Such claims have been the source of much contradiction in the theory of systems subscribing to this belief and have led to some of the most cruel, bloody, and senseless acts by their adherents. Acceptance of these basic standards and making decisions in the light of them, is not to be done out of fear or respect for any authority or force but because it is to each man's advantage to do so.

We believe that no ethical and moral philosophy should contain contradictory tenets; it must not contradict any of the laws of science or oppose the attempt to apply the scientific method in any area. It must not oppose the questioning or testing of its assumptions, and it must condition its adherents so that they will abandon any or all of the assumptions if factual data are discovered which make them untenable. It must have built-in self-correcting devices. I believe general semantics gives us the foundation for a philosophical and ethical system which approaches these ideals.

An Article of Faith

We begin with a basic assertion, a value judgment which in no way can be proved true or false. It is, if you will, an article of faith.

We believe that the survival of the human race is the greatest value, the standard against which all other values should ultimately be judged. An action, process, thing, custom, belief, form of government, is good to the degree that it contributes to man's survival; it is bad to the degree that it opposes it. This is the most general of generalizations and its application to specific cases should be each individual's lifelong task.

The problem, then, in judging any act, custom, etc., is to determine whether or not is is likely to contribute to man's survival, but this is not the only standard by which we will judge. There are an infinity of lesser standards or substandards, which we apply from moment to moment in decision-making; and whether or not, in a given case, we will move up the abstraction levels to apply the more general standard, or down to a more specific substandard, is something each individual must work out for himself. This is his own particular philosophy of life, formed and re-formed from day to day, worked out in the light of experience and the heat of joy and suffering. There are no neat formulae for it, only general guides such as we are attempting to formulate.

We can pose these questions: What kinds or patterns of behavior are likely to promote survival? Against what standards shall we measure them? How can we tell whether or not they themselves are reliable and valid? A partial answer to these questions is to be found, I believe, in the concept of "the effective time-binder."

OUR TIME-BINDING ABILITY

Man alone, of all creatures, is faced with the problem of deciding his own future because of the peculiar and unique survival mechanism he has developed, his symbol-using capacity. Through it he controls and molds and changes his environment to a degree not approached by any animal. It is the one characteristic that clearly distinguishes him from all other forms of life. It is his most powerful tool and weapon, both useful and dangerous to himself and to others.

Through the use of symbols he does something no other creature can do: he can transmit knowledge from generation to generation. He alone does not have to start each generation from scratch. He alone can use the knowledge accumulated in the past, learn in the present, and transmit to the future. He stands on the shoulders of the dead to peer into the future. Think of the vast numbers of speculations, observations, experiments, learnings by millions of men over thousands of years, the arduous, repeated trials and errors, the grand insights of geniuses which, transmitted through symbols, enable a young student to span the learning of centuries and write upon a blackboard the simple, beautiful, elegant equation, $E = mc^2$. Because we are able to span time through the use of symbols, Korzybski called this our "time-binding" ability and man the "time-binding" form of life.

Research to date indicates that all men belong to one species and all have the same time-binding potential, rooted in the enormous elaboration and development of his cerebral cortex and in the neurological structures associated with it. No one group, *as a group,* is inherently superior or inferior to any other. On a statistical basis we expect to find relatively the same percentage of sub-average, average, and above-average in each ethnic group. Superiority in knowledge, technical development, and arts, is presumed to be due to environmental and cultural conditions and not to any heritable superiority in neurological structure.

THE EFFECTIVE TIME-BINDER: A CROSS-CULTURAL ETHICAL STANDARD

Now, argues the general semanticist, if we meet the challenge of living primarily by means of our symbol-using ability, if this is our chief survival weapon, then our chances of survival as a race will depend on the effectiveness with which we use this time-binding capacity. The effective use of this capacity is not inherited, only the potential. It is a learned behavior, the chief concern of man. All our educational systems, our libraries, our communication networks, from the crudest, most primitive cultures to the most complex, center about the transmission of symbols, the communication of knowledge of some kind. We have not yet learned how to use our nervous systems most effectively. Little by little, over the centuries, the knowledge piles up. But not all of this knowledge is reliable, and much of it is false. Through this false knowledge and through ignorance we misuse our symbol-using capacities, sometimes so grossly that we destroy them and become insane, or destroy our bodies in individual and mass suicide and murder.

The effective use of our time-binding capacity, then, becomes, for the individual general semanticist, his life goal. We might say that general semantics is a methodology for learning to use it more effectively. Throughout this book we have tried to demonstrate the ways we misuse it, the harms that result, and ways of correcting it. Effective time-binding depends upon proper use of the abstracting process on all levels of abstraction. It means, therefore, not only the development of "reason," the higher orders of abstraction, but also the proper handling of the "emotions," the lower orders of abstraction, for one cannot function adequately when the other is not.

Since the time-binding ability is so important to man, the general semanticist makes this value judgment: Any form of thought, activity, custom, type of government, or theory is good to the degree that it fosters the development of effective time-binders; conversely, it is bad to the degree that it does not. This value judgment applies to any culture anywhere. Because the nervous systems of all men are essentially the same, any custom which warps the functioning of the nervous system is bad, even if it is accepted by that society, for *in the long run* it will lead to its destruction. If hallucinations, witchcraft, superstition, any kind of false knowledge, is considered good and desirable by any group, it is still considered bad by the general semanticist. Thus we have a cross-cultural standard for proper evaluation based on the scientific study of the human nervous system and how it seems to be designed to function. Note, I am not saying that the general semanticists have made these studies, though some have, but that they have used them as a foundation for the system.

It is most important that we be clear about the term "effective time-binder." Our time-binding ability allows us to transmit all kinds of false and destructive information, but this is bad, not effective, time-binding. A demagogue may effectively delude a mob or a nation through his manipulation of symbols, but although he may succeed very well in his purpose, still he is a bad time-binder, for he has warped the functioning of both his own nervous system and that of others and has lessened the survival chances of the whole race.

Inherent, then, in our concept of the effective time-binder is an attitude, an ethical judgment, a moral precept as strong as any of the Ten Commandments: "Thou shalt not knowingly warp the functioning of any nervous system." Or, stated positively, "So act as to make thyself a better time-binder; so act as to enable others to use their time-binding capacities more effectively." I should like to emphasize that this is not an ethical edict tacked on to the system to make it more palatable, acceptable and "good American." One cannot become an effective time-binder if he hinders, or does not foster, its development in others. We cannot make a practice of deceiving and deluding others without having the deception turn back upon us. The spiritual leaders of mankind have ever proclaimed this and modern psychiatry supports it completely.

The nervous system is designed to act as a unified whole. Any attempt to cut off part of it, to isolate it, ultimately leads to disaster. When this is done unconsciously it is called repression and its effects are documented in any psychiatric casebook. But a similarly corrosive effect upon the nervous system can be produced by the deliberate attempt to cause confusion and identification of the levels of abstraction in others. The politician who thinks of the voters as boobs to be deceived, as animals to be conditioned, like Pavlov's dogs, has lost respect for them as *human* creatures, and inevitably loses respect for himself as a *human* being. It is one thing to see people as humans making mistakes, acting foolishly or viciously or blindly; it is another thing to view them as animals to be exploited.

All of us know of the gratifications that come from belonging to a group. There is a sense of being wanted, an easing of communication barriers, a feeling of kinship and mutual regard—all this despite our awareness of the weaknesses, failings, and pettinesses of the members. And we gain this through our concentration on certain similarities among the members of the group—kinship, occupation, political beliefs, etc.

We hear much talk these days of the shrinking size of the world as communication nets enlarge and become swifter. We hear preached the necessity for a world government, the necessity for choosing between one world and no world. Yet the differences between men and nations—economic, racial, social, educational, attitudinal—seem so enormous and are so real that it often seems that we face a useless and hopeless task. Religious leaders preach the brotherhood of man and the Oneness of God, yet the very existence of different religions serves to weaken their precepts. They preach that Allah and Yahweh and God are but different names for one deity and the different religions simply different paths to the same mansion. I wonder if they really believe this. Probably some of the leaders do, but I have a feeling that the majority of them and their flocks secretly think (not so secretly in many cases) that the others are deluded fools or emissaries of the devil. How else can we explain the viciousness and depth of religious hatred and intolerance?

But there is one similarity among all men which can be used to bridge our differences: we are all potentially effective time-binders, the present crown of the evolutionary tree, the most complex and artfully constructed of all organisms. It is in our symbol-using ability that all of us are brothers, members of the most exclusive clan on earth. When we do anything to damage the symbol-using capacity of any member, we hurt the clan and we hurt ourselves by destroying our sense of clan and belongingness. The damage we do ourselves by debasing the time-binding capacity of others is subtle yet all-pervasive, difficult to describe, yet, I believe, a potent generator of the faceless anxieties which ride the rootless wanderers in Eliot's "The Waste Land."

THE EFFECTIVE TIME-BINDER AND MASLOW'S "SELF-ACTUALIZING PERSON"

We shall begin our elaboration of this theme by a rather detailed reference to what I consider a remarkable book, *Motivation and Personality*, by A. H. Maslow. Maslow postulates what he calls a "holistic-dynamic theory of human motivation." In his view, there is an ascending hierarchy of needs. As each order is satisfied, it releases, or allows to emerge, the needs of the next higher order. The most basic are the physiological needs such as those for food, water, oxygen, sleep, and the physiological aspects of sex.

As soon as these are fairly well satisfied, there arise what he calls the safety needs, after these the belongingness and love needs, then the esteem needs, and finally the need for self-actualization. Tools for achieving the satisfaction of these needs are the desires to know and to understand and the aesthetic needs for order, symmetry, and closure. This is not an inflexible ordering of these needs, nor does it imply that one need must be fully satisfied before the next higher needs can be met. If in childhood the lower scale of needs is never adequately satisfied, they may develop into unsatisfiable neurotic needs in the adult. Thus an adult whose love needs were not satisfied as a child will have an insatiable compulsion to be loved like a child and will not be capable of the more mature, non-compulsive, outgoing love of the person whose childhood love needs were satisfied. Moreover, he will be fixated at that level and will not be able to proceed to the satisfaction of the higher needs of self-actualization.

Some of the differences between the higher and lower needs are:

1. The higher needs came later in evolutionary development.
2. The higher the need the longer its satisfaction can be postponed and the less imperative is it for physical survival at the moment.
3. Gratification of the higher needs produces more desirable and longer lasting subjective results—more profound serenity and happiness.
4. Greater value is placed upon the satisfaction of the higher needs than of the lower by those who have experienced both.
5. Gratification of the higher needs leads to an increased capacity for love and a truer individualism.
6. Pursuit and gratification of the higher needs have desirable social consequences; they are in effect a higher form of selfishness, i.e., unselfish selfishness.
7. The higher the need level, the more effective, and easier, are psychotherapy and self-therapy.

Using Korzybskian terminology, we can say that the higher needs postulated by Maslow are more symbol-dominated and symbol-mediated than the lower. The very lowest order needs can be satisfied only by lower-order abstractions—objects, i.e., food, oxygen, climatic conditions, etc. As we move up the scale to the higher needs, the satisfiers become more symbolic, less immediately dependent upon the environment. The highest needs are almost entirely symbol-satisfied and independent of the external environment. Only the person himself through his symbol-using capacity can satisfy them.

Maslow contends, and he is not alone in this, that Freudian psychologists and most of the other psychologists have built "cripple psychologies." They have studied only the psychologically sick, people who, because of their unsatisfied lower needs, were never able to satisfy or even develop their most human needs and impulses. Consequently, in these psychologies there is little or no place for, or discussion of, altruism, equanimity, ecstasy, joy, creativeness.

Not until recently have studies been made of what psychologically healthy people are like. The implication of the older studies is that mental health is merely the absence of neurosis. But this, as we have seen, is a type of additive, elementalistic thinking. When the higher needs emerge and are satisfied, these are not "just a few more." They are on another level of abstraction and their characteristics cannot be deduced from a study of those of the lower orders.

Consequently, Maslow and his collaborators decided to make a study of people having excellent psychological health. Their criteria were of two types, negative and positive. The negative was the absence of neurosis or a strong tendency toward a psychopathic personality or psychosomatic illness, determined by using standard tests such as the Rorschach. The positive criterion was the evidence of self-actualization. Admittedly this was difficult to define very precisely, but it can be loosely described as the full use and exploitation of talents and potentialities.

The subjects were chosen from among friends, college students, public and historical figures. A screening of 3000 college students yielded only one usable subject and about two dozen possible future subjects, so that the investigators had to depend almost wholly on public and historical figures. All in all, they wound up with a list of 45. I should like to present some of their findings as to the characteristics of these self-actualizing, psychologically healthy people, and try to translate them into g.s. terminology.

1. *They had "a more efficient perception of reality and more comfortable relations with it."* In all areas in which subjects were tested, their powers of perception were above average. They had "an unusual ability to detect the spurious, the fake, and the dishonest in personality." Consequently, their predictions of the future from the facts at hand were more often correct.

One particularly impressive and instructive aspect of this superior relation with reality . . . was [their ability to] . . . distinguish far more easily than most the fresh, concrete, and ideographic from the generic, abstract, and rubricized. The consequence is that they live more in the real world of nature than in the man-made mass of concepts, abstractions, expectations, beliefs, and stereotypes that most people confuse with the world. They are therefore far more apt to perceive what is there rather than their own wishes, hopes, fears, anxieties, their own theories and beliefs or those of their cultural group.[5]

Using g.s. terminology, these people were more efficient in their abstracting processes. They could distinguish more clearly between lower- and higher-order abstractions. What is more, they followed the natural order of abstraction by giving more value to lower orders ("reality") than to higher orders when the problem of verification arose. When they made predictions, they were more often based upon factual knowledge and observation than on the unverified inferences which form the higher-order components of neurotic anxieties, fears, wishes, and fancies.

2. *Acceptance of self and others.* They were able to accept themselves and all their frailties and those of others without real concern. Not that they were self-satisfied. They would like to and did try to improve, but they accepted themselves as they found

[5] A. H. Maslow, *Motivation and Personality,* New York, Harper & Brothers, 1954, p. 205.

themselves *at the moment.* They felt no shame about their bodily functions. They tended to be lusty and hearty, with good "unfinicky" appetites.

Restated, they did not allow their higher-order abstractions to influence unduly what they abstracted on the lower levels. They did not allow theories, fads, names, the unverified opinions of other people—all higher-order abstractions—to distort what they could taste smell, feel. To them bodily functions were not "nasty" or "disgusting," because they did not confuse the levels of abstraction. People who do find them disgusting have built a picture, a map, of the human body that does not fit the territory. According to this map, the body should be free of smells, by-products, etc., and because it is not, they do not change their map to fit the territory but attempt to warp the territory by implicitly denying the existence of these functions by attempting to ignore them, apparently on the theory that if you don't look they will go away. People who abstract in this fashion are said by general semanticists to be intensionally oriented.

3. *Spontaneity.* The behavior of these people is marked by simplicity and naturalness. Very often their behavior is highly unconventional, but it is not a superficial unconventionality. In unimportant matters they will follow conventions even if they seem silly, simply to avoid hurting people. But when it comes to what they consider important, they do what they think is right despite convention. They have "codes of ethics that are relatively autonomous and individual rather than unconventional."

They are the most ethical of people even though their ethics are not necessarily the same as those of the people around them. It is this kind of observation that leads us to understand very assuredly that the ordinary ethical behavior of the average person is largely conventional behavior rather than truly ethical behavior, e.g., behavior based on fundamentally accepted principles.

Because of this alienation from ordinary conventions and from the ordinarily accepted hypocrisies, lies and inconsistencies of social life, they sometimes feel like spies or aliens in a foreign land and sometimes behave so.

Their ease of penetration to reality, their closer approach to an animal-like or childlike acceptance and spontaneity imply a superior awareness of their own impulses, desires, opinions, and subjective reactions in general. Clinical studies of this capacity confirm beyond a doubt the opinion, e.g., of Fromm, that the average, normal, well-adjusted person often has not the slightest idea of what he is, of what he wants, of what his opinions are. It was such findings as these that led ultimately to the discovery of a most profound difference between self-actualizing people and others; namely, that the motivational life of self-actualizing people is not only quantitatively different but also qualitatively different from that of ordinary people. . . . Our subjects no longer strive in the ordinary sense, but rather develop. They attempt to grow to perfection and develop more and more fully in their own style. . . . They work, they try, and they are ambitious, even though in an unusual sense. For them motivation is . . . self-actualization. Could these self-actualizing people be more human, more revealing of the original nature of the species, . . . ? Ought a biological species to be judged by its crippled, warped, only partially developed specimens, or by examples that have been overdomesticated, caged, and trained? [6]

Meanwhile, back at g.s., when Korzybski spoke of following the natural order of abstraction, of not confusing and identifying the levels of abstraction, he asserted that this type of evaluative behavior would lead to a truly *human* form of behavior, would produce what we have called an effective time-binder. These characteristics of the self-actualizing people described by Maslow have a remarkable similarity to those predicted by Korzybski. In effect, Maslow finds that when people do not warp their abstracting processes they approach the ideal of the effective time-binder.

[6] *Ibid.*, pp. 210–211.

Some of the other characteristics of these self-actualizing people are:

1. *They are problem centered, rather than ego centered.* They are not a problem to themselves and therefore can turn to problems outside themselves. Their chief concerns are, "Basic issues and eternal questions of the type we have learned to call philosophical or ethical. Such people live customarily in the widest possible frame of reference. . . . it seems to impart a certain serenity and lack of worry over immediate concerns that make life easier not only for themselves but for all who are associated with them."[7]

Not only are these people better able to order their lives on the lower levels of abstraction so that their perceptual processes are more efficient and reliable, but also they direct these lower-order activities by means of a well-structured set of higher-order abstractions which have a wide range of applicability, and which do not cause confusion of the levels of abstraction. In turn, they evoke a complex of higher-order feelings which in themselves facilitate the orderly and efficient working of their symbol-using capacities on all levels of abstraction.

2. *Continued freshness of appreciation.* "Self-actualizing people have the wonderful capacity to appreciate again and again, freshly and naïvely, the basic goods of life, with awe, pleasure, wonder, and even ecstasy, however stale these experiences may have become to others."[8]

This freshness of appreciation of the most common "moment-to-moment business of living" is, I believe, a product of greater than ordinary consciousness of abstracting, bringing with it greater conscious control of the process. That is, these people can deliberately focus on a specific level of abstraction and thrust other levels into the background. By cutting down on the theoretic, higher-order

---

[7] *Ibid.,* p. 212.
[8] *Ibid.,* pp. 214–215.

abstractions they allow the lower levels to gain in intensity. They do not allow memories, speculations, theories, opinions, to interfere with what they are abstracting at the moment on the lower levels. Thus each sensory perception is seen as it "is," new and different and bright, and this in turn induces the feelings of wonder, awe, ecstasy. When this concentration on differences and uniqueness is replaced by a focusing on similarities through memory and theory, then the sense of newness and uniqueness is lost.

It is important to note that we are not saying that concentration on one level is better than on another. Rather, focusing on the level of abstraction most appropriate to the situation of the moment enables the organism to operate at greater all-round efficeincy and effectiveness on all levels. When theorizing is called for, it is "good" theorizing; it produces inferences of high predictability, gives greater control over the environment, and induces an appropriate set of feelings which implement this activity. When low-order activity is in order, the higher orders are not allowed to interfere or warp it and this also evokes a set of feelings which enhance the processes on all levels of abstraction. Anxieties and tensions thus are not produced which lead, in many people, to the invention of theories and fancies thoroughly untrustworthy for predictive control of the environment, and which, in turn, exacerbate the anxieties and tensions.

In addition to these characteristics, Maslow found that the mystic experience, or, using Freud's term, "the oceanic feeling," was quite common among his subjects, that these people, without exception, had a democratic character structure in the deepest possible sense, that they were strongly ethical and had a philosophical, unhostile sense of humor, and that they had developed the ability to love profoundly.

If this list of characteristics makes these people sound far more saintly than human, we should hasten to add that Maslow found they still had many imperfections. Like all of us, they had silly and wasteful habits, they had their vanities, their stubborn and irritating idiosyncracies. Nor were they free of guilt, anxiety, and internal strife. But according to Maslow, these arose out of non-neurotic sources.

I should like to quote Maslow's summary of his study of these people in some detail because it so beautifully summarizes many of the points we have tried to emphasize throughout this book. He writes:

At this point we may finally allow ourselves to generalize and underscore a very important theoretical conclusion derivable from the study of self-actualizing people. . . . What had been considered in the past to be polarities or opposites or dichotomies were so *only in unhealthy people.* In healthy people, these dichotomies were resolved, the polarities disappeared, and many oppositions thought to be intrinsic merged and coalesced with each other to form unities.

For example, the age-old opposition between heart and head, reason and instinct, or cognition and conation were seen to disappear in healthy people where they become synergic rather than antagonists, and where conflict between them disappears because they say the same thing and point to the same conclusion. . . .

The dichotomy between selfishness and unselfishness disappears altogether in healthy people because in principle every act is *both* selfish and unselfish. Our subjects are simultaneously very spiritual and very pagan and sensual. Duty cannot be contrasted with pleasure nor work with play when duty *is* pleasure, when work *is* play, and the person doing his duty and being virtuous is simultaneously seeking his pleasure and being happy. If the most socially identified people are themselves also the most individualistic people, of what use is it to retain the polarity? If the most mature are childlike? And if the most ethical and moral people are also the lustiest and most animal?

. . . In these people, the id, the ego, and the super-ego are collaborative and synergic; they do not war with each other nor are their interests in basic disagreement as they are in neurotic people. So also do the cognitive, the conative, and the emotional coalesce into an organismic unity and into a non-Aristotelian interpenetration. The higher and the lower are not in opposition but in agreement, and a thousand serious philosophical dilemmas are discovered to have more than two horns, or paradoxically, no horns at all. . . .

. . . It becomes more and more clear that the study of crippled, stunted, and unhealthy specimens can yield only a cripple psychology and a cripple philosophy. The study of self-actualizing people must be the basis for a more universal science of psychology.[9]

A Cross-Cultural Norm of Sanity

Our ideal of the effective time-binder provides us not only with a cross-cultural standard of ethical and moral behavior, but also a cross-cultural norm of sanity. The ideally sane man is one who never confuses the levels of abstraction, who never reverses the natural order of abstraction, who uses all his potentialities. He is the self-actualizing individual whose nervous system acts as an integrated whole without internecine battles among the various levels. Admittedly, probably no such man exists, perhaps never will. Yet this is an ideal which can be approached and through our sciences we can devise methods for facilitating the long journey. It is an ideal founded upon man's psychoneurological structure and is independent of peculiarities of custom and creed. It does not splinter man by focusing upon one segment of his behavior and structure at the expense of others. Sanity, morality, ethical behavior become one; they are an inextricably interwoven pattern of behavior. It does not matter whether a group or culture accepts certain confusions of levels of abstraction (neurotic or even psychotic behavior) as average, and, because prevalent, therefore, sane. A whole culture, according to our ideal of sanity, can be unsane to the degree that its members warp their abstracting abilities.

Accepting these ideals does not mean that we want all men to have the same thoughts, customs, language. Diversity, even more than

9 *Ibid.*, pp. 232–234.

humor, is the spice of life. Without it there would be no challenge, no contrast, no pool of "genes" out of which new characteristics, new ideas, new customs could grow. Let the American eat his meat and the Japanese his rice; only do not encourage warping of their abstracting processes in such a way that each considers his the only food fit for man; do not encourage them to confuse map and territory so that, for example, the label "white" becomes synonymous with "superior," causing both the Japanese and the American to throw away the vitamin- and mineral-filled parts of the rice and wheat in order to have white and, therefore, "superior," rice cakes and bread and, as a consequence, come down with beri-beri and other vitamin-deficiency diseases.

FOOD FANTASY AND THE INTENSIONAL ORIENTATION

We in the United States are considered to be the best fed and most poorly nourished (in light of the quantity of food we eat) of any people in the world. I do not propose to document these assertions about our eating habits and the deficiencies thereof attributable to semantic confusions. This could fill volumes. But consider all the forms of bizarre theories, false information, and outright quackery that we have all around us as, for example, the various food fadists who propound mutually contradictory doctrines on the basis of no scientific observation or experimentation. One group will eat only vegetables and knows for sure that meat is poisonous for man; a larger group will eat only meat and knows for sure that all vegetables, other than potatoes, are for rabbits. Pin one label on a food and they will eat it; give it another name and it becomes nauseous. Call a biscuit "dog biscuit" and it is not fit for human consumption, even though the manufacturer assures us on the box that it is baked under the same sanitary conditions that it uses for its "human biscuits." Indeed, the analysis given there shows it to be a better food for human consumption than any made for humans at twice the price. But the label is more important to us than the territory, so we reject the dog biscuit because of the name and associations built around it, even though the given factual knowledge on the box would suggest we at least try them, or at the very least, be *able* to try them, and reject the sugar- and fat-laden, mineral- and protein-depleted breads and cakes and biscuits we do eat.

Now I am not suggesting that we all run out and buy dog biscuits. My concern is with the reaction I get from students and others when I suggest eating them. Even though they know, verbally, that this is a wholesome, nourishing food, so influenced are they by labels that many cannot even bring themselves to move to the object level and make a sensory test. It is not that they *must* like them after they taste them; rather, they should not be so dominated by the name that they cannot make the test. This intensional orientation acts as a barrier to all forms of more mature behavior and is even detrimental to their physical well-being.

I suggest to the reader that he look through a copy of the *Farm Journal*. The first section is devoted to handling the farm, the second is for the farmer's wife. The contrast is, to me, rather appalling. There are dozens of advertisements and articles on feeds for livestock and almost every ad emphasizes the food balance of the feed, its vitamin, mineral, protein content. The farmer knows his animals sicken and do not reach the peak of development unless their diet is scientifically designed to meet their needs. Then turn to the "human" section. Hardly an advertisement for balanced, nutritious foods. Never have I seen as careful an analysis of a human food, as well-documented and as factually correct, as of an animal food. Indeed, there is much deception in both the advertising and the food itself. Synthetic softeners which have no food value and whose possible long-term toxicity has never been properly evaluated are found in many breads and cakes. The bleached white flour—sublimated sawdust, sometimes "enriched," meaning that they take out many vitamins and put back a few—is still a poor substitute for the whole wheat.

To me, the amazing thing is that the very farmer who is so concerned about, and has so much verified evidence for, the necessity of a good diet for his animals, does not transfer this knowledge to the more important area of his own health and welfare. I am no food fanatic and do not recommend that we worry about the balance and nutritional value of every bit of food we eat. But when we look at the diet of the average American loaded down with denatured food, heavy with much more sugar and fat than he will ever need, it becomes apparent that he has maps of his body and its needs that do not fit the territory.

It is true that cultural conditioning, custom, is a prime factor here. Read almost any woman's or family magazine and you find the most beautiful pictures of luscious cakes and pies which, nutritionally speaking, are not far from poisonous. From childhood we are fed these things and it becomes "natural," the "right thing to do," "common sense," to eat, demand, and have pride in preparing and serving them. Anyone who questions this is seen as "queer" or "cracked." A vast complex of inferences have been made concerning the adequacy and desirability of these foods which have been accepted and offered as factual knowledge, and since they are assumed to be factual, no necessity for checking seems needed.

So the general semanticist, in advocating the concept of the effective time-binder on a cross-cultural basis, is asking, not that all people everywhere eat whole wheat all the time or only organ meats or anything else. Rather, he asserts that the general pattern of confusing levels of abstraction which leads to bad diets and bad health —and this to further bad evaluation—be corrected. Let the Japanese stick to his rice and the American to his wheat, if he wishes, but let them both be concerned with building adequate maps of their bodily needs; when they do not, they are both unsane. Furthermore, by becoming conscious of the abstracting process through education, they would find it easier to break away from their conditioned responses to labels and be able to allow themselves to try new foods and thus broaden the base of their diets.

I realize that this is no simple job and I feel quite sure that the attempt to preach the need for better diets is a most difficult task. General semanticists feel that we are more likely to be successful if we can teach the necessity for proper evaluation on all levels, that is, a generalized pattern of behavior with the choice of proper diet as one example of an extensional orientation. The details of the diet can be left to the individual who will make his choices within the framework of foods available in his particular environment. And what we have said here about food prejudice and misevaluation applies to all other prejudices, customs, and myths. Because of its emphasis on proper evaluation as a whole, the adoption of the cross-cultural concept of the effective time-binder will increase diversity rather than decrease it. One of the most noticeable characteristics of any form of misevaluation is its restriction and narrowing of the choices and alternatives which can be evaluated and held. In the long run, this lessens our chances of survival.

I believe that making our ultimate goal in life the fullest and most effective development of our time-binding ability is the best answer to date to the absolutist-relativist controversy and avoids the dilemmas and contradictions present in both of these positions. It satisfies the absolutists' demand for a cross-cultural standard for evaluating all forms of thought and behavior, one not subject to the whims of fashion, fancy, and custom.

DECISION-MAKING AND THE
CONSTRUCT OF THE EFFECTIVE TIME-BINDER

Decision-making in important situations inevitably involves tension and anxiety which increases a hundredfold when there are no relatively clear, stable, and acceptable standards for judgment. The concept of the effective time-binder offers such a standard, a frame of reference which is free of the contradictions and constrictions inherent in those claimed to be of supernatural origin. It does not clash with any of the findings of science, it puts no limits on thought, it is not, and cannot be, productive of dogmas and creeds which lead to hatred, cruelty, prejudice, and bloodshed, as has every major religion despite preachments to the contrary. Furthermore, it puts the responsibility for his conduct directly on man himself, and he takes it upon himself not because he has been so ordered by some authority, which must be obeyed for fear of punishment, but because to act as an effective time-binder fulfills his highest-order needs, inducing the most long-lasting and satisfying of feelings and attitudes, among them serenity without complacency or smugness, courage without bravado, compassion without contempt, humility without self-debasement, and, above all, a love for mankind which is neither hypocritical nor sentimental nor blind to individual faults.

I am not claiming that acceptance of the ideal of the effective time-binder makes decision-making easy, nor that it gives answers to specific problems, but only that it facilitates and gives direction to our attempts at reaching conclusions. Its acceptance does not automatically make one love his neighbor as himself. This latter is both a cause and effect of our decision to use our nervous systems correctly. Hatred and prejudice are a product of ignorance, fear, and a host of unresolved neurotic conflicts, both conscious and unconscious. We cannot, through learning g.s., directly resolve these conflicts; other techniques are needed for that. But the ignorance and conscious fear can be lessened by direct assault; and to the degree that these are lessened hatred and prejudice are diminished. Furthermore, as these lessen, proper evaluation becomes easier, which in turn, speeds up the elimination of ignorance and the fear it produces, etc. In addition, the conscious knowledge that hatred and prejudice have powerful disintegrating effects upon the normal functioning of our nervous systems moves us to try to eliminate them.

In other words, by being concerned about the healthy functioning of our nervous systems, we can move from being solely occupied with the satisfaction of lower-order needs which are truly "self-ish" —give me, feed me, love me—to the additional concern for the satisfaction of our higher needs which can be accomplished only by being unselfish. By not demanding love, but by giving it, we increase our chances of getting it, because we become more lovable and make it easier for others to love us. Likewise, we see that hatred invites and perpetuates hatred. By reducing it in ourselves we lessen it in others, and when it lessens in others it decreases in us. When this decreases in us, our nervous systems function more effectively and we are able to increase our self-actualizing abilities. Thus, by desiring to acquire the benefits of self-actualization—and this is a form of selfishness—we move from selfishness to selfishness (higher-order) about these lower-order selfishnesses. This second-order selfishness tends to reduce or reverse the first-order, i.e., produces unselfishness. Thus, selfishness on one level leads to unselfishness on another and in this way eliminates the false selfishness versus unselfishness dichotomy.

❈ ❈ 8 ❈ ❈

Semantitherapy

THE basic postulate of semantitheraphy is that an organism acts as a whole at a given date in a given enviroment. For human beings this enviroment is both the external physical world, the interior physiological-semantic reactions to it, and the ongoing reactions to these reactions, all interwoven in a complex, constantly changing pattern. It follows that whatever affects one part of the organism affects all of it. Or restated, one part cannot be affected; the total organism reacts. We may notice that some functions or structures seem to be more influenced by given stimuli than others, but this is likely to be highly deceptive unless we take into account the profound influence of the observer's motivation upon what he perceives. For example, if an adult has a morbid and crippling fear of cats and reacts violently when he sees one, the Freudian psychiatrist may concentrate upon the psychogenesis of this fear and centers his therapy upon getting him to reëvaluate "cat situations" through psychoanalysis, bringing him back to the probable childhood experience which sparked these fears. But the therapist may forget, or not consider important, the fact that these fears are being felt *now* and that the patient's total organism is responding. His heart speeds up and beats irregularly, his body chemistry changes, his viscera are in a turmoil, he is anxious, tense; he feels terrible all over. And his reactions to these feelings, in turn, feed back and reinforce his reactions to cats. These are as much a part of his fear of cats as are the childhood experiences which "caused" them.

Moreover, it will be noted that this fear is not always present in the sense that he is reacting to it. It appears only in times of stress or in the presence of cats in particular contexts. Thus it is apparent that the childhood "causes" are not enough to produce the effects *now*. How he reacts *now* is a function of the whole functioning organism—fatigue, hormonal balance, inferences about his symptoms, the boss' temper, the next installment on the car, life goals or the lack of them, religious beliefs, hopes for the future.

Semantitherapy, being a "rational" approach, is primarily concerned with changing those patterns of behavior open to conscious control and change. We realize that unconscious factors play a large part in behavior, but they are not the only ones. By reducing the misevaluations open to conscious control—all the patterns discussed in this book—we lessen the stress upon the organism and thereby keep from "stirring up" unconscious stimuli; i.e., we let sleeping cats lie. But there is also a positive aspect. By controlling the secondary symptoms, we keep them from reinforcing the primary ones and this in turn, over a long period of time, greatly reduces the potency of the unconscious patterns of misevaluation.

It seems to me that this is a more adequate picture of the functioning of the nervous system than the one which considers the unconscious factors as essentially untouchable and unchangeable by rational processes. This second picture neglects the influence of consciously learned behavior and divides the nervous system into more or less isolated sections or functions. The very language used tends to reinforce this elementalistic thinking. This danger is noted by E. Pumpian-Mindlin:

. . . I speak of the individual as seeking HIS gratifications under the pressure of forces which arise in the id section of his make-up, but which are shaped by compulsive overdrives and phobic inhibitions, which are the products of the activities we call "superego" functions. I take care de-

liberately not to speak of the id's gratification. GRATIFICATION, like FRUS-
TRATION, is an experience that comes only to a whole man not to his
parts. . . . In each case my fear is of allowing a subtle, anthropomorphizing
tendency to inflate these abstractions from the whole personality, endowing
each with a spurious independent existence, which then would allow us to
indulge ourselves in allegorical imagery and figures of speech about strife
BETWEEN them. Whole books have been written in this vein (Cf. Anna
Freud, *The Ego and Its Mechanisms of Defense*).[1]

It is probably true that the more sick a person is "mentally," the
more unconscious factors dominate his behavior and the less he is
able to function in terms of *now,* retreating to the past or future.
Consequently, many psychiatrists, especially the Freudian, since they
come in contact with, and are primarily interested in, the seriously
ill, come to think of the cortical functions as mere thin shells uncer-
tainly containing a boiling lava pool of unconscious drives which burst
out and overwhelm the organism whenever stress heats it or weakens
the shell. But, as Maslow states, this is a cripple psychology. When
the biologist wishes to study an animal species, he selects as a norm
the best and healthiest specimen he can obtain, not the stunted and
sick. Why not do the same for humans?

Studying people who have not been seriously damaged psychologically, we find that consciously controllable mechanisms form a
significant part of the total evaluative process. These people can be
helped by simple counseling, by advice, by deliberate study and application of proper patterns of talking and evaluation. And these
are the ones most likely to benefit from general semantics, both as prevention and cure.

THE "SCANDAL" OF CONFLICTING THERAPIES

In any event, this is not the place to debate the efficacy of one
system of psychotherapy as opposed to another. Indeed, there has

[1] E. Pumpian-Mindlin (ed.), *Psychoanalysis as Science,* Stanford, Stanford University Press, 1952, p. 105.

been too much debate and not enough experimentation and observation, too much defending of theories instead of testing them. For example, one of the "scandals" in psychiatry today is that diametrically opposed systems of therapy seem to get about the same percentage of "cures" and "failures." Some Freudian psychiatrists maintain, as did Freud, that the therapist must not involve himself personally, he must be "objective," while others, such as Whitaker and Malone, maintain he must "enter into" the unconscious of the patient with his own unconscious, both patient and therapist receiving therapy simultaneously. Carl Rogers calls for "non-directive therapy" while others are highly authoritarian and directive. Some hold that we must get at the "causes" and neglect the symptoms, others, like Abraham Low, have devised purely symptom therapies. And, to confound the problem further, we find that in crowded mental hospitals where little more than custodial care is possible, "spontaneous" recoveries occur for which no present school of psychology can account, nor can they account for the action of the various shock and drug therapies.

A number of explanations for these inconsistencies are possible:

1. Each particular type of therapy is best suited for a particular type of mental illness. Consciously and unconsciously, therapists select for treatment those patients most likely to be helped by their particular method.

2. The *methods* of therapy are not necessarily derived from, or implicit in, the psychological structures postulated by each system. Thus most schools accept the Freudian concept of id, ego, and superego functions, but there is little in this theory which postulates methods for dealing with, influencing, or changing these mechanisms. The techniques of free association, the various tests such as the Rorschach and TAT, the objectivity of the therapist, or the interpretation of dreams are largely empirically derived or *ad hoc* explanations. For example, ascribing sexual significance to almost all dreams has become

so generalized, so *ad hoc* in nature, that testing the validity of these interpretations has been made impossible. The male sex member is represented by anything long and slim, the female by anything round, hollow, a container of any kind. Now *any* object can be, indeed must be described in terms of straight or round lines. Consequently every object automatically becomes a phallic symbol. Result: every dream interpretation takes on sexual significance and we cannot tell whether this is truly the case in a given dream or merely our projection, our interpretation. Eysenck has called this "a test-proof theory."

3. All present theories explain the functioning of only limited areas of the nervous system; they are parts of a more general theory yet to be devised.

Techniques for Controlling the Non-Verbal Level: Three Basic Assumptions

I feel certain that other explanations for the inconsistences in conflicting therapies are possible and more probably correct. Be that as it may, we shall drop the matter here and proceed to a description of what general semantics has to offer in the area of mental health. Actually there is no area or field of mental health. All thinking on any subject, in any situation, can contribute to or help destroy mental health. In our view, mental health is synonymous with the proper functioning of the abstracting process at all levels. On the verbal level, the patterns and injunctions are fairly clear and relatively easy to apply: date and index statements, delay reactions, do not confuse factual and inferential knowledge, etc. By consciously doing this, we lessen the chances of falling into stress situations which will excite any "sleeping dogs." Even if there were no repressed conflicts, highly unlikely in our society, stupidity would get us into trouble, causing all kinds of misery. If minding our linguistic patterns can help to reduce this misery, it is worthwhile.

However, our chief concern in this chapter will be the means of influencing non-verbal responses, i.e., feelings, emotions, and attitudes. Our methods all hinge on three assumptions: (1) As we have stated, the organism acts as a whole and what affects one part affects all. (2) A knowledge of the abstracting process enables us to select the level of abstraction at which we shall operate in any given situation at a given moment. (3) The higher orders on both verbal and non-verbal levels are more amenable to conscious control and can be used as "entering wedges" in controlling the lower orders.

GENERAL SEMANTICS AND THE WILL
THERAPY OF ABRAHAM LOW

The late Dr. Abraham A. Low of Chicago, was the founder of a system of group psychotherapy to which he gave the rather quaint name "Recovery, Inc." His is purely a symptom therapy, and since it is designed to be used by patients themselves, alone and in groups without the aid of the attending physician, it cannot involve any form of "cause" removal as in psychoanalysis. Dr. Low claimed that his percentage of "cures" was as high or higher than that of any other type of therapy. His evidence is rather indirect and I do not intend to enter into any controversy concerning its effectiveness, nor is anything written here to be construed as support for his system as a whole. Rather, I shall present those of his concepts which seem to be the most substantial and most relevant to general semantics.

Dr. Low's views are summarized in his book, *Mental Health Through Will-Training.* Having overcome our signal reactions to the archaic term "will-training," we turn to his basic contention:

If the patients are to help and teach one another they must be instructed to use a language which is not confusing. This is particularly important because language, if used glibly, tends to be alarmist and defeatist. By dint of its defeatist insinuations, language frequently engenders tenseness which reinforces and perpetuates symptoms. To avoid the fatalistic implications of the language used by the patient the physician must supply a terminology of his own in matters of health. There are many languages. Features and gestures speak. So do symptoms. Their language is a one-word idiom: DANGER. This is called the "symptomatic idiom." Accepting the suggestions of the symptomatic idiom the patient considers the violent palpitations as presaging sudden death. The pressure in the head is viewed as due to a brain tumor. The tenseness is experienced as so "terrific" that the patient fears he is going to "burst." His fatigue does not let up "one single minute," and "how long can the body stand it?" In these instances, the implications of the symptomatic idiom are those of an impending *physical collapse*. If phobias, compulsions and obsessions dominate the symptomatic scene the resulting fear is that of the *mental collapse*. After months and years of sustained suffering the twin fears of physical and mental collapse may recede, giving way to apprehensions about the impossibility of a final cure. This is the fear of the *permanent handicap*. The three basic fears of the physical collapse, mental collapse and permanent handicap are variations of the danger theme suggested by the symptomatic idiom.[2]

In effect, Dr. Low told his patients, "If you want to get well, you have to learn to use a language which more adequately fits the territory. The very structure of the language you are using helps perpetuate, aggravate and create neurotic symptoms." Naturally, his emphasis on language is what interested us in his method.

Dr. Low's patients, most of them "experienced sufferers" are given a thorough physical checkup to make sure that the "pressure in the head" is not really a brain tumor, that their symptoms are largely psychosomatic. What "originally caused" these symptoms does not interest Low; his concern is to relieve these symptoms so that the patient can lead a happier, more useful life. If it is argued that the relief of one set of symptoms only breeds a new set, Low's answer is that through his system the patient has been given a method for attacking and relieving any kind of psychosomatic symptom which may arise.

If we examine a patient when he is having his "nervous attack,"

[2] Abraham A. Low, *Mental Health Through Will-Training,* Boston, The Christopher Publishing House, 1950, pp. 21–22.

not in terms of causes or theoretical mechanisms, but in regard to what is happening at the moment, that is, on the descriptive level —and this applies to all of us in our bouts with fear, worry, anxiety, panic—we then discover in every case not a simple, static, cause-effect situation, but a dynamic interaction of cause and effect which builds up in a series of what Low calls "vicious cycles." A pain of some kind appears and, instantly, we make inferences about the significance of this pain. We label it "dangerous." Immediately, this inference "feeds back" and increases the pain, which increases the fear which again increases and multiplies the symptoms, and in a matter of minutes, or even seconds, in an exponential build-up, a panic cycle is on, which can and often does lead to "nervous collapse."

Behind every neurotic symptom, behind every worry, is a fear of some kind. In animals, fears are instinctive or, even if learned, are exhibited only when in contact with the feared object or situation. This is a survival mechanism and as such does no harm to the organism. Let us call this "fear$_1$." We also experience this type of fear, and as with animals, it is necessary for our survival and does little harm. But because we have a verbal level we can proceed to a second-order fear, the fear of fear and of the symptoms that accompany it. This "fear$_2$" is highly destructive and serves no useful purpose as far as I can see. It almost inevitably leads to the vicious cycle. But fortunately for us this second-order fear, being closer to the verbal level than the first-order fear, is open to conscious control. It is here that Dr. Low and general semantics make the attack.

Second-order fear can be described in terms of the interaction of two factors, the "idea of danger" and the feelings (mostly visceral) which accompany it. We cannot deliberately say, "Butterflies, depart from the stomach; heart, stop pounding; sweat, stop pouring; intestines, unknot; throat, untense!" At least most of us cannot, excepting some Yogis and those who have perfected the use of some direct methods of relaxation. However, we can control the idea of danger, we can deliberately learn not to make unverifiable inferences about the significance of the symptoms, we can learn not to fear our fears.

THE SPOTTING TECHNIQUE

Dr. Low taught his patients what he called "the spotting technique." The moment a patient feels a symptom coming on, he says to himself, "These feelings are distressing but not dangerous." After a few months of conscientiously applying this technique, along with others, and fortified by his participation in the group, very much as in Alcoholics Anonymous, he learns to avoid the build-up of the vicious cycle. A twinge may appear, a tightness, a giddiness, etc., but as soon as it does the patient "chops off its head" and it soon subsides.

The patient is not told that his pains are imaginary. They are very real. Put in g.s. terminology, he can say, as a statement of fact, that he feels terrible. But to say that his symptoms are dangerous, that he is incurable, that his pains are caused by a tumor or growth or whatever, is an unverifiable, unreliable inference or prediction. In short, the patients learn to distinguish between factual and inferential statements. Quite authoritatively, Low forbids their making diagnoses and prognoses. They are told that only a trained physician can do this. As long as they continue to make these inferences and act as if they were factual knowledge, they will be ill; if they stop, they will get well. And, according to Low, when they do, they do.

THE WILL TO BEAR DISCOMFORT

Perhaps the general usefulness of this technique, even for us normals, will become more apparent if we turn to another of Dr. Low's dicta, "The Will to Bear Discomfort." Discussing one of his patients, Phil, who had developed an inability to write because his hand became tense and rigid when he attempted it, Low wrote:

What seemed impossible to Phil was not the act of writing but rather the necessity to face, tolerate and endure the discomfort connected with it. This is an important conclusion because it describes the pattern which applies to *every* nervous fear. Some of my patients go to bed with the fear of not sleeping. They think they fear sleeplessness because it ruins health. But what actually frightens them is the torture, that is, the discomfort of lying awake in the dreadful stillness of the night. Or, a patient becomes panicky on entering a street car. He thinks his fear is that of threatening collapse. But what actually scares him is the prospect of being tormented during the ride by palpitations, choking sensations, dizziness and sweats. Again, it is the anticipation of discomfort and nothing else that causes the apprehension. I could easily quote hundreds of situations in which nervous patients are convinced that what they fear are certain acts or certain occurrences while, in point of fact, the only fear they experience is that of a discomfort which they conceive of as "unendurable" or "intolerable" or "unbearable." To put it bluntly: nervous fear is the fear of discomfort.

. . . In Recovery he was trained to face, tolerate and endure discomfort and once he learned to be uncomfortable without wincing he gained confidence and passed on to his muscles the assurance that writing was possible though uncomfortable. The muscles, then, swung into action without tremor or delay. The method which was here at work was plainly and simply THE WILL TO BEAR DISCOMFORT. It is the only and authentic Recovery method of making recalcitrant muscles obey directions.[3]

I think Dr. Low makes two very important points here which will bear a bit of semantic analysis and interpretation. In a previous chapter we discussed the "pleasure principle" and decided that we cannot help but choose that action which we infer will produce the greatest pleasure. Even though we may seem to be choosing a more painful course of action, e.g., going to the dentist as against not going, in reality it is selected because we infer that if we do not, even more pain will result in the future, i.e., our teeth will decay further and eventually we will lose them. Low's first point in the above question is the other

3 *Ibid.*, pp. 142–143.

side of the pleasure-principle coin. The only things we can "really" fear are our own feelings and sensations. The man who has claustrophobia and the student who fears getting up to speak before a class—what do they fear? Certainly the man knows there is nothing in the closet to hurt him, and certainly our student knows no physical harm will come when he speaks. What do they fear? They fear the palpitations, the sweats, the shame—all feelings—they infer will occur.

Let us take this situation to an extreme. Here is a poor woman with three young children at the bedside of her dying husband. We say she fears his death. What does she "really" fear? The loneliness, the anxiety, the insecurity, the pain *she infers she will feel* when he dies. Literally, it is impossible to fear anything but our own feelings and sensations. This seems to horrify some people. It seems to make us egocentric, selfish monsters. However, if we index our term "selfishness" and distinguish between lower-order and higher-order selfishness, we escape this dilemma. It is the means of satisfaction that counts. If we seek our pleasures through the satisfaction of our higher-order needs, then this selfishness also implies a selflessness. We cannot satisfy our need for becoming a self-actualizing person, we cannot experience the pleasure which results from our becoming more effective timebinders, without considering the pleasures that we give to others.

To give of oneself, to help others, to give love, to aid others in developing their potentials, gives us a form of pleasure not found in the satisfaction of any of our lower-order needs. If we choose to label this "selfishness" and identify it with lower-order selfishness, we fall into a familiar semantic trap—elementalism. Ends cannot be separated from means, just as effects cannot be divorced from causes, except verbally. Means affect ends and ends dictate means. In any action, the end may be the experience of pleasure, but the means used will determine the character of the pleasure and also the subsequent patterns of behavior. The pleasure principle seems to be an inevitable fact of life and to feel guilty about it is absurd.

We might just as well feel guilty about breathing. But how we seek these pleasures, at what levels we operate, is something about which we can and should feel guilty. Incidentally, it should be noted that we are not saying that *only* higher-order needs should be satisfied; rather, a balanced behavior at all levels of abstraction is the goal of our ideally effective time-binder.

Far from leading to feelings of guilt, I believe that the realization that all we can fear are our own feelings and sensations, that "we have nothing to fear but fear itself," is a tremendously important and even exhilarating map of our nervous system in action. It brings us to the second point in our discussion of the quotation from Dr. Low's book, namely, the "Will to Bear Discomfort." Low was very much disturbed by what he called "the cult of comfort" in this country. He was not against refrigerators, elevators, cars, etc. But we have become so obsessed with comfort that we begin to think of discomfort as primitive, almost as if it were un-American. No matter how many gadgets we invent, we cannot invent away pain and discomfort altogether. They are inherent in living.

INDEXING AND THE ACT OF ACCEPTANCE

We have to learn to index our pain and discomfort. We have to learn to distinguish between the pain and discomfort about which we can do something immediately, and that about which we can do little or nothing. Do everything to change that which can be changed and accept that which at the moment cannot. The act of acceptance, the will to bear discomfort, has an immediate and profound effect upon the intensity of the pain. It becomes much more bearable, less threatening. For, as we have seen in our discussion throughout this book, the organism acts as a whole. Inferences we make about our pains, attitudes we take toward them, feed back and change them for better or worse.

Learning to accept what at the moment cannot be changed produces what I should like to call an enlightened stoicism. It avoids the evils of the one extreme of complete acceptance of all conditions of life, even those which through effort could be changed, as in some Oriental philosophies, and the other extreme of fretful and petulant complaint, the spinning of bizarre and frightening inferences which lead to vicious cycles of panic and ever-increasing fear and incapacity. Knowing that our only fear can be fear of ourselves, of pain of some kind, and that this pain through acceptance becomes endurable, helps breed a quiet courage and sensible serenity which in turn prevents many psychosomatic ills from developing in the future.

I believe that one of the reasons for the relative ineffectiveness of many self-help books on "How to Control Worry," "Peace of Mind," "How to Live 365 Days a Year," lies not in the worthlessness of their messages. On the contrary, most of what they advocate is good, sensible, useful advice. But they begin their attack at the wrong level of abstraction. Their techniques are designed to reduce directly first-order fears, worries, and anxieties. These are quite resistant to direct and rational attack because of their deep roots in the unconscious and their irrational character. Moreover, these are not nearly as damaging to the nervous system as their second-order counterparts—fear of the fear, worry about the worry, anxiety about anxiety. It is the second-order fears which lead to panic cycles, and it is not uncommon for people to inflict upon themselves wounds of great painfulness, or seek painful operations as a means of escaping them. We cannot worry when undergoing great physical pain, and frequently it is found to be more endurable than the terrible anxieties and panic symptoms of second-order evaluations gone wild.

When the reader of these books finds that his first-order anxieties aren't budging much, he is likely to become discouraged and dismiss the whole business as nonsense, or worse, he may begin to worry because he can't control his worrying, begin to fear that his fears will never recede but will increase, and become anxious about his anxiety.

THE LIVING "NOW": PLANNING ACTS AND PLANNING FEELINGS

But suppose we start at the second-order. Take, for example, a group of beginners in a public speaking class who have varying degrees of stage fright. It is worse than useless to say, "Don't be nervous, don't be tense, don't shake, don't let your mouth go dry." This would only increase the severity of the symptoms. Instead, they are told to accept their feelings, that it is normal to feel scared, that even veteran speakers feel some anxiety on getting up to speak. If the hands shake, let them shake. Concentrate on getting the message across and let the body take care of itself. By thorough preparation and practice at home, by selecting material that one knows is interesting, one reduces the hazards to a minimum. When the speech begins, concentration is upon communication and not self-feeling. So in every situation. We change what can be changed, plan to do what we can most effectively, and to the best of our ability prepare, hope, pray. But the moment of commitment, the living moment, the present *now* is accepted. We feel what we feel, and if we must suffer, so be it.

It is most important that we understand the peculiar relationship between acceptance and planned change. It is perfectly legitimate and wise to plan to reduce suffering in oneself and in others, or to build a better desk or house or neighborhood or world. But the feelings and sensations of any given moment cannot be planned because they are involuntary, an end product, a resultant of the total organism-environment situation at the moment. It is this moment as it is happening that is to be accepted and not resented, the saying of yea to life.

Take, for example, a medical student who plans and works hard for his degree. And he dreams. He sees himself walking to the platform to receive the sheepskin, he hears the applause of the audience, sees the radiant eyes of his mother. Oh, ecstasy! Poor soul, he plans that ecstasy, expects to feel it. Comes the great day. Up to the platform he walks, the audience applauds, his mother's eyes beam. He? Ecstasy? Nothing like it! Only a vague diffuse excitement. Suddenly a tremendous letdown. Is this what he sweated and ached for, this moment of nothing at all? Then reaction and despair. What's the use of trying if the reward is a cold bucket of ashes? His mistake was in confusing the planning of plans with the planning of feelings. We can plan doings, movements of the voluntary muscles and higher-order abstractions, but not feelings of the moment or the movement of the involuntary musculature such as the viscera. These latter can be hoped for but not expected, and, having occurred, accepted and not rejected.

The acceptance of one's feelings of the moment immediately breaks the vicious cycle by preventing the unwanted second-order evaluations. Although this will still leave the first-order fears or worries intact, they become bearable and in time may diminish because they are not continuously restimulated by the second-order evaluations. *The acceptance of that which cannot at the moment be changed, changes it.*

GOOD WORRY AND BAD

Consider the problem of worry. Most of us worry over matters though quite often we realize that the worrying does no good, will not help to solve our problems. There are, of course, good worries and bad. If a worry goads us into action which will help solve our problem it is good. But if it does not, or if there is no immediate action we can take which will resolve our difficulty, the worry is bad and useless. Now there are many books on "How To Stop Worrying." Their formulae can be boiled down to a few basic principles. First, we should, as objectively as possible, evaluate the situation to see if any positive action can be taken to solve the problem. Second, having done this, we are to remember that it is impossible to concentrate on two thoughts at the same time. Therefore we are to develop the habit of immediately switching our thoughts from the worry situation to something pleasant, or to indulge in activity which requires our concentrating on something other than our problem, a sort of spotting technique.

There is no doubt but that the system works. The catch is in putting it into operation. Most of us are experienced worriers. We have been practicing it for years and it is a most difficult habit to break. Conquently, success with the "switch game" is mighty small at first and it takes extreme determination to stick with it until the new habit begins to displace the old one. It is easy to become discouraged and quit, especially since these books do not distinguish between first- and second-order worry. The first-order is firmly entrenched and highly resistant to direct attack; the second-order, which is much more destructive, is more easily licked. If a man is worrying about his worrying he can, with relatively little practice, learn to stop, especially if he has learned the art of acceptance. He chooses to accept the distressing feelings which accompany his first-order worry. This has a two-fold effect. First, it immediately reduces the distress of the first-order worry and eliminates the second-order. Secondly, this relatively quick success encourages him to proceed with the more difficult task of "thought switching" to reduce the first-order worrying, for he is always fortified with the knowledge that no matter how severe the feelings, by accepting he can endure them, by choosing to endure them they will lessen. And the more he practices this, the more his successes, the greater grows his confidence in his "self-control," all of which accelerates in a beneficial, non-vicious cycle.

Now most of this is old stuff. The call to courage, acceptance, stoic endurance, is to be found universally and can be traced back for thousands of years. This makes it highly suspect for some "sophisticated" people; it is thought to be naïve, Pollyannish, and unscientific. The answer to this is, first, it works. It has worked to some degree for millions of people. Let us not too lightly explain it away as self-deception, autosuggestion, etc. Merely applying labels explains nothing. If these results do not fit too snugly into our psychological theories, maybe we just ought to do a little redrawing of the maps. Second, as far as I can see there is nothing unscientific about it. It utilizes the principle that second-order evaluations are more easily controlled than first-order, that controlling them feeds back and lessens the intensity of the first-order effects, which is to be expected in a dynamically interconnected organism. It makes use of the common sense procedure of attacking a problem at its weakest point and, through achieving a series of little successes, ultimately securing strength for the major attack on the stronghold—the tried and true process of conditioning and learning by reinforcement through reward.

Dr. Low does not depend solely upon verbal techniques for the relief of symptoms. It is a truism of learning theory that action must accompany thought, that both verbal and non-verbal levels must be involved before effective learning takes place. Dr. Low states, "Muscles can be made to mold and influence mental activity." In practice this turns out to be classical Pavloviana. If a patient is afraid of telephones or closed rooms or cannot leave the house, he is told to command his muscles (meaning the large voluntary muscles) to perform the dreaded activity. He tells himself that he knows that what he is really afraid of is not the telephone but the terrible feelings he will have when he answers it. But these feelings are distressing but not dangerous, he has the will to bear the discomfort and so he proceeds to force himself to use the phone. By practicing this routine he eventually overcomes his dread.

I should not like to drop our discussion of Dr. Low's work at this point without indicating that these are only a few of the techniques he has devised. For example, his patients are taught that "Helplessness is not hopelessness." In g.s. terminology, they learn to date their statements about their feelings. "I feel helpless *now*."

This is a factual statement. "My condition is hopeless." That is an inference only a doctor is capable of drawing with any degree of certainty of being correct. They are forbidden to use that language. There are other devices for controlling temper, for avoiding "sabotage" of the system, for becoming objective, for learning to laugh at oneself. All of them revolve around the elimination of allness statements, of undated, unindexed, level-confusing language.

As we have stated before, we are not concerned with defending the validity and specific usefulness of Dr. Low's methods. Certainly they have their limitations. They cannot be used with psychotics or those unwilling or unable to attend the group sessions. His extreme authoritarianism disturbs some. His total unconcern with causative factors bothers others. No matter; he does get some good results and they seem to be long-lasting in many cases. For one man to be able to do as well as he did with more than 100 patients per year is indeed remarkable. But our concern is with the more general aspects of his system. By correcting the misuse of language, terribly miserable patients feel better; perhaps we non-patients can do still better in handling our run-of-the-mill everyday problems after having seen how the very patterns of misevaluation we have discussed throughout this book have played an important part in making and keeping these people mentally and physically ill. By moving from the limited area of lessening the symptoms of neurosis to the broad plain of learning proper evaluation in all situations, we avoid the authoritarian aspects of Low's system. We choose to use a language whose structure more adequately fits the territory, not because the doctor says we must but because we ourselves wish to become effective time-binders.

Methods for eliminating the idea of danger to the self are to be found in every system of therapy, explicitly or implicitly, directly or indirectly, whether that therapy is offered as a therapy or classed as a religion or philosophy.

1. Theistic religion—trust in, believe in, God. He will take care of you, never fear.

2. Psychoanalysis—relive the experience and reëvaluate it and you will see that your fears are childish and there is now nothing to fear from them.

3. "Be glad you're neurotic" school—everybody has these troubles. Make use of these fears and they will not make use of you.

4. Lose yourself and your fears in "good works" or a great movement. This is a combination approach. When we concentrate on helping others or the Party or the school, we cannot concentrate on our own symptoms and problems. This is the "switch your thoughts" technique. In addition, it helps relieve guilt because the cause is "good." And finally, since it helps satisfy some of the higher-order needs, it tends to redress the previous overemphasis on the satisfaction of the lower-order needs.

THE TRUE BELIEVER

Method four is the most adaptable to general semantics. However, we must point out some of the dangers involved. The most obvious is the danger of becoming a fanatic, a *true believer*. When we seek to escape from the self and its torments through identification with a mass movement, for example, our reasoning goes something like this: "What happens to me does not matter, only the Movement counts. My feelings are of no concern to me, only the welfare of the Movement. I no longer fear any danger because I no longer have anything of value to lose. I do not count. The Movement is all." As Riesman, Fromm, Hoffer, and others indicate, the person loses all sense of personal worth, his thoughts are no longer his own. He becomes the epitome of the other-directed man. Moreover, this escape from the self and the idea of danger is never complete, because there is always the nagging fear that the Movement may die, may be destroyed, may be betrayed, or, worst of all, may turn out to be false. Thus, the frantic search for spies and conspirators and unbelievers gets under way. The slightest deviation from the true gospel is heresy, because the slightest crack in the foundation will doom the whole structure. And if the Movement should die, so would the fanatic believer. His whole inner world would be destroyed. So horrible is this prospect that all contradictory evidence is explained away, all contradictory logic ignored. Physical self-destruction—suicide or martyrdom—is preferred to destruction of the inner symbolic world which revolves around the Movement.

The problem, then, is to select a movement or philosophy or idea which, by its structure, prevents the development of fanaticism and its evils. Needless to say, I believe that general semantics, with its ideal of becoming an effective time-binder, fills this role. I do not see how one could become a fanatic general semanticist, because its whole structure is antifanatic. Yet it does provide the values inherent in a well-structured set of non-contradictory higher-order abstractions which can serve as goals, ideals, and standards for making value judgments.

The Happiness Formula

This complex of higher-order abstractions we call general semantics is reflected in a set of high low-order abstractions we shall call attitudes. One such attitude vigorously endorsed by Alfred Korzybski is found in his "formula" for happiness: $H = 1/E$, or, as modified by Irving J. Lee, $H = M/E$. This is a compact way of saying that we ought to keep our expectations of achieving a goal low and our motivation for working to achieve it high. Korzybski argued that since our knowledge of anything is always limited, and that since the future is an uncertain inference, the proper attitude reflecting this state of affairs is one of keeping the expectations low.

When we keep our expectations high we are not prepared for their not being fulfilled, which, in the light of our limited knowledge and the infinite complexity of the world, is much more likely than the fulfillment of our expectations. Consequently a person with chronically high expectations is a chronically disappointed man. He is likely to become a victim of Wendell Johnson's IFD disease—he moves from Idealism to Frustration to Demoralization. On the other hand, if we keep our expectations low, we have a map that fits the territory. Whatever happens is likely to be better than we expected. Therefore life becomes a series of successes and no matter how minor many of them may be we are much more likely to be happy with this attitude than the other.

There are those who claim that unless we have high expectations of succeeding in a task, we cannot work hard at it, cannot have high motivation. This is not necessarily so. Those who make this claim have never really tried or even thought of thinking otherwise. Thinking of this kind is not a very difficult habit to establish and is well worth the effort in providing an attitude which facilitates more adequate and more realistic evaluation. This does not mean that we attempt to reduce expectations to zero. The man with zero expectations is either in complete despair or utterly cynical. In either case he attempts little, produces less, and is not of much use to himself or anyone else. Nor does it mean that we should be without hope. There is a big difference between high hopes and high expectations. In the former, we are prepared for failure and for success, in the latter only for success. The ideal is embodied in that old chestnut, "Expect the worst and hope for the best."

THE FEAR OF DEATH

One of the most fearsome of fears is the fear of death. The fear of dying is instinctive and seems to be present in all the higher animals and to varying degrees in the lower. The fear of death is nature's dubious gift to man, one of the penalties of our having the capacity to use symbols. Man, like animals, has an instinctive fear of dying; this is a very low-order abstraction and a necessary survival mechanism. Death is a higher-order abstraction, a creation of man. It results from his ability to peer into the future through the use of symbols and his ability to make inferences about his own fate, based upon observation of, and learning about, the dying of others in the past. The fear of dying is present only when the organism is confronted with what it considers a threat to its existence. The fear of death can be present at any time, even in the safest situations. It is possible because we can imagine ourselves being dead. That is, we think we can.

The fear of death has many faces. If a person is religious and believes in what his faith has to say about "life after death," his fears are different from those of the man who has no specifically defined afterlife. The true believer may fear punishment of some kind, but he does not experience—or should not—one of the most excruciating of all fears, the fear of non-being. Our concern in the remainder of this discussion will be with the latter. We have nothing to offer the former other than to tell him to be good, obey the rules, and pray.

I believe that the fear of non-being owes much of its intensity to the fact that it involves a rather violent distortion of the abstracting process, an identification of two different levels of abstraction, an attempt to do what it is literally impossible to do—imagine ourselves dead, non-existent. In our discussion of the abstracting process, we noted that it is literally impossible for us to imagine that which we have never experienced. All we can imagine are new combinations of previous experience. We can picture three-headed elephants and flying mountains and talking trees, for these are merely combinations of previous experience. But we cannot conceive of a color we have never seen, such as ultraviolet or infrared, or of a sound we have never heard.

We also learned that qualities—colors, tastes, shapes, etc.—are a resultant of the interaction of a living organism and its environment. What we see depends upon the structure and state of our eyes and the rest of the nervous system as it responds to what is "out there." Indeed, we decided that there is no "out there" in the sense of there being shapes and colors independent of our nervous system. Now, since the nervous system disintegrates when we die, we cannot possibly feel or sense anything when we are dead. When we try to imagine ourselves dead, we can only do so in terms of being alive. We imagine ourselves being somewhere, feeling something, and these feelings and sensings are inevitably those we experience when alive. Obviously, when the nervous system decomposes, any possible feeling and sensing would have to be radically different from that which occurs in the living state, and this is absolutely unimaginable.

Of course we can postulate a spirit life of some kind, a soul that carries on after death. But even here, unless we give the soul all the properties of a living organism, which in effect would mean bringing a person back to *this* life, whatever this soul would experience must be different from living experience, and hence strictly unimaginable. Indeed, we cannot even imagine ourselves in a dreamless sleep. Always "we" are there, sensing, experiencing.

Therefore, when we attempt to imagine ourselves non-existent, we are trying to make our nervous system do that which it cannot possibly do. All we can know is living. Overcoming this aspect of the fear of death is quite simple but takes practice. It involves using the "switching technique." Every time one finds himself contemplating non-existence he reminds himself that he is warping his nervous system by seeking to make it do that which it is not designed to do. He reminds himself that all he can know is living and to attempt to know and feel non-living is an invitation to psychological disaster. This is not avoiding a problem or a question, for there is no problem or question. What does it feel like to be dead? is a meaningless question because there is no way of getting a verifiable answer.

It may be argued that perhaps some day we will discover a method for answering this question. Perhaps. But at the moment we can be sure that one way *not* to get an answer is by trying to imagine non-being. It cannot be done and the attempt can lead only to a violent malfunctioning of the nervous system. Some radically new form and area of knowledge must be discovered before any reliable answers can be obtained. Until then, speculation of the type used for obtaining answers to meaningful questions will not give us an answer to this question, which by all accepted standards of today's science and logic is strictly meaningless.

We shall have more to say about the differences between meaningful and meaningless questions in another chapter, but it is worth noting, in connection with the question, "What does it feel like to be dead?" how the structure of the language promotes confusion and identification of the levels of abstraction. It centers about our old friend, the verb "to be." To be implies to exist. "Dead" then becomes a state of existence. We "are" dead. But "being" in connection with ourselves can only be in terms of "living," of feeling and sensing. Very subtly, but powerfully, the "to be" causes us to confuse what occurs on the level of living organisms with that of the inanimate level of the dead. Because the language structure identifies the two, we come to think of them as identical. A careful separation of the levels of abstraction leads to this conclusion: A man can die but he cannot *be* dead. And funerals are for the survivors, not for the deceased.

FROM NOW TO ETERNITY

Differentiating between the levels of abstraction helps us to develop the knack of concentrating attention on a particular level, and this can have highly beneficial results, as we have seen. By sharply distinguishing between the non-verbal and verbal levels, we can develop, or rather recover, the sense of "nowness" which is lost when we identify the two levels, or when we concentrate too much on the verbal level. In our discussion of duration and time, we observed that time is a higher-order abstraction obtained when we symbolize and measure our sensing of duration. That is, time is a second-order duration, the measured duration of the sensing of duration. Time is not felt, duration is. We cannot feel or sense an hour, a year, or a moment. These are measurements, symbols, maps of our non-verbal sense of duration. The non-verbal level is timeless; it has only the unmeasured and unmeasurable *now*. At this level there is no beginning, no end, only flow and change. Beginning and end are high-order abstractions resulting from our thinking and talking *about* our feelings and sensings, and like all higher-order abstractions they are static; they are symbols and do not apply at the object level of senses and feelings. Eternity, meaning years without end, is a higher-order abstraction, cannot be felt, and leads to paradox when we try to measure it. But eternity, meaning timelessness, is something that can be felt. When our concentration is wholly upon sensing and feeling without any notion of measurement, without any high-order thinking *about* what we are experiencing on the non-verbal level, there comes to us that feeling of timelessness and eternity which is profoundly moving and utterly mysterious. It is this sense of "nowness" that the artist tries to capture, convey, invoke, and evoke, and it is in this sense that all great art is timeless. The moment we move away from the feeling of immediacy of experience to the higher level of talking about our experience, we no longer feel its beauty, though we may "intellectually" know it is beautiful; we are then in the realm of analysis and criticism. I believe that one reason for the mysteriousness of this non-verbal experience is our confusion of the two levels of abstraction and our unawareness of the differences between them. The verbal level is the level of measurement and analysis. These abstractions are relatively static and are not felt. We do not feel the number 2. Now when we apply higher-order abstractions to the lower orders, i.e., when we attempt to measure and time and, necessarily, stop the flow of non-verbal abstraction (all measurement requires a beginning, an end, and a stopping of the abstracting process being measured) we may fail to realize that these are symbols about the non-verbal level and not the lower-order abstractions themselves. Consequently, we are surprised when analysis and measurement do not yield or elicit the non-verbal experience of timelessness, but destroy it; further, we are amazed and disconcerted by the differences in "quality" of the two levels.

A most serious effect of confusing the two levels occurs when we focus most of our attention and time on verbal levels and not enough on non-verbal. We then get the stereotype picture of the "cold fish intellectual" who knows all *about* life but has very little experience of it. By life I mean the non-verbal level, our most real, most important innermost world of sensing and feeling. This is the most important level of abstraction for each individual. His higher-order abstractions are tools for achieving the satisfaction of his lower-order wants, needs, desires. Our "intellectual" has reversed this natural order and gives more value to the high-order abstractions than the low; and this can be achieved only at the expense of warping the total functioning of the nervous system.

The Immortal Moment

A balancing of attention to both levels enables us to appreciate the values of each; concentrating exclusively on one or the other will destroy the harmonious and effective functioning of the whole. Being able to descend to the non-verbal level and to refrain from theorizing, analyzing, criticizing, enables us to experience the wonderful world of the senses and feelings, allows us to experience the wonders, joys, even ecstasies, that come from concentration on this level of experience. The simplest object can evoke a train of unspeakable unanalyzable feelings; works of art suddenly move us to tears; a profound sense of wonder and a hint of some kind of mysterious meaning to life can be evoked. There is nothing unnatural or supernatural about this. It doesn't mean living in, or going into, a trance. It is an enhancement of the experience of living which comes when we learn to control the abstracting process through an intelligent understanding of its structure and function.

For example, when we are thoroughly aware, "intellectually" and "feelingly," of the differences between the verbal and non-verbal levels, it becomes possible to both understand and feel that each of us, to ourselves, as we live our lives, is immortal. We know verbally, "intellectually," that we were born and that we will die. But at the level of sensing and feeling, life is a timeless, ever-changing dance of impressions, a vast kaleidoscopic onrushing flow with no beginning, no end, only timeless change and an unmeasured sense of duration. I cannot imagine what it feels like to be not-born or not-living. All my knowings are living knowings and each moment of living is timeless eternity. At the non-verbal level I am immortal; on the verbal I have a measured and measurable span. But numbers of years are talkings about life, useful for planning and making predictions and therefore helpful in making the non-verbal level more pleasant. But the living moment, the pregnant moment, the moment as it occurs, as I feel it and sense it NOW as a sum total effect of all the operations of all the levels of abstraction—that moment and each is timeless; in that moment and each, I am immortal.

Just as the attempt to measure and to time non-verbal experience changes and destroys that experience *as we experience it,* so the failure to measure and time at the verbal level produces an equally profound distortion of the abstracting process. When talking and thinking *about* our non-verbal abstractions, it is necessary to date our statements, measure changes, and be prepared to accept and expect change. Higher-order abstractions are static; they need to be pushed; they must be deliberately changed to fit the changing territory they represent. One of the most difficult tasks in counseling people in the 15–25 age bracket is overcoming their tendency to allness statements about their problems. The boy who has been rejected in his first serious love affair knows for sure that he will never be able to love another woman. The girl who is not invited to the senior prom despairs of ever having a boy friend or being popular. Despair, hopelessness come easily in this age group; for one thing, they have had so little living experience with which to compare and evaluate their present problems. For another, the very language in which they state their problems and feelings reinforces their prolongation.

As we get older we learn through sad and sometimes bitter experience that things and feelings and people do change and so we gain the knack of hanging on. We learn the wisdom of the statement, "This, too, shall pass." We learn that even though some conditions now afflicting us may not change for the better and may only get worse, still, by changing our evaluation of the situation, we may make ourselves feel better. We may learn that the acceptance of that which we cannot change, itself changes the situation, that the will to bear unavoidable discomfort eases it, that all we have to fear is fear itself.

But sometimes these things are never learned, or learned too late in life at exhorbitant cost in money, time, and misery. Perhaps by learning some such system as general semantics we can shorten and ease the learning period. Perhaps not.

Invariants Under Transformation

The concept of the effective time-binder is what Korzybski called an "invariant under transformation." This term, borrowed from mathematics, describes a set of higher-order abstractions (constructs) which do not significantly change their basic meanings or structural relationships in any situation to which they can be legitimately applied, as, for example, the laws of nature. Although the law of gravity may not give us a precise answer as to where exactly a given bullet will hit the earth (it will be influenced by wind, temperature, condition of gun, weight of powder, etc.) it does tell us where an ideal bullet would hit under ideal conditions. By controlling conditions to approach these ideals, we can often get remarkably accurate answers. The law of gravity is a higher-order abstraction and like all higher-order abstractions, it is static. Based upon many highly accurate observations, it is a summary and idealization (generalization) of certain invariances in relationships among objects we can discern by ignoring or controlling certain individual differences, such as wind velocity, pressure, etc. Thus we can apply it to falling bullets or falling water or falling leaves; it is an invariant under transformation. On the verbal level these laws of nature, like the equations of pure mathematics, are absolutely invariant under transformation. When applied to the non-verbal world, they are relatively invariant and have a very high degree of probability of being correct and a wide and accurate range of predictability.

We think that the concept of the effective time-binder can be classified as an invariant under transformation because it applies to all men in all cultures up to the present time. In no way does it approach a natural law in preciseness or predictability, yet it is most useful, especially in decision-making, for it provides a structure which guides the process. At the very highest level of abstraction we can lay down sweeping invariants, "biblical" edicts: In every decision choose that course which seems most likely to enhance your time-binding ability! A corollary of this would be the injunction to so act toward every man, in every situation, that the response elicited from him will not warp his abstracting processes. Always seek to promote that response which will represent the most effective use of his time-binding ability no matter how poor it may be.

LEVELS OF SELF AND LOVING

The injunction to act as an effective time-binder also implies a command to love oneself and others. The precept to love thy neighbor as thyself is to be found in every major religion. Often, however, it has been interpreted to mean that one should love his neighbor and despise, or at least neglect, himself, on the assumption that self-love means selfishness. We have seen that if we distinguish between lower-order and higher-order selfishness, this dilemma does not arise. Indeed, it is coming to be realized that one cannot love others if he cannot love himself.

Introspectively we can sense at least two levels of the self. "I told myself not to go," suggests an "I" and "me," with the "I" representing the more "rational" levels and processes of the total personality and the "me" the more "emotional," "irrational" processes. The "me" represents the first-order self, the self of the lower-order needs of hunger, thirst, physical sex, and similar first-order psychophysiological hungers and drives. The "I" symbolizes the second-order self, the level of second-order feelings, emotions, and conscious logical processes. The distinction between the two is most probably not as sharp as our language implies, but for the sake of expediency we shall use this terminology and at the same time realize that it suggests a map whose simplicity is not to be found in the territory it represents.

Corresponding to these two levels of the self we can distinguish two orders of loving. In early infancy there is a deep need for lower-order love. The infant is absolutely helpless and love means life and equals life. His love is the love of "me"; his "I" has not yet developed. According to Maslow, if these lower-order love needs are not satisfied in childhood, he becomes a neurotic and hunts for the love for this lower-order self for the rest of his life. And he never finds it; it is an insatiable, neurotic, possessive, narcissistic love. It is sought as a means of security, for that is what it meant in infancy.

The jealous lover is a fearful lover. His self-esteem and security are bound to his being loved. Therefore he has a profound fear of losing his love. The more he fears, the greater the jealousy, and the greater the uncertainty that he is "really" loved. He can never feel the absolute security his neurotic needs demand; he can never know for sure whether or not his beloved is absolutely faithful to him. And the greater the fear and jealousy, the more unlovable he becomes, thereby destroying the very thing he hoped to preserve. In short, he cannot give love in any deep sense; he can only receive. He can think only of being loved, not of giving it.

As the child matures his cortex develops and the possibility of his experiencing second-order love arises to the degree that his first-order love needs have been satisfied. Now, not only the "me" can love and be loved, the "I" also can produce its variety of love and affection. Second-order love can take at least two forms, one the love of some first-order feeling or emotion, like the love of the love of Mexicans, or the love of the hate of Japanese as previously discussed, or it can be directed toward the act of loving itself. This, in turn, has two forms, the lower, less mature love of being loved or being in love—infatuation, and the second, perhaps the most mature and most noble of all emotions, the love of giving love. But we must remember that this second-order love cannot be achieved if the first-order love needs have not been satisfied, and this includes the acceptance of oneself on all levels of abstraction. We cannot despise ourselves and love others.

More and more psychiatrists are beginning to emphasize the integrating power of this higher-order love. Erich Fromm writes:

What is called love? Dependence, submission, . . . domination, possessiveness and the craving for control are felt to be love; sexual greed and the inability to stand solitude are experienced as proof of intense capacity for love. People believe that *to love* is simple, but that *to be loved* is most difficult. . . . They do not know that the real problem is not the difficulty of being loved but the difficulty of loving; that one is loved only if one can love, if one's capacity to love produces love in another person, that the capacity for love, not for its counterfeit, is a most difficult achievement. . . . There is no more convincing proof that the injunction "love thy neighbor as thyself" is the most important norm of living and that its violation is the basic cause of unhappiness and mental illness than the evidence gathered by the psychoanalyst. Whatever complaints the neurotic patient may have, whatever symptoms he may present are rooted in his inability to love, if we mean by love a capacity for the experience of concern, responsibility, respect, and understanding of another person and the intense desire for that other person's growth. *Analytic therapy is essentially an attempt to help the patient gain or regain his capacity for love.* If this aim is not fulfilled nothing but surface changes can be accomplished.[4]

If our neurotic needs are not so deep that they almost completely inhibit objective analysis and rational control, self-therapy is possible. Again, the point of attack must be at the level of the second-order feeling. We cannot command ourselves to love others or others to love us. We *can* choose to try to love the giving of love without any high expectations of being rewarded in any way by those to whom we give it. The reward will come from the act of giving, from knowing that it represents the nervous system operating at an optimum, that it is good for us in the sense that it is a powerful integrator of all the levels of the abstracting process. This is a higher-order selfishness which is, at the same time, one of the highest forms of altruism.

Moreover, since this kind of loving is so undemanding, it awakens

---

[4] Erich Fromm, *Psychoanalysis and Religion,* New Haven, Yale University Press, 1950, pp. 86–87.

no fears of non-acceptance, for it matters not if it is rejected. Security then does not depend on what someone else does or does not do. Paradoxically, when we do not actively seek the love of another out of a desperate need for it, it is more likely to be offered, for the other person then finds it easier to love us because we do not threaten his security as we do when we jealously demand love. He can feel free to give his self and yet retain his self-identity and self-freedom.

Slowly, very slowly at first, this deliberate giving of love, even in very small ways, gradually builds up into a "good" cycle. Without our directly seeking it, people begin to give more freely the love we once so desperately demanded. There begins a series of small successes, rewards for the giving of love, and these reinforce the act of giving in the typical conditioning pattern. Thus by beginning with a second-order love which we can deliberately choose and direct, we begin to obtain a satisfaction of the first-order needs which could not be directly satisfied.

THE SECURITY OF INSECURITY

Equally important is the development of a higher-order sense of security. Lower-order needs can never be permanently satisfied, for various hungers continually appear; the life of the body is always threatened and always subject to some stress. People who seek security at this level can never find it. There is always the ultimate insecurity of death. But the realization that absolute first-order security is impossible, that pain, suffering, tragedy, and death are inevitable, can lead to a second-order security. The acceptance of first-order insecurity leads to second-order security; it generates the "wisdom of insecurity." The search for first-order security is abandoned and by focusing on the development of the higher-order needs and self-actualization one gains the security that comes from a satisfactory philosophy of life, that is, from the development of the "I." The second-order self, by accepting the necessary insecurity of the first-order self, fulfills the higher-order need for equanimity. Equanimity is a higher-order "feeling good," the equivalent of the lower-order "full belly." It is the good feeling which comes from satisfying a philosophical need, that is, a deliberately formulated need as opposed to an unconsciously formulated need, such as an infantile craving for father and mother. The higher-order need, when satisfied, can feed back and diminish the infantile, neurotic one; but no amount of satisfaction of a lower-order neurotic need can contribute to the satisfaction of the higher-order needs. It is an asymmetric relationship.

Thus the satisfaction of the lower-order needs becomes of secondary importance. They are not to be neglected and are to be enjoyed as freely and deeply as possible, but they are no longer the primary aim in life. The first concern is the development of one's self-actualizing potentials, the satisfaction of the higher-order needs. Instead of living just to eat, drink, lust, and be merry, these become pleasures to be enjoyed along the path whose goal is the development of one's creative and esthetic capacities. Interestingly enough, when the former are not directly pursued as the chief goals of life, they are more likely to be enjoyed because then they are neither indulged in to excess nor thwarted and warped by the fear that one may not be able to obtain and enjoy them.

Pleasant as the satisfaction of the lower-order needs may be, they do not produce the lasting and, in a way, more desirable, effects that come with the satisfaction of the higher-order needs—a profound and pervasive happiness and serenity not to be confused with the full-bellyness and docile peace of mind associated with the satisfaction of the lower-order needs; a true dignity and nobility which comes from a rich inner life quite distinct from the pomposity and arrogance which are the mark of warped and restricted patterns of evaluation.

DETACHED-ATTACHMENT

We can describe two different attitudes toward life and the world of things: attachment and detachment. Attachment is associated with the materialist, the pragmatist, the realist; detachment with the idealist, the saint, the ascetic. Again, these attitudes are incompatible and contradictory only if we attempt to maintain them on the same order of abstraction; but we can decide (second-order self) not to allow our attachment for the satisfaction of the lower-order needs to become stronger than for the satisfaction of the higher-order needs. That is, we can enjoy them and be attached to them as means to the actualization of the higher-order self and be detached from them as ends in themselves. We can be, and must be, attached to the "me" because we would die without it; and we can be detached from it in the sense that it can be looked upon as a trusted servant to be treated as well as possible but never trusted to become master of the house.

This attitude toward the different levels of needs comes very close to the "detached-attachment" Charles Morris describes in his *Paths of Life:*

The ideal attitude is that of generalized detached-attachment. For it would seem as though an attachment to all phases of the self would require at the same time an attitude of detachment to any particular phase of the self in order to prevent it from usurping the active expression of other phases. The resulting attitude would involve both detachment and attachment, generalized to embrace each phase of the self, and extended to the whole self, to the universe, and to the attitude of detached attachment itself.[5]

[5] Charles Morris, *Paths of Life,* New York, Harper & Brothers, 1942, p. 156.

The process of becoming a self-actualizing person—an effective time-binder—is long, difficult, and never-ending, yet withal the most satisfying and truly human way of life. Fromm nicely summarizes it in these words:

The whole life of the individual is nothing but the process of giving birth to himself; indeed, we should be fully born when we die—although it is a tragic fate of most individuals to die before they are born.[6]

Both animals and man are born—physical birth. No animal has a hand in its own development to any great extent. It is born with a set of abilities which usually mature. It does not *choose* to become anything. Only man can choose his life, can determine what he shall become—born$_2$. Within the limits of his hereditarily determined capacities, and if the environment is not so extremely hostile that he must spend all his energies just to stay alive, man can to a large extent decide what kind of human being he shall become.

Sartre, the Existentialist, maintains that man is responsible for himself. He cannot look for help to any outside supernatural agency. And he cannot duck this responsibility without committing psychological suicide. He must commit himself; there is "no exit." Man is free to choose his self and has the responsibility to exercise that freedom. If we flee from this freedom or responsibility we sicken and we never give birth to ourselves. "Man creates himself" and in large part what we create is our own choice.

[6] Erich Fromm, *The Sane Society,* New York, Rinehart & Company, 1955, p. 26.

❊❊ 9 ❊❊

Religion

UNANSWERABLE AND UNANSWERED QUESTIONS

IN this chapter we shall indulge in some rather wild speculation and it might be advisable before we begin to try to define rather precisely what we mean when we say that a statement or question is meaningless or unanswerable. It is commonly assumed that just because we can put a question mark after a series of words we have asked a meaningful, answerable question. This is not the case. An unanswerable question has no answer for it is not a real question, and if answers are given to it we have no way of choosing among them or telling which one is correct, if any.

As a starting point we shall arbitrarily divide questions into two categories: the unanswered and the unanswerable. What are the differences between the two? Let us pose two questions: What does the other side of the moon look like? How many angels can dance on the head of a pin? Most people would agree that the first is answerable but unanswered at the moment. The second is unanswerable. Why? After all, no one has ever seen the other side of the moon because it always keeps the same face toward us. Similarly, presumably no one today can see an angel. So we have ignorance in both cases. What differentiates the two types of ignorance? The difference lies in our ability, in the first case, to define operationally how we would go about getting an answer. We cannot do so in the second.

Even though we have as yet no way of reaching the moon, we can say, "If we were to send up a camera-equipped rocket capable of circling the moon and returning we could find out what the other side looked like." In other words, if we can devise or imagine some *non-verbal procedure*, some experiment, by which we could get an answer, we have asked an answerable, though unanswered, question. If we cannot possibly imagine how we could go about getting an answer which could be verified non-verbally we have asked an unanswerable question. Just how would you go about finding angels?

It does not solve any problems to say that perhaps in the future we will find some means of seeing angels. It is useless to speculate about how many angels can dance on the pin because logic, deduction, theorizing, testimony of other speculators, such as philosophers and theologians, will give you many answers, each one sounding very logical and reasonable. Yet you will have no way of choosing among them.

Arguments involving unanswerable questions are called "intensional." Only verbal procedures can be employed to settle them and they can never be decided satisfactorily. If a decision must be made, one or more of the following procedures are generally used:

1. Force—you shoot your opponent. That proves you are right.
2. Attrition—you talk longer and louder than he.
3. Majority vote—this is the democratic method. 40,000,000 Frenchmen can't be wrong.
4. Agree to disagree—all opponents agree ahead of time they will reach no agreement and no minds will be changed. This is the open-minded method of tolerance which is seen at interfaith discussions of religious doctrines.

With Omar Khayyam you come out the same door by which you entered.

In an extensional argument the point at issue is an unanswered

question. There is talking, theorizing, speculation. But at last someone says, "Let's set up this experiment. If such and such happens
we will get an answer to our question." And they do get *an answer*
acceptable *at a date.* Until new data come along the question is
answered.

To speculate about unanswerable questions and to gain verifiable
knowledge, one should concentrate on devising non-verbal methods
for getting an answer. Of course if one is not interested in reliable
knowledge and wishes to mull over the question for the emotional
excitement its contemplation produces, that is another matter.

We can divide unanswerable questions into two categories: the
ambiguous and the meaningless. Purely ambiguous questions can be
made meaningful and then, in some cases, become answerable; the
meaningless cannot. If we ask, "Is x black?" we have no way of
getting an answer until we fix the variable, i.e., define x. If we
substitute "coal" for x, by observing coal (non-verbal procedure)
we can get an answer, assuming we can suitably define "black." If we
ask ourselves, "Why did this accident happen to me?" we have an
ambiguous question until we fix the meaning of "why." If by "why"
we mean, "What went wrong with the car's mechanism which pre-
vented my stopping in time?" we can get an answer. But if it means,
"Why did fate, or God, do this to me?" Or, "Why am I being
punished in this way?" then, even though the variable has been
fixed, we are left with a meaningless question because there is no
non-verbal procedure yet devised for getting a reliable answer. So
we can say that fixing the meaning of the variables is necessary but
not sufficient for obtaining answerable, meaningful questions.

Sometimes questions which once were considered answerable later
turn out to be unanswerable. Irving Langmuir stated that the question, "Can matter be created or destroyed?" was once answered with
a definite no. Today we don't know what we mean by "destroying"
matter and the question is now ambiguous.

We can divide meaningless questions into two categories. The first is a very special category of questions that do not require non-verbal procedures for obtaining valid answers, that deal with matters purely on verbal levels. For example, "How much is 1 + 1 in arithmetic?" Or, "What is the definition of a circle?" Or, "Does three of a kind beat two pairs in poker?" All of these are purely matters of definition or rules of procedure and have no direct relation to the non-verbal level of things. Here the test of meaningfulness is lack of contradiction in the rules and definitions.

In the second category of meaningless questions are those which would require non-verbal procedures for making them meaningful, and here we meet such old friends as, "What does red look like to another person?" "What is the real taste of sugar?" "What is the color of an electron?" "What does it feel like to be dead?"

With the rules for differentiating between meaningless and meaningful questions we are ready to venture into an area that is fraught with semantic traps, and we enter with the hope that we can elude at least the more obvious ones. We shall attempt a detailed analysis of a question we previously placed in the "meaningless" category: Does God exist?

DOES GOD EXIST?

In one form or another, this question has probably been asked by every member of the class *homo sapiens* who ever existed. Indeed, man has been called the religious animal or the praying animal. The anthropologist Edward Tylor was one of the first to show that if we expand—or contract if you wish—the minimum meaning of religion to "The belief in Spiritual Beings," every people so far investigated, no matter how primitive, has some kind of religion.

In its present form our question is ambiguous. It contains three unfixed variables—does, God, exist. Our problem is this: If we fix the variables, do we get an answerable or an unanswerable (mean-

ingless) question? "Does" implies a necessity for fixing the time of
God's existence. Has it been eternal, will it continue to be? Or doesn't
the concept of time apply at all? "God" requires a fixing of his
attributes, powers, qualities. Or doesn't the concept of qualities apply
to him? "Exist" brings up the problem of the kind of existence—
verbal or non-verbal. Or does no concept of existence, as we know it,
apply?

The different religions have fixed the variables in hundreds of
ways, with all kinds of subtle distinctions. We shall not attempt to
review them all, but rather try to indicate some of the chief lines of
argument and speculation which seem to be common to most religions. We shall not attempt to follow any fixed pattern or order in
our discussion, primarily because all are inextricably intermixed. For
example, discussing the "nature" of God immediately invites the
question of his "timeness" and the nature of his existence.

THE NATURE OF GOD:
CHANGING CONCEPTS WITH CHANGING TIMES

We shall rely on the writings of W. T. Stace for a large part of
this phase of our discussion. Stace points out that the Christian indexing of God's qualities, powers, and purposes has been subject to continuous revision. The early and medieval Christian beliefs were quite
clear and sharp. He writes:

The world-drama was enacted and controlled by purposes in the mind
of God. Everything which happened somehow fitted into the divine
plan. . . .
Not only must the existence and history of the universe as a whole
have a purpose. Every object which exists in the universe, every event
which occurs in it, must have its purpose. And every such detailed purpose
must fit into the grand scheme and the general plan of the whole.[1]

[1] W. T. Stace, *Religion and the Modern Mind*, New York, J. B. Lippincott Company, 1952, pp. 13, 14.

In our discussion of the abstracting process, we found that one of our great limitations is our inability to conceive of that which we have not experienced. Our thinking is hopelessly anthropomorphic. Therefore when we try to conceive of God's attributes we inevitably give him human qualities. Stace puts the problem in these words:

Sophisticated thinkers, whether theologians or philosophers, are aware of the tremendous difficulties wrapt up in this ordinary anthropomorphic conception of God. Hence they have attempted to substitute other more abstruse conceptions, and these may possibly possess very great philosophical merits. But it is impossible that, however sophisticated or erudite, they can ever wholly escape from anthropomorphism. If you think of God as in any sense a person, a mind, or a spirit—however much you realize the inadequacy of such words, however much you try to avoid their ordinary crude meanings as applied to human beings—you cannot help being anthropomorphic, you cannot help conceiving of God in terms of your conception of human minds, because you have no other materials out of which to form your conception of him.[2]

With the coming of modern science a sweeping revision in the fixing of the variables took place, which had drastic consequences for Western religion:

But Newtonian science tended to dry up the springs of a living religion by pushing God back in time to the beginning of the world. Whether this was thousands, or millions, of years ago makes little difference. God created the world, and he also, in doing so, created the natural laws—for instance, the laws of motion and gravitation—by which it was to be run. God was thus the "first cause" of the world, but after he had once created it, natural law, which he had also created, took over the job of running it. After the original creation God did nothing. Gravitation and the laws of motion did everything. God was like a watchmaker who, having once made and wound up his machine, left it to be moved by its own internal mechanism. God differed from the human mechanic only in that he had invented a perpetual motion machine which would go on working for ever by itself without any intervention on his part. Was not this precisely what Galileo's first law of motion implied?[3]

[2] *Ibid.*, p. 17.
[3] *Ibid.*, pp. 86–87.

Does God Matter?

Stace quotes a *Reader's Digest* article of January, 1949, which gave the results of a nationwide poll on religious matters. Ninety-five percent of the people polled stated they believed in the existence of God. When asked why they tried to lead a moral life only 25 percent gave religion as a reason. Only 54 percent said religious beliefs affected their politics and business. Thus, although most people believe in God they do not allow this to affect their behavior to any large extent. Stace argues that a "God who exists but does nothing in the world, who in no way affects the outcome of events, is simply a God who does not matter.[4]

People may not baldly assert these things, but it is a logical conclusion which they consciously and unconsciously avoid.

Modern science has substituted natural causes for the supernatural ones formerly accepted. In effect, God as an explanation for anything is a ploggly theory. It tells us nothing we do not already know and in no way increases our predictive abilities.

Not only has supernatural explanation been ruled out in the realm of science, but it has, in effect, been eliminated from the realm of the moral. The world is no longer a moral order if divine purpose and control are eliminated from the universe. If God cannot directly intervene in human affairs, then all our values must be derived from, and be dependent upon, human purposes.

Stace summarizes the two world-pictures as follows:

The Religious View of the World	*The Scientific View of the World, or Naturalism*
The world is ultimately governed by spiritual forces.	The world is wholly governed by blind physical forces, such as gravitation, the laws of motion, the laws of chemical combination, etc.

[4] *Ibid.*, p. 89.

The world has a purpose.	The world has no purpose. It is entirely senseless and meaningless.
The world is a moral order.	The world is not a moral order. The universe is "indifferent to" values of any kind.[5]

He argues that these propositions are not often stated in philosophy or literature or art, but are dressed up so that they are frequently unrecognizable. But strip away the excess verbiage and that is what remains.

ARGUMENTS FOR AND AGAINST THE EXISTENCE OF GOD

Which world picture shall we choose? Let us take a look at some of the arguments offered to uphold the religious picture and their counterarguments.

1. *The argument from design.*   This argument has an infinity of forms. In essence it runs something like this: If we look at any living organism, even the simplest, the outstanding feature is its organization. The organism is extremely intricate and could not have happened by chance. Think of how beautifully adapted the eye is for seeing and the ear for hearing. Think of the billions of cells all working in harmony and balance. And within each cell we find billions of complex protein molecules whose parts are strictly ordered. Such a molecule may consist of a chain of a hundred thousand submolecules. Change the order of one and you change the whole molecule, which would change the cell, which would change the organ, etc. We see such highly ordered chains in the hereditary "organs," the genes. Vary the order and the whole structure of the developing organism changes. Whether you turn out to be a man or a mouse depends largely on the ordering of substructures in the genetic molecules.

[5] *Ibid.,* p. 143.

Or, turn to the solar system, with its planets moving in stately, precisely predictable order around the sun, and our whole galaxy wandering through the universe according to a complex but ordered plan. Clearly all this could not have happened by chance. It had to be designed, it had to be created. Therefore God must exist.

The counterargument runs somewhat as follows: The argument from design confuses effects with ends or purposes. That is, there is a confusion of inferential and factual knowledge. We can see the complex structures; this is factual. We can only infer that this is the result of deliberate design, and we have no way of verifying this inference. If we argue that this is a highly probable inference because the odds against these highly organized structures being the result of blind chance are impossibly large, we discover a very curious fact, namely, "Whatever happens in the world is almost infinitely improbable." [6]

Suppose you take a bus trip. You meet a stranger from another town. Think of the odds against this happening. If his parents had not moved to that particular town, if his health had been different, if the one particular sperm cell out of the hundred million present at the moment of his conception had been nosed out by one of the others, if the man who was his father had married another woman, if Columbus had not discovered America, if you had not had the bus fare, etc., etc., etc., then this meeting would not have occurred. And if any of these other circumstances had occurred, then what would have happened is equally as much a proof or disproof of cosmic design. That is, *whatever happens,* our inference that it is a result of conscious divine purpose is wholly unverifiable and we can assign no degree of probability to it.

Consider the chances of drawing four aces from a fifty-two card deck. The odds against it are very large, but if we do draw the four aces, does it prove that this was preordained by a cosmic mind, that

[6] *Ibid.,* p. 79.

it couldn't have happened by blind chance? Actually, there is the same chance of drawing any designated four cards, e.g., 2, 6, 9, K. If such a hand is drawn in poker we do not consider it of value simply because by definition it has none. So we are tempted to consider it less "designed," more likely to occur, than the four aces. If we changed the rules and gave that hand a high value and none to the four aces, we would assign it a high degree of improbability of occurrence. In actuality any group of four cards is equally as probable as another, and the same applies to any structure in the universe.

Stace maintains that the hidden assumption in the argument from design is that what is considered good by us is held to be evidence of cosmic purpose:

. . . The argument never selects as proving design those complicated trains of causes which produce blindness in some persons or animals; or the causes which produce, not life, but death. If a city is wrecked by a tidal wave and thousands of its inhabitants are drowned, or any other train of events produces a human disaster, such cases are never chosen as instances which prove design.[7]

If we accept the argument from design, we quickly bog down in the problem of the existence of evil. If God has designed these good things, then he has also designed the evils—flood, pestilence, violence, murder, the pitiful wasting away of an infant dying of cancer. The counteranswer to this is the old argument that evil is man's doing, a consequence of his having been given a free will and with it the possibility of choosing evil. But this is met by the argument that if God is omnipotent and omniscient, why did he design such a frail creature who could choose evil? Why not make one so perfect that it would have sense enough to choose the good? This argument goes back and forth and, like all intensional arguments, ends with an agreement not to change our minds, stated in some fashion as,

[7] *Ibid.*, p. 81.

"God moves in mysterious ways his wonders to perform—but he *does* perform them."

The point is, as Stace indicates, that if we assume the world is ruled by the blind laws of nature, it would be as we see it—an indiscriminate mixture of good and bad. Thus if we have to choose between God and blind chance *as hypotheses* for explaining the nature of things, the latter is better. Suppose I am seriously injured in an accident and hover between life and death for many days. Suppose further that my wife prays for my recovery and finally I pull through, but not without much pain and expense. As we leave the hospital, should we thank God for his help, for his answering her prayer? It could be argued that we should. But it can be equally well argued that we should blame him for causing the accident and the subsequent pain and expense. We cannot logically credit him for the good and not blame him for the bad.

2. *The argument from miracles.* In ancient days miracles occurred quite frequently; today they are quite scarce. It seems rather obvious that the reason for this is the development of science. We use the miraculous as a cause and explanation when we are ignorant and have little or no reliable science to give natural explanations.

But if real miracles do occur, this would in no way prove the existence of God, for the simple reason that we could not recognize a miracle if we saw one. Suppose the Empire State Building should suddenly float away in the sky. Before we could claim this a miracle, i.e., a breach of the natural laws by direct intervention of God, we would have to know all the laws of nature in order to know that this was a breach of one or more of them. That is, we would have to be omniscient, we would have to be God himself. When we view the piles of crutches discarded by the "cured" cripples at Lourdes, all we can reasonably state is that their *faith* in God played a very large part in their recovery. Faith is a natural form of human behavior and we know it has profound psychophysiological effects;

but this in no way proves that God intervened. A faith in the potency of charms and voodoo rites seems to have equally remarkable effects.

3. *Argument from creation.* This argument for the existence of God hinges on the supposed necessity for a Creator. The universe exists. How did it get here? It must have been created. Therefore there must be a Creator, a first cause whom we call God. But if we argue that the universe had to be caused, that it couldn't "just be," then we are forced into an infinite regress. If the universe needed a Creator, then there must be a Creator of the Creator, and a Creator of the Creator of the Creator, etc.

It does no good to say, "God is the Prime Mover. He was not caused." This is simply an arbitrary stopping of the argument, a way of saying, "I believe in the necessity of the universe having a Creator, but not God, because this is the only way I can avoid the infinite regress." It settles no arguments and solves no problems.

4. *Argument from authority.* Any recourse to ecclesiastical authority does nothing to prove the existence of God. Quoting the Bible or the saints or the prophets simply pushes the argument back a little farther but solves nothing. For then we are faced with the problem of determining whether or not they give us factual data. Is the Bible correct? Do the saints speak the truth? Undoubtedly, they were very good people who would not deliberately lie. But how do we know they are not deceiving themselves, or simply speaking out of ignorance of science?

So we see that all the arguments for and against the existence of God are purely intensional. We have no way of choosing among them. Each side has equally valid arguments with no non-verbal procedures for testing the truth of the major premises from which they evolve. We must conclude, then, that the assertions "God exists" and "God does not exist" have no factual basis whatsoever. Not a single solitary fact has been discovered by science to prove or disprove the existence of God.

When Galileo proposed that the earth rotates around the sun it was considered heresy because the Bible, being the Word of God, stated that the reverse was true. Likewise, Darwinian theories of evolution were once taken to be antireligious because they did not agree with the Bible. Yet God could as well have designed an evolutionary world as the spontaneous Biblical one, just as easily have had the sun go around the earth. In other words, no physical facts whatsoever have anything to do with the proof of God's existence.

Now, surprising as it may seem in view of the prolonged warfare between science and religion, this fact has long been asserted by theologians themselves. There is, they assert, a divine order and a natural order. Belief in the first is a product of faith; belief in the latter a product of proof. To quote Stace again: "If God does not lie at the end of any telescope, neither does He lie at the end of any syllogism. I can never, starting from the natural order, prove the divine order. The proof of the divine order must lie, somehow, within itself. It must be its own witness. For it, like the natural order, is complete in itself, self-contained." [8]

Conflict has arisen only because theologians have not been content with faith in God's existence but have attempted to prove it by logic and factual data. But the moment one begins to prove, he moves into the realm of science and must obey the scientists' rules of proof; any other type of proof is worthless if we are interested in gaining reliable, verifiable, communicable, public, highly predictive knowledge. The Biblical assertion that God created the earth and everything on it in six days is a statement about the natural world and therefore is subject to scientific testing. All evidence to date seems to be against it. So some theologians, in desperation, have retreated, as was inevitable, and now proclaim that what the Bible *really* meant is not six of our ordinary days, but six epochs or mil-

[8] W. T. Stace, *Time and Eternity,* Princeton, Princeton University Press, 1952, p. 138.

lenia. This more or less roughly corresponds to six geological ages we can discern when we "read the rocks." But again, all of this is immaterial to proof of the existence of God. Since he is presumed to be omnipotent, he could just as easily have created everything in six seconds as well as in six days or two billion years.

The reasoning behind this theological hocus-pocus seems to be: The Bible states that God exists. It also says some things about this world and its history, e.g., the Jews crossed the Red Sea on foot, manna fell from Heaven, Moses led the Israelites out of Egypt, Jesus was crucified, oily deposits can be found in certain parts of the Sinai Desert. Now we cannot point our finger and say, "There stands God." But we can point to the oily streaks in the rocks today, and there seems to be reasonable proof that there was a Moses who led the Israelites through the desert. Therefore, if the Bible is right about Moses and the oil, it must be right about God's existence. Ergo, God exists.

The following passage from *Time and Eternity* nicely summarizes the fallacy of attempting to prove the existence of God:

These defeats come upon religious men because they take their doctrines to be literal statements of fact, and therefore amenable to proof by argument. It must now be added that these attempts at proof not only fail of their purpose and so do no good to religion, but that they positively degrade it. For their effect is to drag down the divine and the eternal from their own sphere into the sphere of the natural and temporal. As has already been pointed out many times, if we argue back along the chain of causes to a first cause, and call this first cause God, we thereby make Him merely one among other things in the world, that is, in the natural order. All the other alleged proofs have the same effect. They thus make God finite. For the natural order is the order of finite things. If God is related to other things as their cause, then He is finite, since the otherness of these other things limits His being. This is the result of taking God's causality in a literal sense—in the sense, that is, in which we say that heat is the cause of the boiling of water. This also places God in time, because the causal relation is a time relation. But if the causality of God is taken symbolically, then it plainly cannot be proved by going backwards along the causal chain, since this procedure implies the literal understanding of the causal concept.[9]

Stace concludes that all religious language must be taken as symbolic and not literal. Its purpose is not denotative but evocative. It points to a "way." It seeks to provoke the so-called mystic experience, an experience whose meaning is already in us, just as poetry and music evoke what is within rather than describe what is without. This religious or mystical experience tells us nothing about the world of things; it is of another order. This other order will be the subject of the remainder of this chapter.

THE MYSTIC EXPERIENCE

SOME DIFFERENCES BETWEEN ANALYTIC AND SYNTHETIC PROCESSES

Throughout this book we have stressed the importance of differentiating between the different levels of abstraction and the subjective differences of each level. Although the different levels interact, the resultant in each case is uniquely different. The verbal level influences what we see and feel, but the seeing and the feeling are not words. Feelings feel different from words and at each level within the two great levels of verbal and non-verbal we have qualitative differences. Lower-order feelings differ from higher-order ones, descriptions from inferences, names of objects from class terms. In general, the higher the order of abstraction the more static, the more "lifeless," the less "real," it *feels,* "real" in this context meaning the reality we ascribe to the non-verbal level of feelings and sensations.

From a slightly different aspect we might say that we have been discussing two realms of knowledge, verbal and non-verbal. Now

[9] *Ibid.,* pp. 150–151.

we shall face the question, "Is there a third kind of knowledge—
or even more?" In our discussion of symbol-using processes at the
verbal level, we noted at least one important qualitative difference
between analysis and synthesis, between logic and intuition. We have
precise rules for analysis and logic, rules which can be completely
communicated verbally. But when it comes to the intuitive and creative processes, to insight, to the seeing of the whole, to the "Eureka!"
experience, there seem to be no rules at all. We can indicate very
precisely how to solve a mathematical or logical problem, we can tear
apart and analyze a poem or a play according to definable principles,
but when it comes to the reverse—building, synthesizing, creating—
rules fail us. I may memorize the dictionary and learn all the rules
of grammar and still not be able to create a simple story of any
artistic merit. Unconscious processes seem to be involved and we have
not been, and perhaps never will be, able to bring them to a conscious level where they can be adequately symbolized. In the creative
process there seems to be at some point a leap in the dark, a non-
additive factor which cannot be put into words. Analysis feels different from synthesis.

Again, from the standpoint of meaning, meanings at the verbal
level seem much more precise, communicable, and analyzable than
at the non-verbal. Analysis of a poem or painting or piece of music
gives one type of meaning, usually the least important, least mysterious, most exact, and most trivial. It is the unanalyzable meanings
gained by intuitive, insightful, unconscious, and synthetic processes
which seem most important. It is the meaning that is suggested,
hinted at, that cannot be pinpointed or described, which forms the
"message" of any artistic creation.

Yet tenuous, unanalyzable, and mysterious though they be,
somehow we feel that these "messages" are very important, that
they tell us something vital, something we cannot put into words,
yet capable of shaping the course of our lives. Sometimes the feelings

they engender become so overwhelming, so ecstatic, that a conviction arises, an utter certainty that they are telling us about another level of reality, another realm of knowledge. They seem to be signposts to another world, or an open door and an invitation to—what? Are these vistas of a supernatural world or glimpses into the natural, yet mysterious and awesome world of the unconscious levels of our nervous system? When the saint is in ecstasy and the Yogi in trance, what are the meanings of their experiences? Are they the products of the impingement of a supernatural world on their nervous systems, just as colors and sounds and tastes are the products of the influence of the natural world on our receptors? Or may it be that, just as the cortex (and with it the symbolizing processes) is the latest evolutionary development of the nervous system, so perhaps another level of organic development is appearing, a new level of mind, new levels of perception and awareness utterly unimaginable and incomprehensible, which, being in a rudimentary stage, perhaps more advanced in some few than in most others, give us only blurry and tantalizing hints of "things" and "thoughts" to come. Or is it all delusion, self-deception, hallucination?

Of course we can give no definite answers to these questions, which at this stage are, technically, meaningless. But let us indulge in some speculation and see what kind of factual data, if any, are available which may serve as clues, if not answers, to directions which inquiry should, or might, take in attempting to arrive at some reliable knowledge.

The greatest obstacle to getting reliable knowledge in this area is that reports of these experiences are completely unverifiable in the scientific sense. They cannot be communicated, measured, or repeated under controlled conditions. Indeed, any attempt to measure or reason *about* these experiences immediately destroys them and is inimical to their occurrence. This in no way proves that they do not occur, for we are in a similar predicament in regard to "normal" feelings and sensations. However, mystic experiences do not occur with the everyday regularity of the latter and have a queerness about them which sets them apart.

SOME CHARACTERISTICS OF THE MYSTIC EXPERIENCE

William James was one of the pioneers in the attempt to make an objective evaluation of this problem and his *Varieties of Religious Experience* is a classic in the field. I refer the reader to it and to a somewhat similar but more iconoclastic book by James H. Leuba, *The Psychology of Religious Mysticism,* for detailed specimens of reports of people who have had these experiences. James found the following characteristics common to all varieties of them:

1. Ineffability—they are different from all other feelings and sensations and unless one has experienced them it is impossible to know what they are like.
2. Noetic quality—"They are states of insight into depths of truth unplumbed by the discursive intellect. They are illuminations, revelations, full of significance and importance, all inarticulate though they remain; and as a rule they carry with them a curious sense of authority for aftertime." [10]

Two other less sharply marked qualities are their transiency and their passivity.

THE MYSTIC EXPERIENCE AND INSANITY

When one reads descriptions of mystic states by saints and mystics, their similarity to those of certain types of seriously ill mental patients is remarkable. For example, here are some excerpts from a book written by a manic-depressive psychotic during interludes of comparative lucidity while confined in a mental hospital:

The mystic insight seems generally to begin with a sense of a mystery unveiled, of a hidden wisdom now suddenly become certain beyond the

[10] William James, *Varieties of Religious Experience,* New York, The Modern Library, 1902, p. 371.

possibility of a doubt. Its second characteristic is a belief in the unity of all things, in that reconciliation of opposites mentioned by James in connection with the anaesthetic revelation. Other features closely related to these two are a tendency to deny the reality of Time and also to believe that all evil is mere appearance. All these features were strongly marked in the manic phases of my illness, while in the opposite or depressive phases they were to some extent reversed. The most marked was the sense of the unity of all things, including myself as part of the whole, coupled with an inner certainty that good and evil, if not identical, would at any rate ultimately be reconciled.[11]

When the nervous system is thoroughly deranged, the two contrasting states of mind can be almost infinitely intensified. It sometimes seems to me as though my condition had been specially devised by Providence to illustrate the Christian concepts of Heaven and Hell. Certainly it has shown me that within my own soul there are possibilities of an inner peace and happiness beyond description, as well as of inconceivable depths of terror and despair. Normal life and consciousness of "reality" appear to me rather like motion along a narrow strip of tableland at the top of a Great Divide separating two distinct universes from each other. On the one hand the slope is green and fertile leading to a lovely landscape where love, joy and the infinite beauties of nature and of dreams await the traveller; on the other a barren, rocky declivity, where lurk endless horrors of distorted imagination, descends to the bottomless pit.[12]

During the manic phase he experiences "a general sense of intense well-being," intensified sensory impressions, and an "abnormal association of ideas." In addition a "feeling of intimate personal relationship with God is perhaps its paramount feature." Continuing, "in that peace I felt utterly and completely forgiven, relieved from all burden of sin. The whole of infinity seemed to open up before me and during the weeks and months which followed I passed through experiences which are virtually indescribable." [13]

[11] John Custance, *Wisdom, Madness and Folly: The Philosophy of A Lunatic,* New York, Pellegrini and Cudahy, 1952, p. 22.
[12] *Ibid.,* p. 29.
[13] *Ibid.,* p. 46.

Recapitulating the main characteristic features of the manic state, he includes the following: "(1) Intense sense of well-being, (2) heightened sense of reality, (3) breach in the barriers of individuality, (4) inhibition of sense of repulsion, (5) release of sexual and moral tensions, (6) delusions of grandeur and power, (7) sense of ineffable revelation." [14]

Leuba, after minutely examining the lives and statements of saints and mystics, concludes that they show clear indication of hysteria, sexual repression, and displacement to the object of worship. Moreover, it is fairly well established that many of the well-known "outsiders," to use Colin Wilson's term, such as Kierkegaard, Dostoyevsky, Tolstoy, Blake, Gurdjieff were subject at times to epileptic seizures.

What conclusions can be drawn? That these experiences occur must be accepted as fact. According to James, they "break down the authority of the non-mystical or rationalistic consciousness, based upon the understanding and the senses alone. They show it to be only one kind of consciousness." But the crucial question remains, namely, does this different kind of consciousness give us any reliable knowledge about ourselves or the universe, or is it simply a distorted view given by a disturbed nervous system? Although James rejects the assertion of the uncritical mystic that Christ or the Virgin or some saint "really" manifested themselves to him, he holds that the mystic vision tells "of the supremacy of the ideal, of vastness, of union, of safety, and of rest. They offer us *hypotheses,* hypotheses which we may voluntarily ignore, but which as thinkers we cannot possibly upset. The supernaturalism and optimism to which they would persuade us may, interpreted in one way or another, be after all the truest of insights into the meaning of this life." [15]

However, I feel that James was unduly optimistic in his assertion that they offer us hypotheses which may be true insights into the

[14] *Ibid.,* p. 55.
[15] James, *op. cit.,* pp. 419–420.

meaning of life. Even though the mystic experience produces absolute certainty that God or Christ or the Great Spirit exists or was present or appeared, this still is not proof. They are much more reasonably explainable as products of the natural hysterical mechanisms which operate when the nervous system becomes disturbed. The powerful wish to believe becomes father to the vision. The reversal of the natural order of abstraction produces hallucinations. However, these naturalistic explanations still do not prove that the mystics are wrong in their assertion that they were in contact with a supernatural world, because the counterargument can be raised that we can acquire this revelatory knowledge only when the ordinary "normal" functioning of the nervous system is disturbed in some way, be it a powerful wish to believe, Yogi exercises, drugs, fasting, or the like. All these are natural "causes" for putting us in a state in which the religious revelation can occur and no analysis of these causes can prove that what is actually experienced in the ecstatic state is not of supernatural origin. Thus Stace writes:

Now this means that it is impossible for religion to dictate to science, or in general to the conceptual intellect which is concerned with the natural order, what can or what cannot be causes of the divine moment. No doubt it is usually the religious man who discovers these causes. It is he who finds in his experience that prayer, or fasting, or the moral life, bring him nearer to God. But in seeking and discovering causes and effects he is acting as a natural man; he is within the natural order, and is therefore himself a sort of scientist. And it is at least conceivable that a scientist of the ordinary sort might make discoveries which would have a bearing on the causation of religious states, and that these discoveries might come as a shock to the religious man, and have some tendency to undermine his faith—unless he is firm in his understanding that no causes of the religious moment, however materialistic they may seem, can in the slightest degree detract from the divine character of the religious revelation itself. This is but an instance of the general truth that no conceivable scientific discovery could ever destroy religion, if it is true, as is here contended, that science and religion concern two wholly different orders of being, the temporal and the eternal.[16]

There seems to me to be just one weakness in that argument and that is the assumption that what is revealed in the mystical experience is of divine origin, which assumes precisely what is at issue. Stace argues that it is not open to proof because it is of another order or level of knowing and proof applies only to the sensory and verbal levels. But if it cannot be proved, neither should it be asserted. The conviction that it is divine cannot be used as evidence for it in any sense of the word. As Herbert Muller points out, when a man is out of his mind, it does not prove that he is out of this world.

GENERAL SEMANTICS AND ZEN BUDDHISM

However, I feel that this does not end the matter. It still is possible that there may be other forms of consciousness, or perhaps unconsciousness, or consciousness of the Unconscious — a state the Zen Buddhist claims to reach—which may give us other views of ourselves and the universe. Suppose we could find an individual who did not believe in the existence of a divine being of any kind, or of any type of supernatural realm. Could he have a mystical experience, and if he did what would he "see"? Furthermore, what is the use of this kind of knowledge and why should we, as general semanticists, bother ourselves about it?

For an answer to this we shall turn to Zen Buddhism, which has no organized dogma, no transcendental doctrines, no beliefs in a supernatural realm or divine being, yet has worked out a methodology for achieving the mystical experience, variously labeled as Nirvana, Satori, Enlightenment. It is my belief that the mystical experience has great psychotherapeutic value once it is divorced from supernaturalism, and should be recognized as a legitimate view of the world as distorted and undistorted, as restricted and unrestricted,

[16] *Time and Eternity, op. cit.,* pp. 88–89.

as that given by the senses and interpreted by the "intellect." It is one more kind of knowledge, different from, but not in contradiction with, the more familiar avenues of awareness. I would disagree, however, with the Zen Buddhist that this is a better or more real picture of the world. It is simply another, and all views interact and enhance the richness of our lives. But more of this later. What do the Zen Buddhists believe?

At first glance the writings of the Zen Buddhists seem to be the work of madmen. They are weird in a weird sort of way. They seem to be totally irrational and the temptation is great to toss it all off as meaningless nonsense. And Zen Buddhism is irrational nonsense —deliberately so—but it is not meaningless nor is it the work of madmen.

EAST AND WEST AND THE LEVELS OF ABSTRACTION

We can make some sense of it only if we remember that our customary patterns of abstraction are not the only possible and valid ones. We in the West tend to stress, and concentrate upon, the verbal levels of abstraction. We are word-minded, logic-minded, theory-minded. The average man's usage of words may be fuzzy, his logic muggy, and his theories ploggly, nevertheless he bases his conception of what is "real," "right," "sensible," on verbal maps which may or may not fit the territory. Other peoples, notably some in the Orient, seem to concentrate more on the concrete, on the lower levels of abstraction, and neglect the higher levels. The Chinese, for example, (until Westernization sets in) are considered a very practical-minded people. They are not given much to theorizing and have practically no theoretical science. Empirically, they discovered gunpowder and the use of herbs and drugs helpful in curing disease, but no reliable theories as to why they act as they do. "The Chinese," writes D. T. Suzuki, "have no aptitude like the Indians for hiding themselves in the clouds of mystery and supernaturalism. . . . The Confucian verdict that superior man never talks about miracles, wonders, and

supernaturalism, is the true expression of Chinese psychology." [17]
Elsewhere he states: "The Chinese are in many ways great, their
architecture is great indeed, their literary achievements deserve the
world's thanks, but logic is not one of their strong points; nor are
their philosophy and imagination." [18]

ZEN AS A NON-LOGICAL SYSTEM

Zen Buddhism, which had its origins in China, seems to have developed methods for pushing concentration on the lower levels of
abstraction to its very limit. Suzuki stresses that their system is irrational. I should prefer the term non-rational. To us an irrational
man is one who is using his symbolizing processes in an incoherent,
disorganized manner. He uses words and logic but it is a "crazy"
logic. The Zen Buddhists, however, seem to have discovered a way
to stop the symbolizing processes as we know them without producing
unconsciousness. So I think we are more correct in stating that it is
non-logical and non-rational.

We are so accustomed to "making sense" out of a philosophy or
methodology or religion—meaning that we look for the logic in it
—that if we find none we dismiss it as nonsense. But the Zen
Buddhists assert that if we stop attempting to use our symbol-using
processes we can discover a new, and to them more reliable and truer,
understanding of ourselves, the world around us, and our relationship to it. They continually stress that we blind ourselves to reality
by our words. We confuse what we say about things with the things
themselves. The words get in our eyes, the map blinds us to the
"true" nature of the territory.

As nature abhors a vacuum, Zen abhors anything coming between the
fact and ourselves. According to Zen there is no struggle in the fact itself

[17] From *The Collected Works of D. T. Suzuki,* London, The Hutchinson Group,
as selected by William Barrett in *Zen Buddhism: Selected Writings of D. T.
Suzuki,* New York, Doubleday Anchor Book, 1956, p. 48.
[18] *Ibid.,* p. 42.

such as between the finite and the infinite, between the flesh and the spirit. There are idle distinctions fictitiously designed by the intellect for its own interest. Those who take them too seriously or those who try to read them into the very fact of life are those who take the finger for the moon. When we are hungry we eat; when we are sleepy we lay ourselves down; and where does the infinite or the finite come in here? Are not we complete in ourselves and each in himself? Life as it is lived suffices. It is only when the disquieting intellect steps in and tries to murder it that we stop to live and imagine ourselves to be short of or in something. Let the intellect alone, it has its usefulness in its proper sphere, but let it not interfere with the flowing of the life-stream. If you are at all tempted to look into it, do so while letting it flow. The fact of flowing must under no circumstances be arrested or meddled with; for the moment your hands are dipped into it, its transparency is disturbed, it ceases to reflect your image which you have had from the very beginning and will continue to have to the end of time.[19]

Remember the distinction we made between high- and low-order abstractions? The higher are static and lifeless, the lower dynamic and shifting. "The intellect has its usefulness in its proper sphere, but let it not interfere with the flowing of the life-stream." Do not confuse the two levels of abstraction, do not act as if one were the other, do not reverse the natural order of abstraction and allow the higher-order maps (theories about life) to distort the lower (territory —life as process).

For this reason Zen never explains but indicates, it does not appeal to circumlocution, nor does it generalize. It always deals with facts, concrete and tangible. Logically considered, Zen may be full of contradictions and repetitions. But as it stands above all things, it goes serenely on its own way. As a Zen master aptly puts it, "carrying his home-made cane on the shoulder, he goes right on among the mountains one rising above another". It does not challenge logic, it simply walks its path of facts, leaving all the rest to their own fates. It is only when logic neglecting its proper functions tries to step into the track of Zen that it loudly proclaims its principles and forcibly drives out the intruder. Zen is not an enemy of

[19] *Ibid.,* p. 9.

anything. There is no reason why it should antagonize the intellect which may sometimes be utilized for the cause of Zen itself.[20]

ENLIGHTENMENT

The aim of Zen is the achievement of Satori, or Enlightenment. Suzuki writes:

The essence of Zen Buddhism consists in acquiring a new viewpoint on life and things generally. . . . This acquirement, however, is really and naturally the greatest mental cataclysm one can go through with in life. It is no easy task, it is a kind of fiery baptism and one has to go through the storm, the earthquake . . .

Satori may be defined as an intuitive looking into the nature of things in contradistinction to the analytical or logical understanding of it. Practically, it means the unfolding of a new world hitherto unperceived in the confusion of a dualistically-trained mind. . . . Logically stated, all its opposites and contradictions are united and harmonized into a consistent organic whole. This is a mystery and a miracle, but according to the Zen masters such is being performed every day. Satori can thus be had only through our once personally experiencing it.[21]

We have stated that man is the symbolizing creature. We perceive the world through our senses and these lower-order abstractions are immediately modified by words and ideas and theories. Change the symbols and the perceptions change—the world as it appears to the individual shifts with it. Now, consider what would happen if we had a way of stopping the symbolizing process so that only the non-verbal remained. There should be a remarkable change in what is perceived; a new world, a strange, queer world should appear, so different from the ordinary world that it would be absolutely inde-scribable, yet whose reality could not be doubted by the perceiver. This, or something like this, is apparently what happens when Satori is achieved.

We should expect that if this is the nature of the abstracting proc-

[20] *Ibid.*, p. 10.
[21] *Ibid.*, pp. 83–84.

ess involved in achieving Satori, logical principles would be wholly inapplicable, because logic and reason apply only to the verbal level which is absent during Satori. It is quite difficult for us to refrain from applying logic in trying to understand Zen, yet this is what we must do if we are to comprehend it.

Suzuki lists the following as characteristics of Satori:

1. Irrationality—By this I mean that Satori is not a conclusion to be reached by reasoning and defies all intellectual determination. Those who have experienced it are always at a loss to explain it coherently or logically. When it is explained at all, either in words or gestures, its content more or less undergoes a mutilation.

2. Intuitive insight—Without this noetic quality Satori will lose all its pungency, for it is really the reason of Satori itself. It is noteworthy that the knowledge contained in Satori is concerned with something universal and at the same time with the individual aspect of existence. When a finger is lifted, the lifting means, from the viewpoint of Satori, far more than the act of lifting. Some may call it symbolic, but Satori does not point to anything beyond itself, being final as it is. Satori is the knowledge of an individual object and also that of Reality which is, if I may say so, at the back of it.

3. Authoritativeness—By this I mean that the knowledge realized by Satori is final, that no amount of logical argument can refute it. Being direct and personal it is sufficient unto itself. All that logic can do here is to explain it, to interpret it in connection with other kinds of knowledge with which our minds are filled.

4. Affirmation—Though the Satori experience is sometimes expressed in negative terms, it is essentially an affirmative attitude toward all things that exist; it accepts them as they come along regardless of their moral values. . . . Zen is Suchness—a grand affirmation.

5. Sense of the Beyond—Terminology may differ in different religions, and in Satori there is always what we may call a sense of the Beyond; the experience indeed is my own but I feel it to be rooted elsewhere. The individual shell in which my personality is so solidly encased explodes at the moment of Satori. Not, necessarily, that I get unified with a being greater than myself or absorbed in it, but that my individuality, which I found rigidly held together and definitely kept separate from other indi-

vidual existences, becomes loosened somehow from its tightening grip and melts away into something indescribable, something which is of quite a different order from what I am accustomed to. The feeling that follows is that of complete release or a complete rest—the feeling that one has arrived finally at the destination. . . .

As far as the psychology of Satori is considered, a sense of the Beyond is all we can say about it; *to call this the Beyond, the Absolute, or God, or a Person is to go further than the experience itself and to plunge into a theology or metaphysics. Even the "Beyond" is saying a little too much*. . . .

6. Impersonal Tone—Perhaps the most remarkable aspect of the Zen experience is that it has no personal note in it as is observable in Christian mystic experiences. There is no reference whatever in Buddhist Satori to such personal and frequently sexual feelings and relationships as are to be gleaned from these terms: flame of love, a wonderful love shed in the heart, embrace, the beloved, bride, bridegroom, spiritual matrimony, Father, God, The Son of God, God's child, etc. We may say that all these terms are interpretations based on a definite system of thought and really have nothing to do with the experience itself.

7. Feeling of Exaltation—The general feeling, though we are not always conscious of it, which characterizes all our functions of consciousness, is that of restriction and dependence, because consciousness itself is the outcome of two forces conditioning or restricting each other. Satori, on the contrary, essentially consists in doing away with the opposition of two terms in whatsoever sense—and this opposition is the principle of consciousness as before mentioned, while Satori is to realize the Unconscious which goes beyond the opposition.

To be released of this, therefore, must make one feel above all things intensely exalted.

8. Momentariness—Satori comes upon one abruptly and is a momentary experience. In fact, if it is not abrupt and momentary, it is not Satori.[22]

THE MYSTIC EXPERIENCE WITHOUT MYSTICISM

It is worth stressing the essential difference between mystical experience of Westerners and Zen Buddhists. The Buddhists refuse to interpret the experience. Interpretation means symbolizing. It means appeal to logic, to theorizing, and to proof, and inevitably involves

[22] *Ibid.*, pp. 103 ff. (Italics mine.)

a confusion and identification of the two widely removed levels of abstraction, and with it the insane behavior of the people who indulge in it. The line between the saint and the madman becomes very thin. The Buddhist, by refraining from interpretation, avoids this evil. He knows that this confuses two different levels of abstraction. The Christian saint, on the one hand, claims the experience is ineffable and that logic and analysis are not to be applied to it—which is true—yet on the other hand, he himself cannot refrain from doing so. He offers his experience as *proof* of the existence of God. But the minute we set out to prove we move to the verbal level and must use the scientific method for our proof; and of course his "proof" then is seen for what it is—utterly worthless.

I believe that one of the great values in knowing about Zen Buddhism is that it indicates that the Westerner's urge to interpret mystic experience and give it logical explanation is just an urge, and not inherent in the nature of the experience itself. It indicates that interpreting it as a meeting with the Divine, as Stace does, is an arbitrary assumption on our part and in no way justifies the assumption of its supernatural origin.

Here is Suzuki's statement concerning this:

But human life is not like that of other living beings. We do not want to live just an animal life, we like to know the worth of life and to appreciate it consciously. This is, however, the very moment wherein we negate ourselves by deviating from life itself. It is for this reason that we philosophize and become "thinkers." But it is not by thinking that we come back to life, nor is it by "philosophic faith" or by "divine revelation" that we are brought to the presence and the silence of "transcendence." Zen, however, does not like the odour of abstraction which oozes out from even such terms as "Transcendence." For, in fact, as soon as appeal is made to words, we leave life itself and involve ourselves in every kind of "logical" controversy. We construct our own traps and then struggle to escape from them, and as long as we are what we are, we cannot get away from this dilemma. . . .

In the meantime, everyone of us feels an inward urge to effect such an escape in one way or another. The philosophic way is to appeal to Reason, in whatever sense the term may be interpreted, whereas the "religiously" inclined resort to "faith" or "revelation." The Zen way of escape—or, better, of solution—is direct apprehension or grasping "it" or "this."

For example, we create . . . the categories in Western thinking of God and the created, or of God and Nature, or of Man and Nature. These are all of human creation, and we cling to them as if they were absolutely determined, binding us as something inextricably, fatalistically unescapable. We are our own prisoners. We defeat ourselves, believing in defeatism, which is itself our own creation. . . .

Zen, therefore, does not try to disengage us from the world, to make us mere spectators of the hurly burly which we see around us. Then Zen is not mysticism . . . in the sense of escapism. Zen is right in the midst of the ocean of becoming. . . . It does not antagonize Nature; it does not treat Nature as if it were an enemy to be conquered, nor does it stand away from Nature. It is indeed Nature itself.[23]

What is the process by which Satori is achieved? What methods of instruction are used? There is no point to our attempting to explain them in any detail here because they are the epitome of irrationality. They are not to be understood but to be done, to be experienced. The language is used, not to communicate meaning but to point the way to an experience—Enlightenment. Any attempt to analyze the language immediately destroys any chance of achieving Satori. If the reader is interested, I suggest that he read Suzuki's books. He will be in for a frustrating and exasperating experience, for we read philosophical works for intellectual enlightenment, whereas Zen writings aim at suppression of intellectual activity to pave the way for a completely different non-verbal experience.

The chief method of instruction in Zen is through the koan. This is generally some statement made by a Zen master or a reply made by him to some question. These questions and answers are given to Zen initiates to ponder and meditate upon. For instance:

[23] *Ibid.,* pp. 253 ff.

1. "Who is the Buddha?" a monk was asked. "Three bundles of flax," was his reply.

2. What are your original features which you have even before you were born?

3. A sound is made by two hands clapping. What sound is made by the clapping of one hand?

4. A monk asked a master, "Who is the Buddha?" He replied, "The dried up dirt cleaner."

5. When the Many are reduced to the One, to what is the One to be reduced?

6. Here is a man hanging from a high branch by his teeth with neither hands nor feet touching the trunk. Someone asks, "What is Zen?" He must reply, but if he does he falls to his death. What reply would you make if you were he?

The aim of the koan is to stop the symbolizing processes. They can have no logical solution. Suzuki states:

> Technically speaking, the koan given to the uninitiated is intended "to destroy the root of life," "to make the calculating mind die," "to root out the entire mind that has been at work since eternity," etc. This may sound murderous, but the ultimate intent is to go beyond the limits of intellection, and these limits can be crossed over only by exhausting oneself once for all, by using up all the psychic powers at one's command. Logic then turns into psychology, intellection into conation and intuition. What could not be solved on the plane of empirical consciousness is now transferred to the deeper recesses of the mind.[24]

THE ZEN UNCONSCIOUS

In Western psychology the unconscious is simply the unconscious. The Zen Buddhists postulate, or rather seem to be able to experience, a number of levels of the unconscious. Suzuki writes:

> That the process of enlightenment is abrupt means that there is a leap, logical and psychological, in the Buddhist experience. The logical leap is

[24] *Ibid.*, p. 138.

that the ordinary process of reasoning stops short, and what has been con-

sidered irrational is perceived to be perfectly natural, while the psychological leap is that the borders of consciousness are overstepped and one is
plunged into the Unconscious which is not, after all, unconscious. This
process is discrete, abrupt, and altogether beyond calculation; this is
"Seeing into one's Self-nature." [25]

Farther on he states:

In this self-nature there is a movement, an awakening, and the Unconscious becomes conscious of itself. This is not the region where the
question "Why?" or "How?" can be asked. The awakening or movement
or whatever it may be called is to be taken as a fact which goes beyond
refutation. The bell rings, and I hear its vibrations as transmitted through
the air. This is a plain fact of perception. In the same way, the rise of consciousness in the Unconscious is a matter of experience; no mystery is
connected with it, but, logically stated, there is an apparent contradiction,
which once started goes on contradicting itself eternally. Whatever this is,
we have now a self-conscious Unconscious or a self-reflecting Mind.
Thus transformed, Self-nature is known as Prajna.

Prajna, which is the awakening of consciousness in the Unconscious,
functions in a twofold direction. The one is towards the Unconscious and
the other towards the conscious.[26]

To most of us, the unconscious is just that. To become conscious
of anything that was unconscious means we have dredged up material
from the unconscious and made it conscious. According to Suzuki it
is possible to become conscious of the unconscious at the unconscious
level—"a self-conscious Unconscious." For the Zen Buddhist there
are at least four levels of the unconscious and it is possible to become aware of them without being on the level of everyday consciousness. Before we snort and say that this is all a vast contradiction
in terms, we ought to remember that we have made up our definitions of conscious and unconscious on the basis of our experiences.
If the Zen Buddhist claims to have experienced these conscious-
unconscious processes perhaps we ought to think about investigating
further with an eye to changing our definitions.

[25] *Ibid.*, p. 185.
[26] *Ibid.*, p. 211.

When the Zen Buddhist descends into the unconscious he does not fall into a helpless trance or black out. He rigidly controls the process. He uses conscious reasoning processes to direct his awareness to the unconscious non-symbolic levels. He attains the non-rational by use of the rational; reasoning becomes non-reasoning.

What shall we make of all this? Is it utter nonsense, the product of nervous systems warped by excessive meditation upon meaningless statements? If the Zen Buddhist does not allow the intellect, the higher orders of abstraction, to operate, is not this a distortion of the abstracting process? I do not think so, for they do not, as do the Western mystics, attempt to confuse the levels of abstraction by interpreting these experiences. When we try to give them a logical form, we have to attribute to them characteristics belonging to a different level of abstraction and misevaluation is inevitable.

ABSOLUTE THISNESS: NONSENSE OR NON-SENSE

Suzuki quotes a sermon delivered by one of the renowned Zen masters to a group of disciples. Let us examine some lines from it:

When you have nothing disquieting within yourself, do not try to seek anything outside. Even when you gain what you seek, this is not the real gain. See to it that you have nothing disquieting in your mind, and be "unconscious" about your affairs. Then there will be Emptiness which functions mysteriously, vacuity which works wonders. . . . Such words as holiness and ignorance are no more than idle names; excellent forms and inferior shapes are both mere illusions. If you hanker after them, how can you escape complications? But trying to shun them also will bring great calamities upon you. In either case all ends in utter futility.

Both the Buddhas and all sentient beings are of one Mind only, and there are no other dharma (objects). This Mind has no beginning, was never born, and will never pass away; it is neither blue nor yellow; it has no shape, no form; it does not belong to the category of being and non-being; it is not to be reckoned as new or old; it is neither short nor long, neither large nor small; it transcends all measurements, nameability, marks of identification, and forms of antithesis. It is absolute thisness; the wavering of a thought at once misses it. It is like vacuity of space, it has no boundaries, it is altogether beyond calculation.[27]

It seems logical to ask ourselves, "If it has no form how can it be perceived; if it does not belong to the category of being and non-being, how can it exist; if it is neither new nor old, measureless, un-identifiable, how can it be recognized? What in the world is meant by "absolute thisness"? We can begin to make some sense of this if we remember that qualities such as color, taste, form, etc., as we are familiar with them in everyday life, are products of the impingement of the atomic level on our nervous systems and the state and structure of the nervous system at the moment, which includes the symbolic interpretation and meditation of these non-verbal states. More simply put, we see and recognize a tree because atomic processes—which are qualityless (no-form, no-color, etc.) — send out light *waves,* which hitting the eye are then converted by the nervous system into light sensations which are interpreted—given recognition and meaning—by all the experiential and symbolic processes which accompany all nervous activities. If the nervous system is changed in any uncommon way, as for example through nitrous oxide, hashish, mescal, or intensely disturbing evaluational processes such as hysteria or hypnosis, then the tree is a tree and yet not a tree. It seems different, queer; we are at a loss to describe its difference; but we know it is different. Now, think of how much greater and indescribable will be the change if the symbolizing processes are halted. Truly, we will "see" a remarkably different world.

OF WHAT USE IS THE MYSTIC EXPERIENCE?

But we still have not answered the important question, "Of what use is this kind of perceiving?" Isn't it life-denying? Does it have any

27 *Ibid.,* pp. 215–216.

survival value? One value has been indicated by Suzuki: its intensely pacifying, anxiety-reducing, calming effect, among other pleasant qualities, which is carried over to everyday life. But I think there is another very important one. Its very anti-intellectualism has great intellectual value, in that it helps "solve" what seem to be unsolvable paradoxes.

How often are we tempted to ask ourselves such questions as these: What is the meaning of life? How can the universe be finite—isn't there a beyond? How can there be an infinity of space; how can it go on forever? If the universe had a beginning, what was before that? What was it made from and where did that primary material come from? If God created the universe, who or what created God and his creator, in turn? Where was the world before I was born; after I die—what?

We recognize that all of these are unanswerable questions and technically meaningless. There is no possible way of getting a verifiable answer. This is intellectually, but not emotionally satisfying. "How can one escape from the wheel of birth and death?" asked a disciple. "No death, no birth, and no path. Who has chained you?" Another asks, "Is the Way subject to completion and destruction?" The master answers, "If one applies to it such notions as completion and destruction, we can never have insight into it."

Note the answers given: No birth, no death, no space, no end, no beginning. What does this mean? Simply that they are higher-order abstractions; they are products of our symbolizing processes. We have created them. Beginning and end, birth and death, cause and effect, time and space, are man-made abstractions. On the non-verbal level, on the level of things and feelings, there is simply an unending chain. When we stop to *think about* these goings-on, when we proceed to measure and time and name and compare and explain, we are on the verbal level, the level of symbols, and these are words and not the things the words are about. But having generated such notions, such constructs as time and number, we proceed to project these back to the external world and say they exist "out there," in the sense that things exist.

Thus states Suzuki:

The main trouble with the human mind is that while it is capable of creating concepts in order to interpret reality it hypostatizes them and treats them as if they were real things. Not only that, the mind regards its self-constructed concepts as laws externally imposed upon reality, which has to obey them in order to unfold itself. This attitude or assumption on the part of the intellect helps the mind to handle nature for its own purposes, but the mind altogether misses the inner workings of life and consequently is utterly unable to understand it. This is the reason we have to halt at contradictions and are at a loss as to how to proceed.[28]

THE BEGINNING AND THE END

I begin a task, and noting where and when I have begun I call that *The Beginning*. But what is this beginning—a thing? The language forces me to name it and thereby gives it thingness. The same applies to *The End*. But it is I who have created them. Actually the beginning is simply the point where I took notice, that aspect of the infinite complexity around me upon which I chose to concentrate. By an act of awareness I create "a beginning" and act as if it were a thing, as if it had non-verbal existence. Then I proceed to project beginningness upon the universe.

Again, we cannot conceive of colors or shapes we have never experienced, nor imagine what it would be like to have different sensory experiences such as would occur if we were sensitive to x-rays or cosmic rays. Consequently, when we think of God, we can only give him (note how I have to call God "him") human attributes when by definition he cannot possibly have them. As the Christian mystics state, "God is Nothing; He is Utterly Other; He is the VOID." Eckhart proclaims, "Thou shalt love God and He is, a Non-God, a Non-

[28] *Ibid.*, p. 269.

Spirit, a Non-Person, a Non-Form." Tauler describes God as "The divine darkness, the nameless, formless nothing." In Jewish mysticism we find frequent reference to the conception of God as Nothing. It is when these mystics proceed to making affirmative statements about the nature of God that misevaluation occurs. God cannot exist in the sense that we normally mean existence. As with things, whatever we say God is, he is not.

The only escape from these traps is to recognize them for what they are—confusion of the levels of abstraction. The Zen Buddhist, it seems to me, goes a step farther. Not only does he, like the general semanticist, point out that beginning and end, birth and death, are higher-order, static, lifeless abstractions and should not be confused with the lower-order level of our sensory world, but he proceeds to stop the verbalizing process altogether so that he knows this "feelingly" as well as "intellectually."

LIMITATIONS OF ZEN

However, it seems to me that the Zen Buddhist makes one fatal error: He claims that this is the only correct way of viewing the world. As a consequence he undervalues the symbolizing processes and therefore produces no theories and no science. If he were not supported and protected by the common people, he would not survive very long except on a very simple scale and only if not forced to compete with the layman. He is only half a man. The ideal, as I see it, would be to be able to operate on that level of abstraction most suited to the evaluational problem at hand. I do not know whether or not it would be possible to develop both the scientific and the Buddhist methods of evaluation to as high a degree as each can be done separately, but certainly the beginning of wisdom is a realization that there are other paths of life which have a validity of their own and are not to be brushed aside as nonsensical.

THE PRINCIPLE OF COMPLEMENTARITY

If we ask which is the right, the "real" view of the world, I think our reply must be both and neither. For after all, the world as we perceive it is a product of our nervous system, a partial, very partial response to an infinitely complex "out there." A differently constructed nervous system would construct—perceive—a different world. I think that the principle of "complementarity" could profitably be adapted to our purpose.

Since the seventeenth century a large body of evidence has accumulated to support the theory that light travels through space in continuous waves. With the development of the quantum theory there has been an increasing amount of equally reliable evidence to lead to the conclusion that light travels in discontinuous bits called quanta or photons. Atomic particles like electrons and neutrons also seem to have wave-like qualities. Thus we are faced with two contradictory, incompatible concepts. Which is true? Is light a wave or a stream of particles? The answer of Bohr, accepted by most scientists today, is both. When we come to the atomic level we need two sets of equations, two ways of viewing it. Each can be employed separately and will give us reliable information; both must be employed to give us adequate theories about atomic structures, even though logically they are mutually contradictory. As Lincoln Barrett states, "The world is subtler than man's understanding, and the contradictions the scientist uncovers in studying nature lie not in nature itself but simply in man's own inadequate concepts."

WHAT IS THE WAY?

Is the world a timeless, ever-changing flow of things, without beginning, without end, and are we without birth, without death? Yes, that is the way it appears at the non-verbal level. Can the world be timed and will we die? Yes, it can be timed and we can predict that we will die. But do not forget that these are words *about* what our senses give us. As directly sensed and felt, it has duration but no beginning and no end. We must remember that beginning and end apply only to human affairs and abstracting processes and become meaningless when applied to the universe as a whole. If we attempt to go beyond this point, we find ourselves in insoluble paradox which so distorts the nervous system as to produce most distressing anxiety and fear.

Therefore, when we wish to obtain verifiable, communicable knowledge about ourselves and the universe around us, we employ the "regular" sensory and verbal levels. This gives us predictability and control and enhances our chances of immediate and long-range survival. But we must remember that the symbolic processes, especially the higher levels of abstraction cannot handle constant change. They are analytical and they must necessarily distort and kill the world in order to understand it.

On the other hand, the non-verbal level of feelings and sensations is one of constant change and can respond to constant change. If we accept only the picture of the world given us by the higher levels, we then see and feel ourselves as set apart from the universe and everything in it. Remember, the "intellectual" picture is analytical; things are neat, sharp, completely separated from one another, dead. An overwhelming sense of loneliness and isolation is the cataclysmic effect of accepting this set of abstractions as the one true picture of nature and our place in it. Nature becomes something to be conquered and we, the isolated conquerors, are doomed to a losing battle. We may win for a time, but eventually we will die, our universe will burn out or explode, all a vast waste of time; vanity, vanity, all is vanity, and a striving after wind.

But when we turn to the complementary picture given by the lower levels we find that we are not set apart from nature. We work with her and are part of her; she is in us. We flow along, accepting the dance and the tune she plays, for it is our dance and tune as well as hers. There is no isolation, no I and not-I, no birth, no death, no beginning, no end, nothing to be explained, no theories to verify. This picture is equally as valid as the scientific one; it is simply the world looked at from another level. Analytically, the lower-order picture looks nonsensical. And it is, if by sense we mean scientific, verifiable, public knowledge. But it is emminently sense-able at the level of individual feelings and inner life. And it in no way contradicts the scientific view of the world when it is kept at its level and the two are not confused.

The ability to operate at any level as the situation demands becomes the key to a fuller and happier life and more effective time-binding. We can enjoy the sense of belongingness and oneness with the universe given by the lower-order picture and the hints of deep and cosmic meanings which come in flashes like those sparked by a poem or a song or a walk through wet woods or a certain smile. And we can experience the awe and wonder which come with the higher-order picture as we learn of vast distances and tremendous speeds and overwhelming forces and amazingly intricate and complex design and grandiose theories; and these, too, generate a sense of cosmic meaning, not fully comprehended, yet reinforcing them, blending into a sense of reverence, humility, and laughter. Yes, laughter. Only man can laugh. Not the animals, not God. The animals cannot compare what is with what should be and be struck by the incongruity and absurdity of things. And God, being perfect and omniscient and omnipotent, cannot be surprised, and surprise is necessary for laughter, assuming, of course, that there be a God and that he has human attributes, which by definition he cannot have; and by logic he cannot be our "be."

By enabling us to distinguish between levels, consciousness of abstracting makes the non-verbal respectable by placing it, not in opposition to the scientific and logical, but synergic with it. On the non-word level is the magic of things, their queer non-logicalness, their primitiveness and glowingness, their startling realness and secret meaningness, subtle, elusive, unanalyzable, unseizable, unpredictable; evocable and never commanded, the secret in the daisy, and, above all the felt-answered unanswerable. One timeless second of it is infinitely longer than a thousand timed years and it can nourish and enliven and temper the analytical life and encourage the search for the meanings and workings of the measured-answered unanswered.

It should be understood that we are not advocating the curtailment of the cortical processes, but rather trying to channel them into areas proper to them. It is permissible and desirable to conduct scientific investigations of the neurological processes involved at all levels of abstraction. Let us find out what is happening in the nervous system when the mystic is in his ecstasy. Let us try to discover what is happening in the brain and elsewhere when I taste spinach. But let us not try to read logic into the taste of the spinach. Right and wrong do not apply. Similarly, if when I choose to respond to the world in terms of the lower levels of abstraction and experience oneness, flow, timelessness, there can be no questioning of the "truth" of this experience. It happens. If we ask if this is what the world is "really" like, we are asking for verifiable, public knowledge and this can be given only by employing the verbal processes. It is like asking, "Is the Beethoven Moonlight Sonata a true representation of moonlight?"

The only possible reply is, "Keep quiet and listen. You hear what you hear, feel what you feel. It tells you something, but that something is non-logical, unanalyzable. Analysis immediately destroys." Similarly with the mystic response. Be quiet, stop thinking, let it happen, stop looking for explanations. That is what the world is like when you listen to it and ask no questions. You get answers which are no-answers. They are answers which are sensed and felt and in their way as important as the atomic weight of lead.

True wisdom lies in knowing when and how to operate at each level. What is the meaning and goal of life? To make it answerable at the higher levels it must be changed to, "What meaning shall we give it, what goals shall we select?" Our answer would be, "Seek to become an effective time-binder; and the meaning is to be found in the seeking." The answer at the lower level is, "No answer, no goal; it is to be sensed and felt and intuited, not spoken. The meaning of life is the meaning of spinach."

❈ ❈ 10 ❈ ❈

Structure and Function in Cybernetics
and General Semantics

THE verification of a theory in any one field of knowledge by evidence from another is always of prime importance. It is a valuable way of checking self-deception. In our chapter on semantitherapy we introduced the work of Dr. Abraham A. Low as offering some verification for the claims of general sematicists that general semantics can work in pratice. In this chapter I should like to introduce verification for Korzybskian theory that is coming from a new science which is expanding with explosive rapidity and promises a revolution in neurology, philosophy, and psychology: cybernetics. We shall endeavor to present in highly condensed form some structural and functional similarities between basic assumptions in both fields. I refer the reader to the book by Pierre de Latil for an excellent non-mathematical introduction to cybernetics.[1]

Cybernetics was born during World War II of the efforts of the mathematician, Norbert Wiener, and the physiologist, Arturo Rosenblueth, to solve the urgent problem of designing an antiaircraft gun which could shoot down high-speed planes. Before the invention of high-speed aircraft, the problem of aiming and firing at a moving

---

[1] Pierre de Latil; *Thinking by Machine,* Boston, Houghton Mifflin Company, 1957.

target was relatively simple. For one thing, the speed of the target had been so small compared with that of the projectile that it could be neglected, but this was no longer the case. For another, human reflexes no longer were fast enough to aim and fire accurately at so speedy a target. Obviously a machine had to take over the task.

It soon became apparent that the computing machines of the day were not equal to the job, that a machine operating on a new principle was necessary. The new principle turned out to be an old but relatively neglected one—feedback. It had been used by James Watt in his automatic governor for steam engines and by others. Its real significance began to be suspected with the growth of radio in the 1920's, specifically with the development of the vacuum tube and the automatic volume control. In 1932 Cannon coined the term "homeostasis" to describe the self-regulating processes of living organisms and postulated the presence of feedback mechanisms, though he did not call them by that name.

FEEDBACK

What is a feedback system? According to Pierre de Latil, "It is a device which makes an effect act back on one of its causes, thus enabling the effect to carry out its given aim. The differences between the real and ideal effect are transformed into energy which is fed back into the mechanism and tends to cancel out the original differences which set the system in motion.[2]

Perhaps the differences between feedback and non-feedback systems can be illustrated by recourse to the familiar example of the furnace. Suppose we install an oil burner in a house. The only control we have is an on-off switch. When we turn the burner on, the fuel pump forces in oil, the igniter lights it, and the blower forces hot air throughout the house. De Latil calls this an "interactive system."

[2] *Ibid.*, p. 6.

The different parts interact with on another to produce an effect—a rise in the temperature of the house. This effect has no significant effect upon the operation of the furnace. We can neglect the influence of the rise in temperature on the viscosity of the oil, speed of the motor, etc., unless it becomes so extreme as to cause a noticable change in operation.

INTERACTIVE SYSTEMS

What are the characteristics of such a system as far as Korzybskian theory is concerned?

It is an additive, symmetrical system.

A. The relationships among the parts and of the parts to the whole are the same whether the machine is in motion or at rest.

B. No new characteristics arise as a result of the machine's operation except the motion of the parts, which is a non-additive characteristic and this movement is strictly predictable. We can neglect the unpredictable wear on gears, variations in flow of oil, etc., because these are differences which do not make a difference for our purposes. Thus, the whole is equal to the sum of its parts.

C. Aristotelian causality and logic are applicable in describing and explaining the operation and functioning of the system.

D. It is a first-order mechanism. Variations in the operation of the machine can be obtained by varying one of the factors (causes) producing the effect (rise in temperature). We can increase the flow of oil or the speed of the blower and the rate of change of the temperature will change.

RETROACTIVE SYSTEMS

Now suppose we get tired of going down to the cellar to turn the furnace on and off. We build into the system a thermostat which we locate in the living room. The thermostat is set to maintain the temperature between 70° and 74°. We turn on the system, the furnace ignites, and heat comes into the room. Most of it is used to warm the room, but a small part is used to operate the thermostat which "tells" the furnace how it is doing by turning it off and on when it deviates from the set limits. Thus part of the effect of burning the oil is fed back into the system through the thermostat and is used to control the burning of oil. De Latil calls this a "retroactive" system, because part of the effect feeds back—"retroacts"—upon one of the causes of the effect and changes it.

Some of the characteristics of such a system are:

It is a non-additive, non-symmetrical system.

A. The relationships among the parts and of the parts to the whole are not the same when the system is functioning as when it is at rest. There is no feedback until the machine is in operation. The feedback is not a structural part of the machine but a function of it when it is working. Yet this function has the effect of a structure. It is a structuring structure—a function.

B. New characteristics arise as a result of the functioning of the mechanism which are not present when it is at rest. One has just been mentioned—the feedback. Another is the *effect* of the feedback.

C. Aristotelian causality and logic are not applicable in describing and explaining the functioning of the system. They cannot handle feedback effects. Whenever they attempt to they immediately generate paradoxes and unresolvable false dichotomies. It requires a second-order causality to account for second-order effects. In a feedback system one of the effects of the causes of an event feeds back and becomes one of the causes of itself. Thus we have an effect becoming a cause of a cause, a second-order cause. This must be distinguished from a first-order cause of a cause as when A causes B which causes C in a linear system.

D. The retroactive system is a second-order mechanism. In a first-order interactive system regulation is obtained by varying or controlling one or more of the factors in additive fashion. For example, the speed of a car can be controlled by regulating the amount of gas, the brakes, the gears. We have factors acting on factors to produce the effect—speed of the car. An automatic governor on the motor would be a second-order mechanism. The effect, the speed, would feed back and affect the factors, causing a non-additive reaction.

ORGANIZED AND DETERMINED EFFECTS

We note that the furnace-thermostat mechanism is sensitive to and tries to adjust to many variables. The amount of oil being burned varies from moment to moment, as does the quantity of air used to oxidize it. In the house the opening and closing of outside doors and the turning on and off of heat-producing appliances vary the temperature of the room, as does the number of people in the house. All of these and many more result in a final effect, the house temperature of the moment, and this is kept relatively constant between 70° and 74° by the feedback mechanism. Two things are worth stressing here:

1. A new characteristic has arisen as a result of the operation of the system: constancy of temperature. The whole is now more than the sum of its parts.

2. The effect—the house temperature—tends to become independent of the very factors causing it because of the feedback mechanism. What we have, then, is a dynamic structure which tends to become independent of its environment. De Latil calls this an "organized" effect as compared to the "determined" effect of an interactive system. In the latter the effect is "completely" determined by the external factors affecting the system and by the structure of the parts whether at rest or in motion. An organized effect is, of course, a non-additive one and accounts for the "queerness" of holistic characteristics. They disappear the minute the mechanism stops. "Organized effect appears to be a truly transcendental entity; it has no existence, apart from its organization, that could be considered to be linked to its essence. [3]

This characteristic of increasing independence from environmental factors as the feedbacks in a system are multiplied (e.g., a feedback

[3] *Ibid.*, p. 197.

on a feedback hook-up) tends to produce a dynamic constancy of internal organization which is the prime characteristic of living organisms. That is, we have what in general semantics is called "invariance under transformation" on the non-verbal level. It is a second-order invariance produced by variance in the system, as compared to the first-order invariance of an interactive system which can be obtained only by stopping the mechanism. Of course, this invariance is a relative thing, relative to the function and structure of the system. Relative to the rest of the universe everything is varying.

Summarizing, we can use a first-order logic and theory of causality to describe and predict both the structure and functioning of an interactive system and the structure of a non-operating retroactive system. We need a second-order logic and theory of causality to predict and describe both the structure and functioning of a retroactive system.

FREE WILL VERSUS DETERMINISM AGAIN

The free-will-determinism controversy which we discussed in a previous chapter is a good example of a false dichotomy arising from a confusion of levels of abstraction and orders of causality. In our analysis of the problem, we concentrated on the confusion of the levels of abstraction; we shall now take a look at it from the point of view of causality.

We have stated that free will, as we define it, is the feeling of being free to choose and is on the non-verbal level of abstraction. Determinism is an inference, a theory of causal connection. In order to operate successfully, we have to infer (with perhaps certain exceptions in the case of single atomic phenomena) that everything is causally connected. The whole of science is founded on this assumption which cannot, in principle, be proved.

We have to assume, for example, that all of a man's behavior is strictly determined; nothing he does "just happens." One of the effects of this determined behavior is his feeling free to choose; the feeling is caused. But the feeling of freedom of choice then feeds back and becomes one of the causes of his behavior. That is, because he feels free to choose he looks at menus and plans papers proving that free-will does not exist. Thus the act of choosing helps to cause his be-havior—a second-order causality; but this act of choosing is strictly determined—a first-order causality. So now it is no longer free will versus determinism but free will *and* determinism.

NEGATIVE AND POSITIVE FEEDBACK

Not all feedback mechanisms serve to maintain an equilibrium in a system. Mechanisms which tend to destroy equilibrium are called positive feedbacks. Those which tend to maintain it are called neg-ative feedbacks. It would be possible to rig up a thermostat-fur-nace system so that as the temperature in the room rose, the thermo-stat would increase the size or heat of the flame in the furnace. Then, the warmer the room the higher the flame, the higher the flame the hotter the room, etc., until something gives way—the house catches fire or the furnace blows up or breaks down.

We have seen the psychophysiological counterparts of this in the runaway panic cycles common to the "nervous breakdown" and ex-treme stage fright. It is interesting to note that the means for rational control of these cycles is through the regulation of second-order feel-ings. That is, by choosing not to fear the fear, worry about the worry, etc., we change the system from one of positive to one of negative retroaction. Conciousness of abstracting enables us to choose the variables or factors which will determine the program of the "thermostat."

The Program

The program is the set of directions inserted in the control mechanism. In the negative-feedback furnace-thermostat system it was: Maintain the temperature between 70° and 74°. In more complex mechanisms such as the giant electronic computors Univac and Eniac, the program is much more complex, but the degree of complexity is of the same order as that of the machine—second-order. In a second-order machine the program does not vary as a result of the machine's operation. In a third-order mechanism it would. This machine would change its program on the basis of its "memory" of the results of repeated application of the original program. It would be a goal-seeking machine controlled by a program of programs. The second-order program, in effect, would say: Vary your original program in the light of your experience with it. Such a machine has been built—a chess-playing machine which can play a fair game and beat the average player; it can be beaten by experts.

Animals, and especially man, have third-order mechanisms. In man even higher-order programs are possible. A very high-order program corresponds to an overall philosophy and life goal. The subprograms represent the day-to-day means of achieving or moving toward this goal. As we move higher and higher in our orders of programs we become more and more independent of the immediate environmental factors which help determine our behavior. These are our invariants under transformation on the verbal level.

It should not be thought that all positive feedback systems are detrimental to machine or animal. Positive feedbacks are what de Latil calls "tendency effectors," as opposed to the "constancy effectors" of negative feedbacks. Positive retroaction changes the program in third-order and higher mechanisms and is responsible for goal-seeking activity. It can be modified by experience. Negative retroaction maintains the program and cannot be modified by experience. We need both to function adequately.

In setting up the various programs of our lives we must use the multivalued approach to make as certain as possible that we have investigated as many of the variables and alternatives we can in the time allotted. Then when this is done we carry the program out in a two-valued fashion, making use of the negative feedbacks to maintain the system and achieve the goal. At the same time we build into the program positive feedback mechanisms which will shift or change both goal and program if new data and new experience warrant it. In effect, when we formulate the program we act through a set of conditional responses. When we carry it out we try to act through conditioned responses. But inserted in the program is the order to watch out for important new data while carrying it out— a conditionally conditioned response.

By building both constancy and change into the program we maintain the stability that comes from order and the stable instability which comes from internally organized change, as opposed to the unorganized instability which results from the unplanned breakdown of a given organized state.

Corresponding to the orders of causality and mechanism are the orders of complexity. An adding machine having a thousand billion parts would still be a first-order interactive mechanism producing additive, "certain," predictable results. It would have a first-order complexity. When a feedback mechanism is added we produce a second order of complexity. It may be a very simple machine from the point of view of number of parts, yet it can then produce effects that the most complex first-order mechanisms could never achieve. It is a complex simplicity. If a number of feedbacks are inserted, especially if we have feedbacks of feedbacks, we get a complexity which expands with exponential acceleration—a complex complexity. As an example we have the synthetic "turtle," Elsie, built by Grey Walter. Elsie seeks out a source of light and moves toward it. If she runs into an obstacle she works her way around it. If she sees herself in a mirror she waltzes about as if admiring herself. If she meets her brother, Elmer, they begin a strange dance, a sort of mating quadrille. When she gets hungry (low batteries), she returns to her hutch to eat (recharge). According to Walter, although in theory her actions can be predicted (first-order causality), in actuality she always produces some unpredictable reactions.

Despite this complexity of behavior, behavior which can never be programed in detail, Elsie is a rather simple machine in number of parts. She is about $18'' \times 18'' \times 8''$, with fewer parts than the average television set. Essentially she consists of a photoelectric cell hooked up to two motors which steer and drive her, and a shell which is sensitive to the contacts when she runs into an object, and which is also wired to the motors. Aside from the amplifiers, resistances, coils, relays, etc., needed to run the photoelectric cell and motors, that is about all there is to her construction. Yet because of her feedback systems her behavior is more complex than that possible for any first-order machine having a million times as many parts. The differences are essentially qualitative, just as they are when we move from one level of abstraction to another.

Most interesting to me is the element of unpredictability in her behavior. Operating at a second level of complexity, Elsie "chooses" between varying light sources and obstacles. Is this not a very rudimentary "free will" or "purposeful" behavior? It should not surprise us when we observe a tremendous elaboration of this in animals, seemingly well-defined, purposeful behavior. But while they may not be aware of their behavior, and therefore not "actually" purposive, man most certainly is. Through awareness of his awareness he has developed his feeling of being free to make choices and the ability to seek the purpose of purposes.

And so we come to the end of our journey. We have spoken of many and diverse things. But through all their differences ran one unifying thread, one invariant under transformation, the structure of the language used to describe and define them. Now our portion of the tapestry is woven. I hope the design is clear, the pattern appealing, and I hope this weaving is not the end.

Bibliography

Bruner, J. S., Goodnow, J. J., and Austin, G. A.. *A Study of Thinking,* New York, John Wiley and Sons, 1956.

Custance, John, *Wisdom, Madness and Folly, The Philosophy of a Lunatic,* New York, Pellegrini and Cudahy, 1952.

de Latil, Pierre, *Thinking by Machine,* Boston, Houghton Mifflin Company, 1957.

Frankel, Charles, *The Case for Modern Man,* New York, Harper & Brothers, 1955.

Fromm, Erich, *Psychoanalysis and Religion,* New Haven, Yale University Press, 1950.

Fromm, Erich, *The Sane Society,* New York, Rinehart and Company, 1955.

Hayakawa, S. L., *Language in Thought and Action,* New York, Harcourt, Brace and Company, 1949.

Huxley, Julian, *Heredity East and West,* New York, Henry Schuman, 1949.

James, William, *Varieties of Religious Experience,* New York, The Modern Library, 1902.

Johnson, Wendell, *People in Quandaries,* New York, Harper & Brothers, 1946.

Korzybski, Alfred, *Science and Sanity: An Introduction to Non-aristotelian Systems and General Semantics,* International Non-aristotelian Library Publishing Company. Distributed by the Institute of General Semantics, Lakeville, Conn., 1st ed. 1933, 2nd ed. 1941, 3rd ed. 1948, 4th ed. 1958.

Lee, Irving J., *Language Habits In Human Affairs,* New York, Harper & Brothers, 1941.

Low, Abraham A., *Mental Health Through Will-Training,* Boston, The Christopher Publishing House, 1950.

Maslow, Abraham H., *Motivation and Personality,* New York, Harper & Brothers, 1954.

Morris, Charles, *Paths of Life,* New York, Harper & Brothers, 1942.

Muller, Herbert J., *The Uses of the Past,* New York, Oxford University Press, 1953.

Platt, John R., "Amplification Aspects of Biological Response and Mental Activity," *The American Scientist,* vol. 44, no. 2 (April, 1956), pp. 180 ff.

Pumpian-Mindlin, E. (ed.), *Psychoanalysis as Science,* Stanford, Calif., Stanford University Press, 1952.

Rapoport, Anatol, *Operational Philosophy,* New York, Harper & Brothers, 1953.

Stace, W. T., *Religion and the Modern Mind,* New York, J. B. Lippincott Company, 1952.

Stace, W. T., *Time and Eternity,* New Jersey, Princeton University Press, 1952.

Suzuki, D. T., *The Collected Works of D. T. Suzuki,* The Hutchinson Group, as selected by William Barrett in *Zen Buddhism: Selected Writings of D. T. Suzuki,* New York, Doubleday Anchor Books, 1956.

Weinberg, Harry L., "Some Functional Patterns on the Non-Verbal Level," *ETC.: A Review of General Semantics,* vol. IV, no. 3 (Spring, 1947), pp. 196–212.

Zirkle, Conway, *Death of a Science in Russia.* Philadelphia: University of Pennsylvania Press, 1949.

Index

Absolute terms, 79
"Absolute thisness," 245–246
Absolutistic philosophy, *see* Relativist-absolutist controversy
Abstracting, consciousness of, 96–143, 252, 253
  and beauty, 129–135
  and conditional response, 126–129
  and control of irrational processes, 96–98, 261
  and free will vs. determinism, 102–121
  and happiness, 137–139
  and love, 136, 137
  and multiordinality of terms, 98–102
  and pleasure principle, 121–125
  and time, 140–141
Abstracting, process of, 51–76, 182
  and amplifier theory, 52–55
  and causality, 105
  distortion of information, 52, 55
  limits of, and fear of non-being, 198–200
  and nature of God, 218
  and mental health, 181
  and perception, 51
  reversal of, 76, 81, 91
  and self-actualization, 164–168
  and time-binding, 158
    See also Abstraction, levels of; consciousness of
Abstraction, levels of, 56, 247
  differentiating between, 200–204, 227, 237
    and detached-attachment, 211–212
    and satisfaction of needs, 206–211
  and invariants under transformation, 204–206

and multiordinality of terms, 99
and principle of complementarity, 250–254
and process thinking, 77–95
semantic confusion of, 56–60, 249, 260
  and beauty, 130
  and empiricist vs. skeptic, 59–60
  and free will vs. determinism, 120
  and hedonist—non-hedonist controversy, 123
  and intensional orientation, 173–174
  and paradoxes, 92–93
  and time, 141, 200
and value, 151–152
and Zen Buddhism, 235–236, 237, 240–241, 245
  See also Non-verbal levels; Verbals levels
Acceptance, act of, 188–191, 204
"Allness" pattern, 46, 194, 204
  in higher level abstractions, 78
  in syllogistic reasoning, 88–91
  and two-valued orientation, 83
Ambivalence, 99
Ames experiment, 52
Amplifier theory, 52–55, 109–110
Analysis vs. synthesis, 227–230
Anxiety, 1, 85, 189
Aristotelian thought, 48, 66, 81–83, 88–90, 92, 112, 114, 149, 150, 151, 257, 258
Atomic level, 56, 60, 72–74, 94, 246, 250
  See also Event level; Non-verbal level
Attitudes, 196–197

Index